Poor-Bashing

For less Nola
our very nice
neighbours.
Jean

Poor-Bashing
The Politics of Exclusion

Jean Swanson

Between the Lines

Toronto, Canada

Poor-Bashing

First published in Canada in 2001 by
Between the Lines
720 Bathurst Street, Suite #404
Toronto, Ontario
M5S 2R4

National Library of Canada Cataloguing in Publication Data

Swanson, Jean, 1943-
  Poor-bashing : the politics of exclusion

Includes bibliographical references.
ISBN 1-896357-44-X

1. Poor. 2. Poverty. 3. Social Policy. 4. Economic policy.
5. Discrimination. I. Title.

HC79.P6S92 2001   305.'69   C00-933342-8

Design by Margie Adam, ArtWork
Printed in Canada by union labour

Between the Lines gratefully acknowledges assistance for its publishing activities from the Canada Council for the Arts, the Ontario Arts Council, and the Government of Canada through the Book Publishing Industry Development Program.

THE CANADA COUNCIL | LE CONSEIL DES ARTS
FOR THE ARTS | DU CANADA
SINCE 1957 | DEPUIS 1957

ONTARIO ARTS COUNCIL
CONSEIL DES ARTS DE L'ONTARIO

Contents

To people who are poor and keep fighting for justice
despite the discrimination, the hate,
and the hardships.

Acknowledgements

The executive of the National Anti-Poverty Organization (NAPO) helped me decide to write a book on poor-bashing. I had just finished my term as president and, as I only work half-time to support myself, wanted a half-time volunteer job. I proposed to the executive that I write either a regular newsletter for the organization or a book on poor-bashing. They wanted a book.

My anti-poverty work started when Bruce Eriksen hired me to work at the Downtown Eastside Residents' Association (DERA) in Vancouver in 1974. I had been slinging beer at the Patricia Hotel on East Hastings to support my children. At DERA, Bruce and Libby Davies taught me about politics and organizing and perseverance. My children Paul and Lora had to put up with my obsession with work. I hope they will forgive me for a decade of not getting as much mother's attention as they should have.

My special partner Sandy Cameron loves books and is always telling everyone to write one, even me. After I started, he read virtually every draft of every chapter, talked me out of tough spots, and got me going again. Sometimes his excitement about the book would pull me out of depressing writing times.

Nancy Pollok volunteered to use her editing skills and faithfully scoured every proposal and every chapter, making numerous practical suggestions. This was before the publisher or official editor even saw the book. Nancy, too, kept up the encouragement.

Besides Sandy and Nancy, the people who have helped me the most are Bev Brown, Linda Moreau, and Rose Brown. All three have read book proposals and several drafts of various chapters, as well as a whole first draft. Their thinking has shaped my thinking and their support and encouragement have kept me going. Nandita Sharma has also helped a lot, challenging my words and pushing my thinking about racism and sexism.

Both the National Anti-Poverty Organization and End Legislated Poverty have helped too, NAPO with research help, and lots of moral support, and ELP by allowing me to use its equipment and giving lots more moral support. I especially want to thank Mike Farrell, Tara Nollet, Liz Sutherland, Joanne Louisseize, Rosemary Spendlove, Madelaine Roy and

Lynne Toupin on the NAPO staff, and Ken Wyman, a NAPO volunteer. NAPO board members helped out by letting me interview them and allocating time at meetings for this, and by their enthusiasm for a book on poor-bashing. My eight years on the NAPO board allowed me to travel throughout the country, meet many dedicated poverty fighters, and get a more national perspective on the issue of poor-bashing.

I especially want to thank all the people who allowed me to interview them, mostly in hopes that something good for poor people could come out of it. They include: Dave Ross, Leigh Donahue, Pam Coates, Barry Schmidl, Marlene Vieno, Cathy Hebein, Arlene Mantle, Debbie Ellison and Mila and Mikey, Elisabeth Ziegler-Simmons, John Clarke, Nandita Sharma, Sara Torres, Shelley Bird, Jo Grey, Pia Shandel, Susan Learoyd, Mr. Berhane, Todd Cunningham, Sue Bruce, Deborah Graham, Michelle Forrest, Aline Akeson, Claire Beland, Colleen Dingwell-Corbin, Deb Andrews, Donia Naffaa, Fay Blaney, folks at the Gathering Place in St. John's and Abbott Mansions and the Dodson Hotel in Vancouver, Mike Harcourt, Linda Lalonde, May McIntyre, Roman Gerschack, Sandra Pronteau, Marie Wadden, and Jean Trickey. Several of the people I interviewed didn't want me to use their names, so I haven't. Thanks very much to all of you for taking the time to talk with me and let me learn from your experiences and thinking.

Other people who helped out include Mary Ann Cantillon, David Northcotte, Rolf Auer, Marjorie Bencz, Harold David, Ellen Woodsworth, Georgina Wilson, Deborah O'Connor, Edna Doiran, Diana Ralph, Neil Brooks, Sheila Baxter, Nancy Hannum, Andrew Martin, Elaine Briere, Robert Clarke, Maureen Davis, Karen Boyes, and Pat Chauncey.

My grandson Devon helped out too by playing with me for a couple of hours every day, giving me something to look forward to after a day of struggle writing the book.

I also want to thank my editor, Julie Beddoes, the book's designer, Margie Adam, and Paul Eprile and Peter Steven of Between the Lines for their work on the project. I am grateful to Between the Lines for being willing to publish a book about social and economic justice.

Of course, just because a person or group helped me out doesn't mean they necessarily agree with the points I've tried to make. To everyone who supported this work, I hope this book will help in our fight to end poverty and poor-bashing and build a just society.

Jean Swanson,
Vancouver, fall 2000

Introduction

Ken Wyman was on his way to work at the National Anti-Poverty Organization (NAPO) office close to Ottawa's Byward Market area in January 1996. Wyman, a retired civil servant, volunteered at NAPO researching, among other things, trends in welfare law. He walked into the building, pushed the button, and the elevator doors opened to greet him. But this morning the greeting was vicious. "Kill the poor" was scrawled in black letters four inches high across the back of the elevator.

Ken Wyman wasn't a poor person himself, but "I felt a mixture of anger, horror and shame," he said. "Shame that our society has come to this. If one group of people can be singled out, anyone can."

Wyman called the building security guard and asked him to remove the graffiti. He also told the rest of the staff at NAPO. "They were afraid," he said to me.

Joanne Louisseize was one of the staff who was afraid. Louisseize, a mother of two, was NAPO's secretary, the one who first greeted visitors to the organization's third floor office. "I wasn't comfortable staying at work that night," she told me. "I worried that some wacko was going to come in, with me sitting out front, and say, 'You represent poor people,' and take it out on us."

"I'm not afraid of people who are poor," Louisseize added. "I am afraid of people who say, 'I'm a taxpayer and I don't want to pay for welfare.'"

NAPO had a solution that's not available to Canada's five million poor people. They moved their office to a new location with better security. "We're blessed," Louisseize said.

Dennis was not so blessed. I first met him when he was hauling a bag from the food bank up to his tiny second-floor room on East Cordova Street in Vancouver. He didn't want me to use his last name because his family might find out he was on welfare. He subsisted on $500 a month in the Downtown Eastside, one of the poorest neighbourhoods in Canada. With rent at $350, it was hard to have enough money left for food and everything else, unless you went to the food bank. I asked Dennis if he'd ever experienced poor-bashing. He got right to the point. A friend of his was walking along East Hastings Street. "They killed him and got a few bucks out of it," Dennis told me. "I've been mugged three times. It's the ones called skinheads who do it. I've heard them say, 'Let's roll a few drunks' and they think anyone who lives in this area is a drunk."

When I first got the idea of writing a book on poor-bashing, I thought I had a definition of it: poor-bashing is when people who are poor are humiliated, stereotyped, discriminated against, shunned, despised, pitied, patronized, ignored, blamed, and falsely accused of being lazy, drunk, stupid, uneducated, having large families, and not looking for work.

Before talking to Dennis I thought that poor-bashing was similar to racism and sexism because all three involve stereotyping, discrimination, and unequal power. After talking to Dennis I realized that poor-bashing, like racism and sexism, can also include threats, and even murder.

Dennis, who was fifty-eight when I interviewed him, had worked in the hardware business, then in a milling company until he was over forty. The milling company, his last employer, was bought up by a competitor and eliminated. He admitted that he hadn't been in contact with his family for years. "I keep saying tomorrow I'm going to try to contact them," he said. "Let's say it. I'm ashamed. In two years I won't be on welfare." Dennis was thinking he might try to contact his family when he became sixty and his income could be called a pension. Then he wouldn't face the stereotyping, the discrimination, the hate, that people on welfare face, even from their own families.

Dennis was one of millions of casualties of a war against the poor in Canada, a vicious war taking place on three fronts in one of the richest countries in the world. On the economic front, there were simply no jobs for Dennis. In June 2000, with the Canadian economy ostensibly booming, a Statistics Canada official told me by telephone that there were still over a million people officially unemployed. The exact StatsCan number for May 2000 was 1,028,000. Many of the jobs that do exist pay very low wages and are part-time and short-term.

On the political front, in 1996, the federal government cut funds for welfare, and ended rights for people in need by eliminating the Canada Assistance Plan. It also gutted unemployment insurance. (Throughout this book I'm going to use the term unemployment insurance, or UI, even though the government is now calling it employment insurance. This is because I hate to use the language of people who are trying to manipulate me and others.)

On the attitude front, Dennis, like others on welfare, was stereotyped, discriminated against, ignored, hated, threatened, and even beaten. Three months after I talked to Dennis, he was dead, a typical fate of poor people in Canada whose life expectancy (for men) is, on average, 6.3 years shorter than for richer people.

This book is about the war of exclusion, prejudice, and hate against the poor in Canada. More and more anti-poverty groups have started to call this poor-bashing. Poor-bashing is one part of classism–discrimination against people because they are thought to be in a lower social class. Poor-bashing is the part that hurts people on welfare and unemployment insurance. It hurts people who can't get either welfare or unemployment insurance, people who are homeless or have to panhandle for money to live on; they are also being poor-bashed and criminalized.

Poor-bashing is a very intense and personal experience when it happens to you. So it's natural to want to challenge poor-bashing in a personal way, to say that the vast majority of individuals who are bashed, like Dennis, are trying hard, are "deserving," don't have a chance to get paid jobs that don't exist. I believe this is all true. But I also believe that we shouldn't let this kind of individualized thinking about people who are poor insidiously reinforce individualized "solutions" to poverty. This is a kind of poor-bashing itself: it ignores the many ways in which poverty is actually legislated by our governments, and it demands a higher standard of behaviour and sacrifice from people who are poor than from people who are not.

As American writer Michael Katz says, "Poverty ... is about distribution; it results because some people receive a great deal less than others." He points out, "Descriptions of the demography, behavior, or beliefs" of people who are poor "can't explain inequality."

Too often these so-called descriptions of the behaviour and beliefs of people who are poor are themselves nothing but poor-bashing. To think about poverty in a way that doesn't blame people who are poor, we have to use language that doesn't suggest they are to blame; we have to consider government and corporate decisions that impoverish hundreds, thousands, and millions of people throughout the world.

Ending poor-bashing isn't just a matter of being nice, of not using certain words that don't respect people who happen to get their income from welfare or unemployment insurance, or people who live on the street. Ending poor-bashing means asking questions about the unequal distribution of wealth and income. Rose Brown, one of my co-workers in Vancouver at End Legislated Poverty (ELP), a B.C. coalition of anti-poverty groups, has lived in poverty nearly all her life. She works organizing low-income people, and has done a lot of thinking about poverty and wealth. She believes that simply allowing poverty to exist when our society has the means to end it is a form of poor-bashing. "It's forcing one segment of society to live in horrible conditions. Our society knows how to make bombs and go to the moon," Brown explained to me. "We have humungous financial resources, so why isn't it a priority to end poverty?"

Having the term *poor-bashing* to describe what happens to us can be very powerful. In a speech at the 1998 Vancouver People's Summit on Asia Pacific Cooperation, anti-poverty organizer Linda Moreau, a woman I've worked with for over a decade, explained that fighting against classism today is like fighting against sexism in the 1960s. Back then women were oppressed, but the word sexism didn't exist. "In those times it was common to blame a woman who was raped for being raped. 'What were you wearing? Where were you? ' people would ask of the raped woman," Moreau said. When this attitude was identified as sexism it was easier to resist.

Now people who are poor are beginning to use the phrase poor-bashing to resist the treatment and policies that corporations want and governments have created. DJ wrote to me from Newfoundland about being poor-bashed when she tried to cash a welfare cheque at a bargain shop. She had been to a workshop on poor-bashing sponsored by the St. John's Women's Centre before this incident. The manager told DJ she would have to get her social worker to sign an affidavit before the store would cash the cheque. DJ told the manager he was poor-bashing. Using the word helped DJ name her experience and take the blame for poverty off herself. It might have even taken some of the blame off her in the manager's eyes. He relented and cashed the cheque.

Poor-bashing has existed in Canada from the beginning of colonization, but in the 1990s it became more intense and relentless. Politicians rarely use the words poverty or welfare unless in the context of "fraud and abuse" or forcing poor people to take low-wage jobs with crummy conditions. Poverty is a problem worthy of political lip service (not real action) only when children are involved. The interests of the elite are served by the media through columns, commentators, news stories, and entire sections of newspapers, as well as by TV and radio programs devoted to business news and littered with information on how to use tax loopholes. But most news media ignore government actions that increase poverty. Instead they focus on the behaviour of individual poor people whom they pity, patronize, or bash with lies, gossip, stereotypes, and fraud accusations. Or the media do stories on measures designed to change the poor people themselves so they won't use welfare or unemployment insurance but will still be poor.

While poverty is studied a lot, people who are poor are seldom consulted; reports often discuss hypothetical or anecdotal people, not real ones. This book differs from others on social issues in that it incorporates and is based mostly on the thinking and experience of people who are poor and fighting for changes that will reduce and—one day—end poverty. I begin with stories about how some poor people are thinking about poor-bashing, and how they experience poor-bashing in their daily lives, and in their work. I think it's important to read their words.

This book is mostly about poor-bashing in Canada today, but it also looks at poor-bashing as part of a long European and Canadian tradition of considering some human beings as inferior or superior to others because of characteristics such as race, gender, income, and other categories. It also offers practical suggestions for how people who are poor and their allies can challenge poor-bashing.

The more I worked on the book, the more I realized that it's just a beginning at exposing and challenging poor-bashing in Canada. I would have liked to talk to poor people from more provinces and territories, and poor people who speak languages that I don't understand. I think it would be useful to explore the similarities and differences among racism, sexism, poor-bashing, and classism more than I have. I hope this book will spark more thinking, talking, and writing about these important issues by the people who have experienced them, as well as by their allies.

My interest in poor-bashing was sparked by reflecting on over twenty years of work in the anti-poverty movement at the Downtown Eastside Residents' Association and ELP in Vancouver, and as a board member of NAPO for eight years, ending in 1998. Why were we able to make small gains in the 1970s and even the 1980s that we couldn't make in the 1990s? By 1995, as president of NAPO, I was learning that poor-bashing was epidemic in Canada. Participating in meetings and workshops and giving talks and speeches from St. John's to Victoria, I found that talk about poor-bashing, and especially connecting poor-bashing to policies that corporations were pushing for, could take a huge weight off people who had been blaming themselves for their own poverty. In 1995 I watched in disbelief as the New Democratic Party, which I had once joined because of its stand on ending poverty, refused to even mention welfare except in the context of "fraud and abuse." I noticed that both federal and provincial politicians, when they talked about social programs, always noted health and education and left welfare out. In the spring of 1996, I was one of over three hundred people across the country who fasted (hundreds of others used other activities) to protest the Canada Health and Social Transfer when the new act (see Chapter 7) took effect on April 1. This was the end of the legal rights of Canadians to an adequate income when in need, and to not have to work or train for welfare. As NAPO president, I spent long days on the phone trying to get the media to cover this issue, which they largely ignored.

As the decade wore on, important issues for people who were poor became of less and less interest to the media and to politicians. But the poor still had a use. In Red Deer, Alberta, I discovered, the hospital wanted workfare workers to replace laid-off nursing assistants. The New Brunswick government was using people in welfare programs to replace nursing and teaching assistants at half the usual wage. The ignored and despised poor were being used to undermine the wages and working conditions of people who already had jobs.

At End Legislated Poverty in British Columbia, we started using a hundred-inch length of string cut in five pieces, each representing a fifth of the Canadian population, to illustrate the disgraceful distribution of wealth in Canada. The pieces were wildly different in length. According to a 1984 Statistics Canada study, the richest 10 per cent of Canadians had more wealth than the poorest half. What is more, the study didn't include the very richest people in the country, people like the Irvings, the Bronfmans, and the Westons. As Lars Osberg says, they probably wouldn't answer a survey if they were asked. Even so, the 1984 findings are crucial for understanding poverty in Canada. I've put them in a chart at the end of this introduction. Lars Osberg also reports that researcher J.B. Davies has estimated what the distribution of wealth would be if the very richest people were included in the Statistics Canada survey. He calculated that the richest 1 per cent of households in Canada had 28.7 per cent of the wealth and the richest 5 per cent had 46.5 per cent in 1984.

Anti-poverty workers suspect that StatsCan hasn't updated its wealth study for so long because it would reveal an even greater gap between rich and poor. Armine Yalnizyan of the Centre for Social Justice calculated that by 1997, just one man, Ken Thomson of The Thomson Corp. and The Hudson's Bay Company, had more wealth than the poorest third of Canadians. Three families, the Thomsons, Bronfmans, (whiskey), and Irvings (oil), had more wealth than the poorest half of Canadians. Another study, reported in Thomson's newspaper *The Globe and Mail*, said that the number of millionaires in Canada tripled between 1989 and 1996 to 220,000, and predicted that number would triple again by 2005.

StatsCan claims to be producing a new wealth study, but the report has been delayed at least once and wasn't available in time for the production deadline of this book.

I was also a member of the Action Canada Network that was fighting corporate rights agreements (also called free trade deals) with other countries. I learned from other members and from solidarity trips to the U.S. and Mexico how corporations were moving from city to city, province to province, country to country, in search of the lowest wages and taxes. What would happen to the people who had to work for these wages, I wondered? How could anyone justify paying such low wages anywhere in the world, knowing how much people would suffer because of it?

As I thought about all this and talked with other people who were fighting poverty, the role of poor-bashing kept getting more important. It wasn't just that poor-bashing was hard on poor individuals. The owners of the big corporations were actually using their think-tanks to promote and justify it. The free trade deals these corporations wanted were giving more and more power to transnational companies that wanted lower and lower wages. How could they take the blame off themselves for the hardship and suffering their system was creating? Poor-bashing was at least part of the answer. It blamed the poor for policies they didn't create so the people who did create the policies didn't have to be accountable for them. And, as we'll see, it cheapened the labour of other working people, leaving more profit for corporate owners.

This book is for people who are poor-bashed. I hope it helps us understand that poverty is caused by laws and corporate decisions, not by individuals, and I hope it gives us the courage and some strategies for not taking it anymore.

This book is for working people who have felt angry because they pay taxes to support people on welfare—working people who deserve the security of decent social programs to help them survive if they happen to lose their jobs, health, or spouse. I hope this book can help you see how poor-bashing, like racism and sexism, undermines your own security and livelihood. I hope it will help you ask questions about poverty and wealth, questions that will help you figure out how poor-bashing cheapens everyone's labour.

And this book is for people who want to live in a fair and just society. How do we end poverty in this country and the world? So many supposed attempts have been failures. One necessary step is to end the kind of thinking that puts people into groups like, "the poor," or those "on welfare," or "immigrants," or "Third-World people," or "Indians" to justify treating them badly and/or blame them for poverty. If we stop blaming poor or other oppressed people for poverty, we can expose the policies, laws, and economic system that force millions of people in Canada and around the world to compete against each other, driving down wages and creating more poverty. With a clear view of what's really going on, we have a better chance of winning the struggle for a just society.

The distribution of wealth in Canada

Poorest 10 per cent (of households) owned minus 0.4 per cent of Canada's wealth (i.e. they were in debt)

Second poorest 10 per cent owned 0.1 per cent (virtually nothing)

Third poorest	0.6 per cent
Fourth poorest	1.8 per cent
Fifth poorest	3.6 per cent
Sixth poorest	5.7 per cent
Seventh poorest	8.2 per cent
Eighth poorest	11.6 per cent
Second richest	17.5 per cent

Richest 10 per cent .... 51.3 per cent, over half of all the wealth in Canada

Source: the most recent survey of household wealth, done by Statistics Canada in 1984 (Catalogue 13-580,1984), reported in Armine Yalnizyans's *The Growing Gap*.

Chapter 1

What poor people say about poor-bashing

Mr. Berhane felt guilty even though he knew he wasn't. He was very focused on his computer and a stack of reports when I met him at the Low Income Families Together (LIFT) office in Toronto about a year and a half after the Mike Harris government came to power using a campaign that attacked people on welfare. He had lost the business he owned during the recession years of the early 1990s, and was surviving on welfare and working at LIFT on an incentive program. He asked me to use his last name only. Jo Grey, a well-known Toronto anti-poverty activist, introduced us, then left us to talk.

"I came from Ethiopia in 1981," Berhane began. "I had a banking background. I didn't just walk into Canada to be a burden to taxpayers." He explained why he didn't have a paid job: "It's because there are no jobs, regardless or race or age, no jobs available," he said.

"Governments accuse you," Berhane continued. "They say you are a lazy bum. That's how they classify you. You hear that message in the papers, on TV. They don't go to your background," he said.

"Potentially I'm a person who can work. That's what the government says. But the employers on the other side don't want me," he said. "I hate this [Mike Harris] government. It's a dehumanizing government.

"They discourage you by bringing in so-called workfare, to make you work freely for employers," he noted, pointing out another consequence of poor-bashing. Workfare forces people to work or train in order to receive their welfare cheque. Workfare is a euphemism for forced labour or forced training. Workfare policies are based on the poor-bashing stereotype that people on welfare won't look for work on their own and have to be forced. "[Employers] are happy because they will save a lot of money if it is introduced and enforced," explained Berhane. Then if other workers don't cut their hourly rate, they may be asked to work thirty hours a week or take a day off," he said.

"I would say to the Minister [of Social Services], 'Please try to understand their situations. Talk to them. Listen to what they say.'"

Berhane summed up his contradictory feelings and thoughts: "I never chose to be poor. I'm ashamed of what I am now, but it's beyond my ability to change things. I'm still alive. I haven't committed suicide. I'm living with hope. Although I know with all my heart that it's not my fault, the system makes you feel guilty. Society makes you feel guilty." Berhane had looked for jobs; he would work if he could find a job. He *was* working at LIFT. He knew it wasn't his fault that he was on welfare, but he still felt guilty.

He picked up a napkin and covered his eyes. I realized he was crying and tried to reassure him. "It's not your fault," I said. But his rational self knew that. Jo tried to console him too. "There's one example of being poor-bashed for you," she said to me.

As a Black man, Berhane is a target of racism as well as poor-bashing, multiplying the impact. He is an intelligent person who understands that there aren't enough jobs for everyone; that employers benefit from a strategy of blaming people on welfare; that all humans are equal in worth and dignity. He sees who his accusers are—the government, media, and population in general—and knows they are stereotyping him falsely. He knows why he feels the way he does. But poor-bashing and racism are so relentless that, like many of the people I interviewed, he began by defending himself. He talked about people on welfare as "they" not "we." His discouraged, hopeless feelings were so powerful that he saw it as a good sign that he had not committed suicide.

Raised to poor-bash

I interviewed Mary Smith (not her real name) in a hotel in Ottawa in 1997. As a representative of low-income people from Saskatchewan she, like me, was attending a NAPO board meeting. She told me she was raised to poor-bash: "I think poor-bashing first affected me when I was about five years old and I could hear my dad sitting at the kitchen table talking to his neighbours, saying, 'We should just go on welfare like the rest of those sons 'a bitches, quit working so hard,' and so on. I think he was a person with an attitude about the poor, that they are all lazy, useless, and good-for-nothing people. To be on welfare would be the ultimate form of degradation to him."

Smith's father's "attitude" rubbed off on her, she admitted. "I've been guilty myself of snubbing [people on welfare]. In Estevan when I was a nice little middle-class mother, we had a problem relating to a single parent who was on welfare," Smith related. "We used to wonder what *they* did with their time, going to bars and what not," she said.

"Then I became a single parent and a poor person, someone who had to go on welfare. I think the hardest thing in my life was walking through that welfare door being full of shame and degradation and personal failure and looking at suicide because I couldn't support my kids in a way that they deserved to be supported and seriously feeling that to take my own life would be the best possible solution." A good friend stopped Smith from suicide and helped her realize that she wasn't to blame for not having a paid job.

Many of the people I talked to observed that it is often those who are most at risk of needing welfare in the future who carry around a lot of society's hatred for people who already receive it. But they may face a crisis—their job ends, their spouse leaves, their health deteriorates—and when they have to resort to welfare their feelings about people on welfare are transferred to themselves with devastating personal consequences, like Smith's suicide attempt.

For Smith, the poor-bashing continues, even in her own family. "In my siblings I think there's poor-bashing by ignoring the fact that we don't have as much as they do. They don't want to know, and they can be very critical. For example, last time I went to a NAPO board meeting, my sister heard how much my babysitter was paid. [NAPO pays low-income board members child-care expenses so they can attend meetings.] So she said, 'Oh, welfare must pay pretty good.' She doesn't even know the difference between welfare and NAPO.

"I still find it hard to get away from the shame of my own poverty,". Smith said. "This past month I signed up for a new careers training program and the teacher is a poor-basher. She told me how she feels that the food banks are grossly misused. She doesn't want her taxes going to people who smoke and drink booze and I'm sitting there smoking with her, but I'm not one of them?"

When Smith learned that she wasn't to blame for her poverty, that it was mostly due to a lack of decent jobs, she became "a defender of the poor." She started anti-poverty groups in her community and got involved with NAPO. During the Ottawa meetings she encountered, in a hotel lobby, another prairie resident talking about street people. Smith and Barry Schmidl, another NAPO executive member, heard the man say, "The kindest thing would be to get them all drunk and then just put them to sleep. Nobody would know the difference. Nobody knows them. They'd never be missed." Like the people I talked about in my Introduction, Smith learned that poor-bashing can go as far as death threats. She interrupted the man's poor-bashing, telling him that many street people would rather have homes and jobs and that there are good reasons for not wanting to go to shelters. People are afraid of being beaten up, getting their things stolen, or getting diseases like tuberculosis that are rampant in shelters.

Smith's story shows how parents teach their children to poor-bash. She has fought the "shame of her poverty" even though she, too, knew it wasn't her fault. But she was also working to organize people who are poor and to challenge poor-bashing. *Poor-bashing means ignoring facts and repeating stereotypes about people who are poor.*

Consultation: another kind of poor-bashing

From Newfoundland to British Columbia, Canadians who are poor face poor-bashing when they try to participate as citizens in their community or to consult with government about laws that cause poverty. Anti-poverty activists Linda Moreau, Bev Brown, Deb O'Connor, and Jacquie Ackerly told me how the poor are often ignored by the people they're working with, and consultation ends up being just another kind of poor-bashing.

Former B.C. NDP Premier Mike Harcourt took a lot of pride in consulting the people affected before enacting government policies. He says so in his book *A Measure of Defiance.* In office from 1991 to 1995, Harcourt claims, he "wanted all the players, business, unions, workers, academics, public servants, First Nations citizens—to take part in this process of consensus building for our future." So he set up a number of premier's summits to include, not exclude, "the people most affected by a government's deliberations."

Except for poor people. The "summit" for poor people, called the Premier's Forum on Living and Working Opportunities, was set up in 1994. It had thirty members from business, unions, universities, and some community groups. Some members worked in government and there were even several cabinet ministers. Its purpose was, to use its own euphemism, "to renew the social safety net." Its main topic was welfare, but it excluded people on welfare or anyone accountable to them. The forums on other issues, however, did include people with a direct interest in the issues.

In 1997, after he was no longer premier, Harcourt willingly agreed to an interview with me. I asked him why he excluded representatives of people on welfare from the Forum. "I think it was probably an oversight rather than conscious. I just ask that the work be done and expect the minister and staff to make the appointments," he told me.

I asked him if it was easier to have an oversight that would exclude poor people than one that excluded corporate people. "Probably," he replied, "because poor people are less organized, have enough of a struggle just to survive, let alone be involved as activists, so in that sense they're less visible."

B.C. at that time had two anti-poverty coalitions, both partially funded by Harcourt's government, as well as at least fifty organized groups of low-income people around the province working hard to get government to recognize their concerns about increasing poverty. *Poor-bashing means leaving poor people out of discussions on issues that are crucial to their livelihood.*

Women's and anti-poverty groups mounted a campaign to be included in the Premier's Forum, and Linda Moreau of End Legislated Poverty was appointed to the Forum, after two meetings had already taken place. She had been on welfare herself as a single parent, and she was accountable to the ELP board of low-income people and groups. After adding Moreau, out of thirty-one people the Forum on welfare now had one who represented people who were poor. *Poor-bashing is about making tokens of people who are poor.*

Moreau and Rose Brown, her colleague at ELP, have done a lot of thinking about classism and poor-bashing so I talked to them about the Forum. When I asked Moreau if poor-bashing happened at the meetings, she replied, "The whole premise was that there was nothing we could do about the federal cuts to provinces for health, education, and social assistance, except cut welfare. There was a huge range of responses the government could have taken in terms of how to deal with federal cuts. But the first and only solution [that government considered] was to cut the very poorest."

"There's this new language of the right," Moreau explained. "They say, 'increase people's attachment to the labour force,' as if people get unattached because of their own bad attitudes or not wanting to get up in the morning or that welfare is such a wonderful free ride." The Forum didn't consider that the official unemployment rate at the time was 9 to 10 per cent; and that many jobs with part-time hours didn't pay even enough for a single person to live on. "It was very hard to fight against the assumption that poor people are to blame for their poverty," Moreau told me.

"Bashing of single parents was very bad," she recalled. "People would say, 'Why were all these women on welfare when they get all this help?' They assumed that everyone got the amounts that people could get from welfare if they were in the worst possible situation and had the most generous social worker. Five hundred dollars' worth of dental work, school start-up fees, crisis grants—they actually counted those in terms of money and then said, 'This is what people get. Why aren't they getting off their butts?'" In fact, people on welfare have a hard time getting the benefits that the rules say are available. Maybe if their house burned down, Moreau thought, they could get as much money as government officials claimed they were getting, but that didn't happen to many people.

"Bashing of youth was very bad," Moreau continued. "'How can we keep them attached to school and then attached to the labour market?' That was the big thing. 'These lazy louts are dropping out.'

"This was an NDP government. They could have done public education. They could have really pushed the federal government like they did when the Americans were catching Canadian fish. But all they could think of was to save money by blaming people for having to go on welfare. People on the Forum acted like gods saying, 'What if we took this person's food? What if we reduced welfare to force people to take a $6.50 an hour job?'"

Every once in a while, Moreau told me, she'd rally herself and say, "This is outrageous. There's a range of possibilities and you're the government. I can't believe that you're talking about taking food out of people's mouths in such a detached way. You're talking about real people here and the economy is not their responsibility. They can't tinker with it like you can as the government.

"Then there would be this embarrassed silence," related Moreau. "And someone who was trying to be sensitive would say, 'Well Linda certainly has given us something to think about while we have lunch.' Then we'd go to this lavish lunch at the Hotel Vancouver and the bureaucrats would be scooping up the shrimp and saying 'I think it's outrageous that these people [on welfare] double-dip, taking welfare and UI at the same time.'" (In

1997, in B.C., people who were in need and waiting for their UI cheques to start could get interim help from welfare. When their UI cheques came, they would go off welfare, but if what they had received was for some of the time that the UI cheques covered, they didn't have to pay it back. That has now changed and people who get welfare while waiting for UI have to pay it back, sometimes leaving them in crisis situations.) *Poor-bashing means assuming that the rich are entitled while the poor must do without.*

"They are totally calm and secure in their rightness," Moreau said, reflecting on the attitudes she encountered at the Forum. She tried to think of a time when she had been so confident of her rightness that she ignored what others were saying. "The only way I can relate to how I was treated at the Premier's Forum is around the adultism that I had with my kids: this young person must go to bed; they must go to school. I was correct. They were having a temper tantrum or were out of control if they questioned me. I could not see the situation from their point of view, or think their feelings were worth considering. And I can see maybe that's how they thought of me."

As Moreau spoke, Brown was thinking about the problem of how people who are poor and have something crucial to say can get middle- or upper-class people to really listen to them, especially when they are only one or two among many. It's hard to get the courage to speak out, when years of experience tell you will be dismissed or ignored because of your class, your poverty. Brown calls this the "weight that you're going against," a heavy pressure keeping you from saying what you need to say. "What do you say to make them focus on what you're saying when you're speaking about something that you know about and they don't? What can you say to them to make them not distance you? Or can you say anything?" asked Moreau.

"The closest allies I had were the union people and that was a bit scary because they were experiencing discrimination and classism them-selves," said Moreau. "Every once in a while one of the business people or the bureaucrats—not the politicians—would have a little zing about union wages being too high. You could see [the union people] were deal-ing with that oppression too."

When I first talked to Newfoundlander Bev Brown, she was a sin-gle parent to her teenage daughter and an anti-poverty and human rights worker on the NAPO executive. "Often I'm the only unemployed person sitting around tables dealing with human rights and welfare," she told me. She had been on welfare in St. John's, looking for work in an economy that the St. John's *Evening Telegram* said had a real unemployment rate of 47 per cent. Being the only unemployed person at meetings on community issues "feels dispiriting because people who haven't experienced being of that low an income don't have the same attitude that you have," Brown said. "Instead of being militant, they're more charity oriented and patronizing."

For example, a group was formed to figure out how to spend some federal money on a "child poverty initiative." Brown was asked to join as the NAPO representative. "But everyone sitting around the table was employed except for me. They made silly off-the-wall suggestions about how to use the federal money to address child poverty," she said. "For example, set up a clothing bank of really good clothes for people to borrow to look for work. Another was to give *Chickadee* magazine to all the kids on welfare. I proposed a project designed and run by the youth and it wasn't even considered at all." *Poor-bashing means ignoring people who are poor when they propose what they need.*

"When I went to the meetings, the people involved in the board were bashing people on welfare all the time. When I tried to address it, I was told 'Oh it's not that bad.'" *Poor-bashing means having your reality and your perceptions denied by people with more money than you have.*

The group produced a binder to be used in schools containing information about how teenagers could become entrepreneurs. "The project was not very useful," Brown said. *Poor-bashing means that projects supposedly designed to help people who are poor, don't.*

"It just felt like I was nobody and invisible and I was nothing. And I was the only one volunteering my time too," Brown added. "The others were paid. So after that I thought, why am I the only unemployed person who gives my time when nobody else does? Not one policy change I've ever suggested has been made. I feel as if I end up helping government manipulate poor people just by showing them how their words are offensive. Then they use less offensive words to describe the same poor-bashing policies. I'm wondering if I'm doing the right stuff."

When poor-bashing keeps people who are poor out of citizen groups designed to solve problems, or isolates and makes tokens of them and their ideas, what are the consequences? The projects or policies produced are based on the stereotypes that the non-poor people have of people on welfare and UI. With the experts on poverty excluded from designing solutions, the solutions usually don't work.

Deb O'Connor has years of experience organizing for social justice in the Ontario town of Cobourg. She was working in a community law office as a paralegal when she joined other NAPO board members to talk to me about poor-bashing. A single mother of two grown children, she had recently become a grandmother. "Most of my experience with poor-bashing has been from the early days of running the Help Centre in Cobourg when I was on mother's allowance," O'Connor told me. "It was becoming fashionable to include low-income people in committees and groups and consult with them, so I was a perfect target for this kind of thing. I certainly don't think that consulting with low-income people is poor-bashing because it's appropriate and we need more of it. Where the poor-bashing comes in is when it's phony. It might take a meeting or two for it to sink in but you realize you are there as the token poor person and they're not the least bit interested in what you have to say. All that matters to them is that they can say, farther down the road, 'Oh, but we consulted. We had Deb over there to represent poor people.'

"There was a group called the Community Services Group, made up of the senior-level people from Children's Aid, the family counselling place, the boards of education, the women's shelter, the welfare place," O'Connor related. "The way they handled me was to ignore me. When I'd go in, no one would speak to me. When we had a smoke break, I'd be at the edge of whatever group because I was never made to feel welcome or included. One time I made a fairly strong statement; I don't remember what it was about, but I spoke for a few minutes and when I stopped there was dead silence from about twelve people in the room, just dead silence. And it went on for a little while and then the chair said, 'Well, moving on to the next agenda item ...' It was as though I wasn't even there and they wouldn't even give me the dignity of saying I was full of shit."

Jacquie Ackerly and nine other Canadians went to Geneva in 1998 to tell the United Nations Committee on Economic, Social, and Cultural Rights that the government of Canada was passing laws that increased poverty and violated the human rights of poor Canadians. On December 4, Ackerly, vice-president of NAPO and chairperson of ELP, held a news conference in Vancouver with Shelagh Day, who had also been to Geneva, representing the National Association of Women and the Law.

Day is an expert on human rights and a good ally to people who are poor. She began the news conference speaking strongly and excitedly, telling reporters that the report was "stunning and an extraordinary wakeup call to Canada." She said it was the "first time that this

Committee has ever taken so critical a view of a developed country."
She reported some of the things that the Committee said Canada
should do to stop violating the human rights of its poor citizens:
restore national standards to welfare; restore unemployment insurance
payments; build housing for the homeless; protect poor people from
discrimination in human rights laws; make it illegal for provinces to
deduct the child benefit from welfare (see Chapter 7); and expand
human rights laws to include economic and social human rights.

Then it was Ackerly's turn. Ackerly has struggled on welfare for
years, raising her four children and volunteering in the anti-poverty
movement. Over the years she has written briefs, organized demonstrations, met with politicians at all levels of government, always trying to
get them to reduce poverty with jobs, decent wages, higher welfare rates,
and changes to welfare regulations to benefit those who need it. Despite
all this work, conditions were still getting a lot worse for poor people in
Canada, even in B.C., with a provincial NDP government that she had
hoped would make a difference. For Ackerly, it was a different kind of
emotional moment than it was for Day. She took a deep breath that
pushed the tears back and said simply, "The [UN] report validated all
those messages that no one listened to in Canada." *Poor-bashing is being
ignored.*

The UN experience helped Ackerly realize how, in Canada, "If
you're poor, you don't experience much validation from politicians or the
media. Being ignored is the ultimate poor-bashing," she explained to me
later. "You're not acknowledged in the results and usually during the
experience, there's this sick condescension." The condescenders are polite
and nice, said Ackerly. "You just leave with the feeling that they don't
believe you; they think you are out of your depth and don't understand
the complexities of the issues, nor do they expect you to." At the UN,
Ackerly said, "we were treated as experts in the field." The chair of the
Committee allowed her to continue her presentation after lunch because
of the "stature" of the group she represented, NAPO. "We hung around in
the lounge with people from the World Health Organization. There was
no differentiation in status," she said in a sort of amazement at being
treated like a regular human being.

Because the UN didn't ignore Canada's poor in its *process*, Ackerly
noted, the concerns of the poor were actually reflected in the *content* of
its report, which made numerous recommendations on how Canada
could stop abusing the human rights of its poor people.

Poor-bashing a neighbourhood

The Neighbourhood Helpers Project (NHP) is part of a long history of struggle for justice in Vancouver's Downtown Eastside. The group organizes low-income people to fight for their neighbourhood, sometimes called "the poorest postal code in Canada." Income there comes mostly from pensions, welfare, unemployment insurance, and low-paid work. Most of the ten thousand or so residents live in single rooms, ten feet by ten feet, with one window, sometimes looking out on an air well, not a street or even an alley. They use communal washrooms, and communal kitchens if they are lucky.

Neighbourhood Helpers rents rooms like this in rooming houses and hotels. It takes the bed out, puts in a couple of tables, some chairs, a little fridge and a hot plate and a phone. Most of the building's residents don't have phones. A building resident is paid a small honorarium to open the room every morning, put the coffee on, and welcome people who come in to chat. NHP staff deliver donated baked goodies every so often, along with local newsletters and information about community events. Some of the NHP people are getting involved in stopping the demolition of affordable housing, and working as volunteers on other neighbourhood issues.

NHP staffer Ellen Woodsworth took me to meet the folks at the inappropriately named Abbott Mansions, which was then a typical Downtown Eastside cockroach-ridden rooming house. It was early December 1996. Mike, Vince, Kim, and Gwen were in the NHP room drinking coffee and chatting when we arrived. Later Frank and Ray arrived. I didn't ask for their last names. They all seemed to be in their thirties or forties. Most of them, I learned later, have health problems. Vince had a hip infection. Mike had two bad knees. Gwen had osteoarthritis. Woodsworth introduced me as a person writing a book about poor-bashing .

"People confine you." Mike started right out with his poor-bashing experiences. "'Oh, you belong to the Downtown Eastside.' Not too many will say 'Hi' to you. 'Go back to your own area,' they say." *Poor-bashing is being told you aren't free to go where you choose.*

Mike made an important point: poor-bashing is more than name-calling; it can be laws that assume it is acceptable to treat poor people inhumanely. "[Social Services Minister Joy] MacPhail made the three-month waiting list. Even a guy in his sixties, she gave him a bus ticket and shipped him to Quebec." Mike was talking about the NDP government, which had just changed welfare polices to exclude people who hadn't lived in the province for at least three months. Since a lot of people come to B.C. looking for work, the policy was having devastating effects, with many more people forced to live on the street, and even people who were sick being denied welfare when they got out of hospital. The policy was eventually revoked after pressure from anti-poverty groups and the federal government.

"If there was work," Frank said, "I'd be working. If you've never been on welfare, then you don't know what it's like. If you've been on it, then you know. The mayor [Vancouver's Philip Owen] has gotta be the worst," said Frank. "He said that people live on the street because they choose to. I was disgusted when I read that. Narrow-minded people." *Poor-bashing is repeating myths such as "People choose to live on the street."*

Ray came in to use the phone, but I asked him first about poor-bashing. "If you get a job and go in the lunchroom, they'll tell you what they think about welfare people. They say they gotta work to support lazy bums collecting welfare. 'They all get too much money, drive a big car, and they even eat.'

"There's no reason to be angry at the poor just cause you gotta work," Ray continued. "You could quit and go on welfare yourself if it's so damn good. It's not something they consciously believe. It's just something they hear a lot from the media I suppose," said Ray, naming another poor-basher. "That and they resent people for not working," he explained, picking up the phone and dialing a number. "Any word on the welders job? OK, well call me. You've got the number—if you hear. Thanks."

"Because I live in this neighbourhood people automatically assume I'm a skid, a down and out, a drug user, even though that isn't the case," explained Mike, who was probably in his thirties. "So, automatically it's a no when I go for a job. *Poor-bashing is being denied work because of being on welfare or because of the place you live, probably the only place that you can afford because your income is so low.*

"My brother and I make $15 to $20 an hour as painters," Mike continued. "Lately we've had to work for minimum wage. If you had any idea how hard we work for that money—and there's people who call us low-lifes. We're painters. It's winter, and we get laid off." That's another part of being poor-bashed, always having to justify things about your situation that others who have paid jobs or live in more wealthy neighbourhoods don't. "I know in my heart I'm a good worker," Mike added.

"I'm not gonna let the street win. I've got my health, my brother." Mike's brother was in the room with him, quietly drinking a coffee.

The way Mike told his story, unconsciously defending himself for not having a job, got me thinking about the yachts not far away in the harbour. Writer Peter Newman says that Ted Rogers, the multimillionaire cable-TV owner (he has recently extended his media holdings and bought the Toronto Blue Jays), has a "35-metre, $10-million floating palace with all the goodies." He also bought the house next door to his Toronto home so he could tear it down and build a tennis court, and he travels in a $40-million Challenger jet. Who should feel the most need to defend himself—a printer who gets laid off in the middle of winter or a guy who uses up so many resources in a world where many are starving?

"I'm heading off to Rice World to see if I can get a job today," Mike said as he took off with his brother.

NHP has another room at the Dodson Hotel on East Hastings Street in Vancouver. I went there that same week with Georgina Isaacs, an NHP volunteer. Rick, Maggie, Eldon, and Gavin were there.

"What we do at NHP is bring people together to talk about problems and do something about them," Isaacs explained. "I took some city hall people down here, down to the Argo Hotel. Coffee was ready and they wouldn't sit down to drink it. They were dusting their chairs off." *Poor-bashing is thinking that people who are poor are dirty, or that they are too unimportant to drink a coffee with.*

"Outsiders look at this community and see it as a bunch of garbage," said Eldon, "but they've never been on this side of the fence. People who stereotype us don't see the good side of us, the volunteers. I've been up in front of city council twice. They just scoff at us. Their attitude is, we'll sit here while you speak because we have to." *Poor-bashing is not listening to people who are poor.*

Eldon said that people who are uneducated and inexperienced are among those who poor-bash. "I've got a bad back," he said. "You try and explain it to someone that's still strong. They don't realize that things like this happen. Before they open their mouths they should look at the situation. It's not that you choose to be on welfare. It's what you have to do to survive." *Poor-bashing is making up your mind before you know the situation.*

Leigh Donahue came in and again I heard that poor-bashing includes actions as well as words. "The government claimed B.C. had higher welfare rates. Then Premier Glen Clark cut welfare. But rents didn't go down. Food didn't go down. That's poor-bashing." Clark had cut B.C. welfare rates for single people from $546 a month to $500 a month, about 39 per cent of the poverty line, while the official unemployment rate was still over 9 per cent. Poor-bashing made it okay to the electorate to cut rates. *Poor-bashing makes it okay to force people to live on miserable amounts of money.*

"I'm convinced that a lot of [drug overdoses] are suicides of people with no hope," said Leigh. *Poor-bashing and the policies that go with it take hope from people.*

Maggie asked us if we'd like some soup she made. Some of us took some in bowls or in our coffee cups. It was delicious soup, made with vegetables because one of the people there was a vegetarian. Everyone complimented her on her cooking. Then Eldon washed up the dishes in the small bathroom-type sink in the room and put them on the clean white towel on top of the dresser.

Poor-bashing gets mixed up with racism

Fay Blaney is one of the Homalko People, the most northern of the Coast Salish people from the B.C. coast and Vancouver Island. "That's how the Department of Indian Affairs spells it," she says. "We've never spelled it in our language." She was raised with her foster family at Surge Narrows, on the mouth of Bute Inlet.

When I talked to her, she was the vice-president of the National Action Committee on the Status of Women and active in the Aboriginal Women's Network, as well as a teacher. As we sat on lawn chairs in my front yard, Blaney talked about her experiences with poor-bashing and racism.

"All my life I've been really poor," she told me. "I remember in my childhood—and it's partly racial, partly cultural—the embarrassment whenever white people came to our home. We would hide things like our bannock. One time I made a mistake and pulled it out. It was our custom to have tea and bannock sometimes for breakfast and sometimes late in the afternoon if we got hungry. So these people were there and I pulled it out and put it on the table and I got into big trouble for doing that from my foster parents. Bannock was food that we were ashamed of. It was poor food. All families were like that. It was normal back then. I never thought of it being strange the way I do now."

Blaney said that it's hard to tell whether discrimination is based on poverty or racism. "But we always knew our place," she recalled. "We always knew that we were less than other people in some ways." Blaney said that the "white people in the area like the teacher or the Christian people sometimes came by and donated clothes to us. You could tell if it was their first time at our home by the way that they behaved. We always had a lot of shame around our cleanliness. Today I recognize what it is. [In the city] we have sidewalks. We don't have dirt. There you track dirt into the house and it doesn't matter if you wash it every day, you always have dirty floors. So I knew there was a lot of shame around that in my childhood. I still feel that way today. With my busy schedule, I have that gnawing feeling [that] I'm never clean enough. I will be judged when people come into my home." Racism plus poor-bashing "affect the way that you live your life into adulthood," Blaney explained.

Blaney has been on welfare a few times in the city. "I've tried my hardest not to be. I've really hated dealing with the system. I find it so dehumanizing," she said.

"You try to talk to the workers in the welfare office and they treat you like you're less than other people. Right off the top when you're phoning to make an appointment, they're so rude to you on the phone. They treat you with suspicion, like you're trying to pry their last penny off of them. The level of controlling over your life that they exercise is unbearable for me, so I've really struggled to change my own condition so I can do something about that." *Poor-bashing means welfare officials feel they have the right to control you.*

Blaney told me another story of poor-bashing and racism. She had left her partner, who had an addiction problem, and was desperate to find a place to live. She rented a place only to find that it was full of cockroaches and leaked. In fact, all the possessions she had moved in, including her kids' clothes and bedding, were soggy from the leaks. While Blaney was trying to fix the leaks and keep the cockroaches from getting in everything, the landlord came down and called her a "dirty Indian." When Blaney took the children to stay somewhere else and didn't return until 8:30 in the evening, the landlord said he was going to phone welfare because she was keeping the children out too late. "He lived upstairs from us and he was dictating what we could do," said Blaney. "We were out because there was such a horrendous situation in our home." *Poor-bashing plus racism means some landlords feel they have a right to judge and condemn your activities.*

Someone who knew her called for help because they thought Blaney might commit suicide because she was in a crisis. "And rather than offering any kind of support, they sent two police officers in uniforms and a social worker to my door. They banged like they were gonna break the door down and then they wanted to take my children then and there.

One of the privileges of education is the way that I talk. From being abused I operate best when I'm under stress and pressure. So my survival skills kicked in and I just told the people off and told them to leave and managed to keep my children, but I think they were really anxious to do that child apprehension and I think that if it had been another Aboriginal woman without that privilege of education and these words that I have, they would have taken the kids then and there." *Poor-bashing means constantly being afraid that someone will take your children.*

Even though Aboriginal people made up 8 per cent of British Columbia's population, the province's Child and Youth advocate admitted that 35 per cent of the children in government care were Aboriginal. *Poor-bashing plus racism means absolute terror that someone will take your children.*

"What I needed right then was some support to deal with the landlord," Blaney said. "I went to city hall and asked for help and the guy that they sent was racist too. He just really gave me a rough time and asked me why I was picking on my landlord. He said that he was a sick old man and I shouldn't be picking on him and what was the matter with us Indians anyway, we're asking for so much all the time and not willing to do anything on our own and on and on. I complained to the office at city hall and nothing was ever done about that man." *Poor-bashing and racism mean not getting the same services that others are entitled to.*

Poor-bashing stops communication

Jean Trickey helped me understand that poor-bashing is similar to racism in that it keeps non-poor people from finding out the truth about people who are poor. Instead of asking questions, they believe stereotypes. Jean Trickey worked to integrate Little Rock High School in Arkansas as a teenager. She was the director of the Tungasuvvingat Inuit Centre in Ottawa when I talked to her in the spring of 1997. "One look at a Black woman and people make all these assumptions about who you are, where you've been, what your experiences are, what you've done, and all kinds of things. Communication stops. I don't make assumptions about what people's experiences are by looking at them. I'm curious. But with inherent racism, people cease to be curious and think they know what you've experienced. I went to a party once and one woman, perfectly sweet, very friendly, came up to me and started telling me about all the Caribbean events happening in the city. Did you go here? Did you go there? She was so sure that I was a newcomer of Caribbean birth, that she didn't even ask me anything about myself. On the face of it I can handle it, but when a whole bunch of people start behaving in that way, it's very serious and it's very dangerous. It seems like nothing on the surface, but it's a very very important and damaging kind of thing."

"A Taxpayer" wasn't interested in real communication with Velma Wells. Wells had been working with other parents at Macdonald School in Vancouver for several months to create public support for their goal of two trained adults in every classroom. Macdonald had a high number of children with special needs in each class and the provincial accreditation team had made that recommendation a year earlier but no action had been taken. The parents began fighting for more staff, holding public meetings, and speaking to the media. They set up a tent city at the school board office. Wells, a First Nations woman from the Mt. Currie Band near Pemberton, had been quoted in the papers. Then she received this letter :

> I read with interest of your struggles with life in East Vancouver. I also notice that you are 28 years old with five children, one only four months old. Where is the children's father? Why do you keep having children? What do you have to offer these children except poverty and despair? Get wise and have your tubes tied. No more children please. I feel very sorry for the children you are bringing into such a life.

The letter was signed, "A Taxpayer." *Poor-bashing and racism mean being the subject of ignorant hate messages from people you don't know who accuse you of being every stereotype they ever associated with poverty and people of colour.*

While Wells read the letter to me in the parent room of the school at lunch time, her chubby baby was smiling and showing off her two new teeth, as a cousin who attended the school played lovingly and carefully with her.

Poor-bashing and racism stop curiosity. Taxpayer didn't try to communicate with Wells. He or she didn't leave an address for a reply. Poor-bashing stops communication. Taxpayer figured he or she knew what Wells's life was like without having to ask.

Wells wrote a reply even though she couldn't send it because Taxpayer didn't leave a name or return address:

Dear Taxpayer,

I've read your letter with a lot of heart and emotion. I would like to invite you to MacDonald Elementary school to see all our beautiful, wonderful and talented children besides mine. My dream was to have five wonderful children of my own. I take special care of them. My children have a very caring, loving father who cares for all of us, loves us as a family, cooks and cleans house while my three oldest and I are at school. Don't judge me on how many children I have. It's how much patience I give to my children and all children at the school.

I'm well known at this school as a loving parent. I have a lot to offer my children and other students. I never leave my children's side. If they're at school, then I'm at the school. I teach a number of different courses at the school: beading, painting, mask making, card design and other arts and crafts classes for students. This is unpaid volunteer time that I willingly donate to society.

My dream is to be a pre-school teacher. To be honest, I want more than that but there is only one of me. I have a lot of responsibility, which means my whole life goes out to my children and other working people's children too. How much volunteer time do you give back to the community? Do you spend time at your child's school? How much quality time do you spend as a family?

I don't judge you on only having two children, not having the guts to sign your letter, or making a lot of assumptions and accusations about my life when you don't even know me. Do you feel insulted by me asking you these judgmental questions?

Yes, I would like to have a job. That's why I'm doing upgrading classes. Once I go home and help cook, clean, take care of our children, I spend hours working on classes and helping my husband with his school work. Yes, I realize how hard life is. I've been around for the last 28 years. I wish my parents were there for me like I'm there for my children.

I never want you to feel sorry for my children. They're happy and healthy. My children are a gift that I'm thankful to the creator for every day of my life. I hope you are happy with yours.

Wells signed her letter, "a quality parent and volunteer worker."

Poor-bashing children

It's very hard to get children to talk about being on welfare because they know they will be poor-bashed. In twenty-six years there have been many times that anti-poverty groups I worked with wanted to set up panels of poor high school students to tell forums what it was like. Only twice did we succeed even partially. Once was with the son of a fellow activist; the other time a teacher asked his students to be on the panel and the middle-class students were extremely supportive of the one panel member who was on welfare. At the forum, she "exposed" herself for the first time. It took tremendous courage. So the only young people I was able to interview for this book were ones I already knew, whose parents were active in anti-poverty work.

Mila was fifteen and Mikey thirteen when I talked to them. Their single-parent family had lived on welfare for years but is now off, thanks to co-op housing, a shrinking family (two children have grown and moved out), and a mother's determination to get off welfare. Debbie Ellison and her children sat with me at their kitchen table.

Debbie and Mila recited the stereotypes about people on welfare they had heard so many times. "Drunks, lazy, all Natives, bad parents, unmotivated, uneducated," said Debbie.

"They want to be on welfare; they dress like bums," added Mila.

"You have lots of time and money to do whatever you want," chimed in Debbie.

"You don't have electricity or a phone; you have to drink powdered milk," said Mila. "They say our school's on welfare cause it serves powdered milk."

"People don't talk about being on welfare," explained Mila. "If they asked me, I'd probably lie cause they'd make fun of me and I wouldn't want sympathy from other people. Friends think it's like harsh bums on Hastings Street."

Mikey didn't say much as his mother and sister talked. He did say that jobs ought to pay enough to live on. Near the end, he said, "I don't know anything about [welfare]. It was just you guys. I told my friends I wasn't poor. I put all the poor stuff in [Debbie's] room." *Poor-bashing means children living a lie.*

Denial was a tactic that Donia Naffaa used as well. Naffaa was a twenty-year-old mother of an "awesome" seven-month-old son when I talked to her about her childhood in Vancouver. She told me that she simply denied being on welfare. "I've always been in denial. I've always had a story to back me up. I never told my friends I was on welfare. I never admitted it. I always said my mom was an English teacher and my dad was a vet, which was all a crock. My dad studied to be a vet.

"I denied it because I didn't want to be poor-bashed," she said directly. "Kids get pushed around, called names, bums, welfare.

"Poor-bashing is worse now," Naffaa continued, "because the expectations to fit in now are much higher. I couldn't keep up with the other kids' style; everything's appearance. Nothing else matters. You get different treatment if you're on welfare. They make you wait, you're not the first on their list. The attitude just changes."

Sometimes people who are poor question the poor-bashing they experience: "We don't even know what's going on and we're always checking, are we crazy, am I making this up, is this real, am I a whiner?" explained activist Jean Trickey. But poor-bashing is real.

To me, the remarkable thing about poor-bashing is not that it seeps into so many aspects of daily life from so many levels, but that so many people who are poor do survive, don't commit suicide, are fierce in their dignity, and see a place for themselves helping others survive and challenging an unfair system.

Chapter 2

History: Making the rich better than the poor

It seems to be a law of nature that the poor should ... fulfil the most servile, the most sordid, and the most ignoble offices in the community. The stock of human happiness is thereby much increased, whilst the more delicate are not only relieved from drudgery, and freed from those occasional employments which would make them miserable, but are left at liberty ... to pursue those callings which are suited to their various dispositions.

Rev. Joseph Townsend, 1785

[The relief recipient's] situation on the whole shall not be made really or apparently so eligible [desirable] as the situation of the independent labourer of the lowest class.

English Poor Law Commissioners, 1834

In 1529 the French city of Lyons was a lively international centre with a growing population of over forty thousand. It was a rapidly developing trading centre for the European money market, textiles, printing, and metalworking. As Lyons prospered, people came from the countryside and from other parts of Europe to work and live there. But not all was well.

The population of the whole region was increasing because disease was taking a smaller toll than it had in previous centuries and there was a temporary interruption in the killing from wars. The increase meant

many people were looking for work. Wages often dropped below the cost
of living. When harvests were poor, the price of grain would double or
quadruple in a matter of days so working people in the city couldn't
afford bread. The rich in the new trading centre would buy and hoard
grain, waiting to sell it when the prices were high.

In the countryside, bad harvests forced peasants to borrow against
the next year's crop, then fall behind in payments and have to give up
their land to moneylenders. The "destitute peasant, racked with hunger,
would take his family off to town hoping to sell surviving livestock and
to scratch a living from charitable doles, casual labour or begging," writes
Janine Garrisson in her book on sixteenth-century France.

There were many years of bad harvests and famine in that century.
In 1529 the starving people of Lyons took over the city, forcing the
wealthy to flee to a monastery for their own protection. They looted the
homes of the rich and sold the grain from a public and a church granary.
In 1530 the poorer people of Lyons armed themselves and marched
through the town, and in 1531 starving peasants from the countryside
overran the town again.

The riots "shook the Lyons elite to the core," says Garrisson. They
responded to the chaos and to their fears by creating a welfare system.
They taxed the well-off to supplement church contributions for the poor.
Every Sunday, food and money were distributed to the needy who were
on an official list.

The system of dealing with poverty in sixteenth-century Lyons,
anticipated many of the elements of Canada's welfare system today. It
was a system designed to keep the poor from looting the rich, not a system to promote any kind of equality. It was a system that ensured that
the poor would still be forced to work cheaply.

The poor people of Lyons were divided into what we now call
"employable" and "unemployable" categories, the "employable" being
healthy adults for whom no regular work exists. The officials in Lyons
ensured that these people would either work for their food or be kicked
out of town; they subsidized employers to take on poor boys as "appren-
tices" and put poor girls to work as servants and silk weavers.

This welfare system judged and stereotyped the poor instead of
looking at the low wages, famines, and high prices that were causing
their poverty. In Lyons it was assumed that people who administered
relief were justified in visiting the homes of the poor, making judgments
about their morality, and ensuring that they didn't spend their dole on
gambling or alcohol. Begging was outlawed.

Medieval ideas about poor people

In the Middle Ages, before the sixteenth-century and the revolts in Lyons, people had assumed that both rich and poor owed their positions to the grace of God, not their own individual efforts. "If anything, the poor were thought to be morally superior to the rich. Monks, nobles, and wealthy people would wash the feet of paupers and invite them to dine," writes F. Allan Hanson. Poor people "represented a Christ-like way of life." This doesn't mean that the medieval poor had an easy time. It was a hard life that included forced labour. But, according to Max Weber, who wrote a famous book on the connection between Protestantism and capitalism, begging was tolerated and even "glorified" because it gave the wealthy a chance to give alms and thus increase their chances of getting into heaven. Almsgiving was a religious duty, as important as prayer or fasting, wrote Beatrice and Sidney Webb. They quote Clement of Alexandria, who said the givers weren't supposed to judge the receivers because it might cause them to neglect "some who are the friends of God."

In medieval times, usury and greed were sins. Moneylending for interest was illegal in some parts of Europe, and usurers were denied Christian burials, according to R.H. Tawney.

By the mid-sixteenth century, however, wealth stolen from the colonies started to appear in Europe. Even as business and merchant classes prospered, the thirteen famines between 1520 and 1600 created tremendous hardship and suffering for the poor. Attitudes of the rich towards the poor began to change. "The idea that the poor were in the image of Christ ended when bad harvests, famine, plague, and runaway inflation" created bands of starving people who begged and stole to meet their needs, writes Hanson. The Webbs quote John Calvin, a prominent Protestant theologian of the times, who called beggars "petty brigands." Garrisson says that a whole literature of the "cheating beggar" became common in Europe.

While the medieval poor lived a hard life, they were at least part of a system of work and religion, and helping them was a religious duty. By the mid-sixteenth cetury, however, begging had become illegal in many places.

Witch hunts as poor-bashing

As the new capitalist economic system developed with its confusion and inequalities, accusations of witchcraft, torture, and killings were also increasing. About a hundred thousand women were killed between 1560 and 1760. About 80 per cent of the people accused of witchcraft were women, and often they were "the poorest of the poor, dependent on [their] neighbours to stave off starvation," according to Anne Llewellyn Barstow.

Barstow explains that women fell into poverty because they had supported themselves from their gardens and dairies, which were being lost to wealthier landowners. Men in these circumstances could sometimes get waged work, but women couldn't compete with men for paid jobs. This, she says, accounted for an increase in women beggars who were often accused of witchcraft. The torture and killing of so-called witches were undoubtedly a form of sexism. Barstow's book opens up the possibility that the sexism was also mixed with poor-bashing.

Martin Luther's contribution to attitudes about poor people*

In 1523 the German religious reformer Martin Luther developed a plan for aiding the poor in Saxony. His plan forbade begging and set up a "common chest" for the elderly, the weak, and people who had worked hard but still didn't have the means to survive. The able-bodied poor for whom there was no work were forced to seek whatever employment they could find at whatever low wages or terrible working conditions. Their only alternative was starvation.

Martin Luther's plan to help the poor was an expression of the newly developing Protestant ethic that is still embedded in the way many Canadians think nearly five hundred years later, even though they may not be Protestant or religious at all. Luther was angry at the Roman Catholic Church for its corruption. In a way he was sticking up for the poor. He didn't think priests should tell the rich they could buy their way to heaven by giving money to the Church, but taught that all people should work hard, as the poor did, and wait to see what God would do with them when they died.

Luther developed the idea of a calling as the highest form of moral activity and the only way to live acceptably to God. Every legitimate calling, or occupation, from manure movers to milkmaids to writers and teachers, had equal value to God, said Luther. Begging was not a legitimate calling, though. Luther thought it should be abolished. People who

---

* My sources for the section on Luther are Bainton, Piven and Coward, and Weber.

couldn't support themselves because they were old or sick should be supported by the community. The rest should work, he said. He just assumed that jobs were available.

While Luther did not approve of high interest rates or greed, his theories lent support to the idea that begging or the poverty that drives people to beg was a sin of the individual; an idea that just happened to benefit the owners in the changing economy, people who wanted hardworking, disciplined, industrious workers.

Racism in the sixteenth century

While Europeans who were prosperous in the sixteenth century were beginning to stereotype and poor-bash the unemployed of their own countries, they also reached out on a grander scale to stereotype and dehumanize the people of other continents. As they changed their ideas about the poor, seeing them as more and more inferior, they were also creating ways to portray themselves as better than the poor and working people.

Robert Miles argues that the model for racism began in Europe as discrimination against the poor. At first feudal rulers changed their behaviour; they made their bodily functions more private, for example. They did this to "contrast the refinement of their behaviour with that of the 'inferior' people whom they ruled." Miles says that people in the business and industrial classes imitated this so-called "civilized" behaviour and began to assert that their polite values had been inherited, rather than built up by social custom. The purpose of this "civilization project" was to construct and justify a social system in which some had more power than others.

In Spain, the most powerful European country of the time, the missonary and historian Bartolomé de Las Casas persuaded the king to reconsider expeditions to the so-called New World until moral issues about the rights of its inhabitants could be resolved. A debate on this topic took place in 1550 at the University of Valladolid. Thomas Berger relates that Las Casas argued that the Europeans had no right to enslave the Indians, that the peoples of the Americas had a right to live. But Juan de Sepúlveda said Aboriginal people "require, by their own nature and in their own interests, to be placed under the authority of civilized and virtuous princes and nations so that they may learn from the might, wisdom, and law of their conquerors to practice better morals, worthier customs and a more civilized way of life."

As Sepúlveda's words indicate privileged Europeans convinced themselves that they were better than the people they ruled. Miles says that colonial racism like this can't be explained without understanding "domestic racisms" within Europe. Although his book doesn't mention the witch hunts or use the phrase poor-bashing, it seems to me that these could be two examples of "domestic racisms." Such racism was not an abnormality of the sixteenth century, but deeply ingrained in how people thought.

While the European poor-bashing of that century was justifying laws that enforced low-wage work, Sepúlveda's denial of the humanity of indigenous people helped to justify theft of land in the new colonies and the slavery and murder of tens of millions of people there.

Puritan thinkers

By the mid-seventeenth century, Martin Luther's ideas about work, wealth, and morality were being modified by Puritan thinkers in Europe and North America. Weber says the Puritans developed Luther's idea of a "calling" to mean that if God gave someone the opportunity to profit, a pious person had to take advantage of that opportunity. If you became wealthy by continuous work in your calling, you were favoured by God, they thought. John Calvin, according to the Webbs, often quoted St. Paul, who said, "If any would not work, neither should he eat."

Richard Baxter, an influential English writer on Puritan ethics, reinforced ideas from the previous century that "begging on the part of one able to work is not only the sin of slothfulness, but a violation of the duty of brotherly love." Poverty, he said, was a "symptom of sinful slothfulness."

As Protestantism spread in England and North America, the doctrine that work as a discipline could help people reach a high moral and spiritual state took hold more firmly with refinements that made the great wealth and poverty produced by capitalism seem acceptable. According to Weber, the writing of almost all Protestant denominations is "saturated with the idea that faithful labour, even at low wages, on the part of those whom life offers no other opportunities, is highly pleasing to God."

Weber concludes that the Puritan values of the seventeenth and eighteenth centuries helped turn workers and employers into their own slave drivers. Work in any calling was seen as a means of being acceptable to God. Employers who accumulated wealth were also thought to be working in their calling and favoured by God. Although the Puritans didn't approve of spending money on personal luxury, they did think it was acceptable, even morally required, to accumulate wealth if you were given the opportunity.

Even though there probably aren't too many Canadians nowadays who would say that people should have a paid job to please God, the idea remains that work is virtuous and that rich people deserve their wealth. People who receive welfare or unemployment insurance, even when no decent jobs are available, are seen as non-workers, scroungers, or undeserving and are often despised because of it. What Weber wrote in 1904 is just as true nearly a hundred years later: "The idea of duty in one's calling prowls about in our lives like the ghost of dead religious beliefs."

The English Poor Laws

The English Poor Laws of the eighteenth and nineteenth centuries became the inheritance of the men who made policy about people who are poor in what is now Canada. These laws, like those in Europe, grew out of the economic and religious turmoil of the sixteenth and seventeenth centuries mixed with the self-interest of the ruling elite. By 1598 English parishes were supposed to provide almshouses for people who were old and sick, workhouses or work materials for the able-bodied poor, houses of correction or jail for the able-bodied who refused work, and apprenticeships for children of the poor. But often, as the parish tried to cut costs, all these people were thrown together in poorhouses, "one of the most depressing institutions ever devised by man," according to Dennis Guest. And while "apprenticeships" were supposed to train pauper children in the virtues of discipline and regular work habits, they were often "thinly disguised slavery" in cotton mills and mines, and as chimney sweeps.

Beatrice and Sidney Webb quote a Middlesex judge who ordered, "every person committed [to a house of correction] shall be set to labour, and have no other nurture than he or she shall get with their labour," unless they were sick. The Webbs give an example from 1615 of a man branded with an R on the shoulder (for "rogue incorrigible") and sent to a House of Correction, and another in 1616 who was committed to be flogged and detained until the illegitimate child he fathered died. That punishment may not have been as harsh as it appears: conditions in the workhouses were so horrible that a House of Commons study found that only seven of a hundred infants born or taken into workhouses in 1767 survived for even two years.

How enclosures created poverty

By 1750 a growing English population and more manufacturing increased demand for food for the urban population and wool for the cloth manufacturers. New methods of agriculture made big farms more efficient than smaller ones. By the end of the century most people were landless. They subsisted by hiring out to larger farmers and using common land for firewood, grazing, and hunting to supplement their wages. The government passed laws (Bills of Enclosure) privatizing the common land, depriving many people of their livelihood but enriching the big landowners. Employers changed how they used labourers, according to E.P. Thompson; instead of taking them on year round, they would, in keeping with the new market system (much like the new market system of today), hire them for the part of the year when they were most needed and lay them off for the rest. Thousands of people were turned off the land and away from the farm work they needed. Hungry people rioted for bread and food in almost every town and county from the late part of the century until about 1840. In short, the poverty of the period had little or nothing to do with individual morality, or willingness to work.

How the privileged blamed the poor for poverty

But that isn't the way everyone saw the situation. By the late eighteenth century, the privileged English had gone beyond simply seeing themselves as different from the poor. In 1785, for example, the Rev. Joseph Townsend wrote a popular pamphlet (quoted by the Webbs) on the English Poor Laws claiming:

> It is a law of nature that the poor should be to a certain degree improvident, that there may always be some to fulfil the most servile, the most sordid, and the most ignoble offices in the community. The stock of human happiness is thereby much increased, whilst the more delicate are not only relieved from drudgery, and freed from those occasional employments which would make them miserable, but are left at liberty ... to pursue those callings which are suited to their various dispositions.

Miles shows how the use of words like "breeding" suggested that what was seen as the superiority of the rich and the inferiority of the poor resulted from biology, not from circumstances. One definition of "breeding" is "civility, culture, good manners, refinement." Another is "biological reproduction." Such language made it hard to talk about manners and refinement without assuming they were biologically inherited traits, that the poor were somehow less than human.

Thompson observed of the same period that "most men and women of property felt the necessity for putting the houses of the poor in order." More police, Bible tracts and Sunday schools, and the Society for the Suppression of Vice and Encouragement of Religion (for the poor) were ways that the rich sought to "help" the poor. The Webbs show that some were more interested in punishing the poor than helping them. Philosopher John Locke wrote that all able-bodied men between the ages of fourteen and fifty who were caught begging should be put on ships for three years under strict discipline. If they were over fifty or disabled, they should be put in houses of correction and "subjected as slaves to a Master" while paying for their own keep. Boys and girls under fourteen who begged should be "soundly whipped," Locke added.

Thomas Malthus, famous for his book on the need to limit population, sounds very much like a combination of a seventeenth century Puritan and a 1990s corporate think-tank author with his claim in 1798 that people who had employment were "industrious" and "more worthy" than those who didn't. "Dependent poverty ought to be held disgraceful," he asserted. "The labouring poor," continued Malthus, with an early version of the modern prejudice that people who are poor cannot "delay gratification," "seem always to live from hand to mouth. Their present wants employ their whole attention, and they seldom think of the future.... All that is beyond their present necessities goes, generally speaking, to the ale-house."

If the poor were portrayed as drunkards, spendthrifts, lazy, promiscuous, and insufficiently religious, even subhuman, then it was easier to believe that they deserved the conditions awaiting them in English factories and poorhouses.

How the Poor Laws cheapened labour

In 1782 a new Poor Law ordered local officials to find jobs for the able-bodied or give them relief in their own homes. In other words, the poor didn't have to go to the hated poorhouse to get help. This was called out-door relief and was much preferred by paupers. But even this improved way of helping the poor was designed mainly to help employers. It was prompted, the Webbs say, by the "double panic of famine and rebellion" and turned into a regular system of relief that subsidized low wages. It was assumed that employers had no responsibility to raise wages to livable levels.

Piven and Cloward note that, in 1795, Poor Law officials in parts of England began supplementing the wages of farm workers, based on family size and the price of bread, if wages fell below a certain scale. This was called the Speenhamland Plan. By 1834, writes Thompson, the biggest part of the local labour bill was being paid by taxes intended to support the poor. Employers with workers who were not subsidized by the poor rates would fire them and apply for workers who were on the dole. Workers said that the farmers "keep us here [on the poor rates] like potatoes in a pit, and only take us out for use when they can no longer do without us."

The Speenhamland Plan was the origin of various proposals of today, such as the Negative Income Tax (NIT) and the corporate version of the Guaranteed Annual Income (GAI) (more on this later). In one way the plan "guaranteed the right to life," but, by helping to keep wages low, it also guaranteed poverty for workers who received it and those who had to compete with them. This system of using poorhouse workers for seasonal labour benefited the larger farmers by keeping a batch of desperate people that they could call on whenever they needed them without having to pay wages in off-seasons. "It had a single tendency: to destroy the last vestige of control by the labourer over his own wage or working life," observed Thompson. The Speenhamland Plan happened at a time of excess labour supply, like the 1990s in Canada, yet it still forced people to work for their benefits. The use of people from poorhouses helped to stave off union organizing in the mills. Piven and Cloward note that laws preventing unions were passed at the same time, further undermining workers' ability to earn a life-sustaining wage.

By the early nineteenth century, they note, children were being ordered from the poorhouses and shipped to remote textile factories that used water power from streams. The children would usually have to work until they were twenty-one years old, if they lived that long, in terrible conditions; thirteen hours a day was one of the more humane work days of the time.

Thompson writes about labour markets in Manchester and Leeds where poorhouse officials would almost auction off families to mill owners. The officials would list the characteristics of the family, such as age of children, moral character, and health, "like stock for sale."

By 1832 the number of poor people as well as the taxes that paid for their relief was soaring. The rich didn't want to pay the taxes but they also didn't want any big rebellions of the poor. So they set up a Royal Commission to report on the Poor Laws. Nicholas Edsall describes how the commissioners travelled around the country investigating the operation of the old poorhouses and laws. They examined reports from poorhouse officials and various citizens (not the poor, of course) from all over England and Wales.

The Royal Commission tackled the problem from the perspective of the well-off; could a country have a system of poor relief that didn't give workers any extra bargaining power? The commissioners decided that this was possible if the amount of relief was lower than the lowest wages and if able-bodied people were forced to work in a degrading workhouse. They abolished outdoor relief and built over six hundred new workhouses, writes Ben Carniol. The new Poor Laws and their prison-like workhouses embodied Puritan beliefs about discipline, work, and poverty.

Piven and Cloward quote the Poor Law Commissioners as they described the purpose of their new workhouses in 1834:

> Into such a house none will enter voluntarily; work, confinement, and discipline, will deter the indolent and vicious; and nothing but extreme necessity will induce any to accept the comfort which must be obtained by the surrender of their free agency, and the sacrifice of their accustomed habits and gratifications.

This statement contains the stereotypes we still hear about people who are poor being lazy, even "vicious," and prone to fraud. And it has the gall to assert that the poorhouses "abundantly relieved" people in need, just as today's corporate think-tanks claim that welfare is "generous."

Conditions were so horrible, and the people in the poorhouses so despised, whether "deserving" or "undeserving," that people would take any work at any wage to avoid having to go there or send their family there. "The workhouse was designed to spur men to contrive ways of supporting themselves by their own industry, *to offer themselves to any employer on any terms. It did this by making pariahs of those who could not support themselves,"* explain Piven and Cloward (emphasis in original). In 1837 British Prime Minister Benjamin Disraeli said that the change to a workhouse system "announces to the world that in England poverty is a crime."

Attitudes about the poor had changed quite a bit since the Middle Ages, when the poor were seen as close to God. The Puritans had treated the poor as sinful, and by the time of the new Poor Laws in 1835, the poor were treated as criminals, the political equivalent of sinners.

By the late eighteenth century, relief officials began to openly state an important principle, which they had already been implementing: relief should never amount to more than what the lowest-paid worker could earn—even if that was not enough to support a healthy person. Piven and Cloward quote the 1834 English poor law commissioners' announcement of this principle: "The first and most essential of all conditions, a principle which we find universally admitted, ... is that [the relief recipient's] situation on the whole shall not be made really or apparently so eligible [desirable] as the situation of the independent labourer of the lowest class." In Britain this was called "The Principle of Less Eligibility." The commissioners did *not* say, "The first and most essential of all conditions, a principle which we find universally admitted, is that the relief recipient should be given enough to maintain a decent standard of living." For nearly five centuries, governing and business elites have realized that if this humanitarian principle took precedence over their desire for cheap labour, workers would have more power to demand life-sustaining wages.

The Principle of Less Eligibility is often accompanied by another unstated rule: that the wages of the lowest-paid workers, even when they are too low to provide a reasonable living standard, cannot or should not be increased. Workers must be forced to do with less, and the unemployed with even less than that.

According to Piven and Cloward, the English Poor Laws of the nineteenth century, like the new Canadian poor laws of today, "reinforced the coercive structure of labour law and to some extent came to replace it." The English Parliament forbade any efforts to regulate the supply of labour in 1543; in 1563 it required the unemployed to work for any who wanted them and gave justices of the peace the authority to fix *maximum* wages and to penalize any employer who paid more than the maximum.

Because of this, workers in the sixteenth and seventeenth centuries "could not organize, they could not refuse work, they could not exploit labour shortages to demand higher wages, and they could not move to new localities to find better working conditions." The Poor Laws, with their requirements that paupers be county residents and do any kind of paid work, and with their horrible poorhouses, served the same purpose.

It wasn't enough that the English poorhouses were actually sources of cheap labour for the manufacturing businesses of the time. It wasn't enough that poor-bashing and terrible living conditions made the poorhouses a symbol of degradation that kept the English working poor straining at hard labour for low wages. The British ruling class wanted still more cheap labour and searched beyond their borders, expanding their "internal racism" against the poor in their own country to "external racism" against Aboriginal people and people of colour living on other continents. David Korten quotes the famous British colonizer Cecil Rhodes, known as the "founder" of Rhodesia (now Zimbabwe), who said, "We must find new lands from which we can easily obtain raw materials and at the same time exploit the cheap slave labour that is available from the natives of the colonies."

The poor fight back

The poor of the British Isles fought back continuously through the late eighteenth century to about 1840, trying to get enough to eat and a decent living standard. There were bread and food "riots" in nearly every town and county. Thompson says that these were "popularly regarded as acts of justice and their leaders held as heroes." What the police called riots were often disciplined and purposeful actions by working people demanding prices they could afford. In James Town, Ireland, for example, businessmen had bought up all the corn in the area and loaded it on a Dutch ship. The so-called mob took the corn off the ship, brought it to the market, and sold it for the owners at the common price.

The Luddites were skilled workers in the English wool industry who staged their own rebellion during the years between 1811 and 1816. New machines like power looms were taking their jobs. They wanted government to regulate industrial growth to meet human need. They wanted a minimum wage, better working conditions, and the right to organize unions. Sandy Cameron writes that there was no legal means of protest, not even voting for the working class, so the Luddites destroyed machinery that was used in places where wages had been reduced. While the Luddites' struggle was crushed, the vision of their movement lived on in the fight for a ten-hour day and for people who didn't own property to be able to vote.

A movement against the Poor Laws of 1835 spread turmoil, especially to the northern part of England in 1837-38. Assaults on assistant Poor Law commissioners, attacks on workhouses, and blockades of guardians' board rooms prompted action by local police and the military. The movement involved paupers, handloom weavers, factory hands, agricultural labourers, overseers, and ratepayers.

While the well-off were using poor-bashing and racism to justify brutal treatment of the poor, low wages, slavery, and the theft of entire continents, they understood that the poor did have a use. The Webbs report that, in 1806, police reformer Dr. Patrick Colquhoun wrote, "[Poverty] is the source of wealth, since without poverty there could be no labour; there could be no riches, no refinement, no comfort, and no benefit to those who may be possessed of wealth." Reflecting the thinking of his class, Colquhoun explained, "Poverty is therefore a most necessary and indispensable ingredient in a society, without which nations and communities could not exist in a state of civilisation."

The people of property were secure in their belief that they were a superior "race" and that the poor in England, as well as the indigenous peoples of other continents, were somehow less human and deserved their poverty. For them, low wages for the poor, slavery, and colonization became legitimate, even preferred, elements in the continuing quest for accumulation of wealth.

Chapter 3

History: Keeping the myth alive

Mary Dowding 514 King St. E and husband. No children. says can't get work. fancy they don't want it. no reason why they should be in want. Recommend a little starvation until self help engendered, probably drink.

Volunteer visitor's note, Toronto, 1882

Recognition of the inherent dignity and of the equal and inalienable rights of all members of the human family is the foundation of freedom, justice and peace in the world.

United Nations Declaration of Human Rights, 1948

[The poor] are the losers in the race for material sufficiency.

Senate report on poverty, 1971

By the mid-eighteenth century, a way of thinking that categorized people as inferior and superior according to their wealth or "race," as well as other attributes, was firmly entrenched in the British colonies that were to become Canada. The class structure of the immigrant society echoed that of their countries of origin, according to John Porter: "Within the cities and larger towns the upper class English as officials, administrators, professionals, and clergy attempted to reconstruct an aristocratic way of life, while the bottom layer was made up of large numbers of destitute immigrants from the factory cities."

The Protestant religion contributed to judgmental, victim-blaming ideas about people who were poor by defining poverty as a moral problem caused by a sinful life, not by economic and social conditions. As well, many newcomers believed that Canada was a land of opportunity and all who were willing to work could succeed. These attitudes merged with the individualism of the new occupiers, who were often isolated on small farms and dependent on their own labour to get crops planted and harvested and to acquire the necessities of life.

For the first 150 years of occupation, roughly from 1600 to 1750, the European population was relatively small and the primary economic activity was fur trading. European and Aboriginal people "believed themselves to be benefiting from an exchange which allowed both cultures to better meet their own needs," according to Aboriginal activist and author George Manuel. During this period, "The governors of the European settlements, whenever ... a misunderstanding arose, considered it to be in their interest to ensure a conciliation rather than to fan the flames of hate."

By 1749, however, white people were fanning the flames of hate against Aboriginals. A British-government-appointed governor of Newfoundland, for example, called on the colonists to "annoy, distress, take or destroy the Savages ... wherever they are found," which is pretty much what happened, according to Douglas Francis and his co-authors. The Beothuk people of Newfoundland were wiped out by disease, murder, and starvation.

While poor white people were thought to be deficient in morals and discipline, Aboriginal people weren't even considered to be human by the time John A. Macdonald became Canada's first prime minister. Manuel notes that Macdonald's Indian Act defined a person as "any individual other than an Indian."

Earlier, in 1779, United Empire Loyalists who came north from the new United States were promised land and provisions by the British government. It turned out that Black Loyalists got either nothing, or inferior land in smaller parcels than white Loyalists. Conditions were so harsh, according to Francis, that many Blacks moved to Sierra Leone after a few years.

During the late eighteenth century, Nova Scotia and New Brunswick passed their versions of the English Poor Laws, and some villages actually had auctions where they sold paupers to the lowest bidders. While the law stated that the paupers who were sold shouldn't be treated inhumanely, the rule wasn't enforced. Hundreds of paupers were auctioned in just one county in the hundred years of pauper auctions. Sometimes the sickest people fetched the highest bids because buyers kept their money if the pauper died—a system designed to promote neglect for profit. Children were auctioned off for cheap labour. Women were auctioned to buyers who used them for sex.

Dennis Guest writes that at the same time in Quebec the Catholic Church provided help to the poor, and there was a system of licensed begging in Montreal and Quebec. The three largest Quebec towns had a Bureau of the Poor for relief and jobs.

As the poor from Europe arrived in Canada, various institutions were set up to try to meet some of their needs while at the same time blaming them for their poverty. In 1828 a public welfare agency in York (later renamed Toronto) changed its name from the Society for the Relief of Strangers to the Society for the Relief of the Sick and Destitute. Francis notes that this shift reflected more closely the attitude of the time that only the sick and destitute should get help, not unemployed people who were supposed to work. Ben Carniol writes that Lieutenant-Governor Sir Francis Bond Head introduced English-style workhouses to Upper Canada in 1830, saying, "Workhouses should be made repulsive ... if any would not work for relief, neither should he eat." In one workhouse, "Whipping, shackling, starvation, and other necessary inducements were used to correct the behaviour of the idle, vagrant, or incorrigible inmates." In places with no alms or workhouses, the homeless and people with mental disorders were put in jail.

Richard Allen's book says the social gospel movement in the 1880s and 1890s was beginning to suggest that poverty was not caused by individuals. In an 1884 book, *The Gospel to the Poor*, B.F. Austin argued that churches should challenge the system that causes poverty and abolish pew rents so the poor could attend church. But the old view that some are better than others continued. As immigration increased, the Methodist, Presbyterian, and Baptist churches saw themselves as national churches working to "teach all these babbling tongues of the earth the language of the Anglo-Saxon race, and bring them into line with the march of our Christian civilization."

Canadian cities doubled and tripled their populations between 1900 and 1910 as more factories were built. Private charities also multiplied. Montreal, for example, had fifteen houses of refuge, thirteen outdoor relief agencies, fourteen old-age homes, eleven orphanages, and eighteen "moral" and educational institutions as well as other charitable agencies. Carniol writes that upper-class Canadians imported the Charity Organization Society model from England to Toronto. The COS motto was "not alms, but a friend." They carried this out by sending middle-class and wealthy people to visit the poor and check out their morals, but not to relieve their poverty. The COS stated in 1901 that "the welfare of souls and characters is of more concern than freedom from physical suffering." Not only was the COS perpetuating poor-bashing myths about morals and work habits, but it was also assuming that its middle- and upper-class volunteers had the right to make judgments about the "souls and characters" of the poor. Of course the "souls and characters" of the rich who had so much while others suffered in poverty were not questioned.

In 1896 Herbert Ames, a Montreal manufacturer with a social conscience, did a house-to-house survey of low-income people in Montreal and came to what was then (and is now) a revolutionary conclusion: "Want of employment was believed to be the cause of distress in as many cases as sickness, intemperance, and shiftlessness combined." Guest notes that Ames was one of the first to suggest reforms like winter works programs at minimum wages, higher housing standards, better public sanitation, and the building of low-rent housing.

While some people were beginning to understand that individual poor people didn't create poverty, most people's attitudes were still based on stereotypes from the old Protestant religion and English Poor Laws. Guest says that until 1914, most help to the poor was provided by charities or municipalities in the form of grocery hampers, fuel, or used clothing. The assistance was on an emergency basis and did not continue over time. The givers avoided handing out cash, because, then as now, poor people were seen as being unable to budget.

When relief was provided, the old "principle" that welfare payments couldn't be more than what the lowest-paid worker could earn, while not formally written in Canadian law, was the basis of setting rates of payment. Guest says that in some cases the payments were so low that they threatened the health of the people who received them. In addition, the English workhouse test came to Canada as a work test. In 1915 the House of Industry in Toronto told relief applicants that they had to break 650 pounds of rock a day. If people in need refused to saw wood or break rock for their assistance, they were considered frauds.

In its 1912 poor-bashing report, the Associated Charities of Winnipeg provided a comprehensive list of the usual rubbish about people who were poor:

> Unfortunately, the large majority of applications for relief are caused by thriftlessness, mismanagement, unemployment due to incompetence, intemperance, immorality, desertion of the family and domestic quarrels. In such cases the mere giving of relief tends rather to induce pauperism than to reduce poverty.

But the next year the Industrial Workers of the World, a radical union organizing in British Columbia, was trying to warn its members about poor-bashing. Mark Leier reports that the union's paper, *The Industrial Worker*, wrote that a person who was unemployed was "a worker before he was a tramp. A machine took his job and he left for another city to seek employment. The machine got there first ….The march of the machine is steady. It is even now upon you. Tomorrow you may be a tramp."

In the early twentieth century, more Canadians and people around the world began to realize that individuals were not responsible for their own poverty. Business recessions in the years 1873-79, 1884-87, 1893-96, and 1914-15 revealed that unemployment wasn't caused by laziness. Meanwhile more workers were organizing for jobs and wages. In the Winnipeg General Strike in 1919, thirty-five thousand workers walked off their jobs to demand the right to collective bargaining, an eight-hour day, and a living wage. During a silent protest parade the police attacked strikers and their supporters, and two of the protesters were killed, over thirty injured and over one hundred arrested. News reports, says Ben Swankey, claimed hysterically that Winnipeg was under "red rule" during the strike, and suggested it had become a "soviet republic." The idea that there could be an economic system different from capitalism, with its extremes of wealth and poverty, was sweeping Canada and the world following the Russian Revolution of 1917. For decades afterwards communists were elected to Winnipeg civic government.

The mothers' pension movement

With over sixty thousand people killed in the World War I and about thirty thousand in the flu epidemic, Canada in 1918 had a lot of widows. In addition, the women's movement was strong, and women of European descent had won the right to vote federally in 1918 and provincially between 1916 and 1920 (except for women in Quebec, who got the right to vote provincially in 1940).

The mothers' pension movement has an interesting place in a discussion about poor-bashing. Its supporters wanted a pension for mothers so they could avoid the stigma associated with traditional relief. Guest says they also defined the problem of poverty in a way that took the blame off the individual and put it on social and economic factors.

First Manitoba, then all provinces from Ontario west, passed mothers' pension legislation. In B.C. the pension was for poor mothers of European descent with one or more children under sixteen who were widows or deserted wives, wives of men in jail or asylums, mothers whose husbands were ill, or any other person the superintendent thought should be included. The applicant had to provide two reference letters, an example of the judgmental attitudes of the time, which often disqualified mothers in need.

To avoid stigmatizing mothers, the pension was administered by the workmen's compensation board, not local or charity relief organizations. The mothers' pension also recognized the value of poor women's work in the home, a recognition that was being abandoned by the 1990s. On the other hand, by excluding Aboriginal women, women of non-European backgrounds, and women whose husbands weren't citizens, the pension reinforced, once again, the racist idea that it was acceptable to exclude people because they belonged to a group that was looked down on. The pension drew poor white women and their children into an economic and political system that was excluding other poor women based on their colour, origin, or Aboriginal ancestry.

Even with its exclusions, the pension was too rich for business interests. They pressured the provincial government, which ordered a review by the Canadian Council on Child and Family Welfare, Guest reports. The Council's director, Charlotte Whitton, had a more poor-bashing attitude than the original pension supporters. Writing at the beginning of the Great Depression, which forced so many Canadians into unemployment, she suggested that the mothers' pension was "destructive of personal effort, and self-dependence and so disruptive of the very basis of initiative, enterprise, and strength of character that must be the greatest resource of any people."

Whitton thought that social workers should oversee everyone receiving the "allowance" to ensure that those recipients escape "dependency," using the poor-bashing language that still permeates provincial welfare bureaucracies. This attitude was typical of the growing group of mostly middle-class social workers in the first part of the century—a group Whitton worked to establish firmly in the emerging provincial welfare systems. While many were caring people, and some understood how the economic system caused poverty, most members of the new profession held the poor-bashing view that the poor needed the services of social workers rather than a job at a decent wage or a good pension.

Attitudes towards the poor during the Depression*

The Great Depression hit people who weren't expecting to be poor or to have to endure the humiliation of Poor Law-type relief. About one-quarter of the labour force couldn't find a job and roughly a fifth of the population was on relief, according to the 1938 Canadian Conference on Social Work. In a letter to Prime Minister R.B. Bennett in 1931, P.W.L. Norton of Sherbrooke, Quebec, wrote:

> I've been going and regoing to the City to get work: all I get is We will see what can be done: Our rent is back from Nov. Dec. 1930 and this month God only knows where are going to get it from: I have asked & asked the City to help, and they say its been turned down for some reason other reason they wont tell: Today I went to get 3$ to keep us for a week and Mr Valcourt of the City Office said I couldn't get it because someone said we had a radio: We have never had a radio: He sent Mr. Lesseau from the city Office to search our home from top to bottom bedrooms and bathrooms under and over: Then he says he don't have to give us help if he don't want to: I ask you Sir ... is it for a man to crawl on his hands and knees to get a loaf for his family?

Norton signed the letter "A disheartened Man." At this time, tens of thousands of disheartened, unemployed men roamed the country looking for work. The government set up a sort of Canadian version of the English Houses of Industry: the relief camps for single homeless and unemployed men paid twenty cents a day for eight hours' work, such as building roads or airports or reclaiming land. Workers would get their work clothes, three meals a day, soap, a towel, and a place to sleep. By 1936, when they were closed, over 170,000 men had been taken in by the camps. In 1935, fifteen hundred camp workers went on strike, moved to Vancouver, and, two months later, took a train they hoped would get to Ottawa. They were turned back by police at Regina after three months of continuous publicity, and a lot of public support. The leader of this On

---

* The source for this section is Grayson and Bliss, *The Wretched of the Earth*.

to Ottawa Trek, Slim Evans, was a Communist organizer. According to writer Ronald Liversedge, although Evans said that Communists didn't control the movement, some Canadians had become Communists, hoping that a different economic system, similar to the one they read about in Russia, would provide a better life. The Trekkers organized to fight for relief when they couldn't get work. They demanded jobs, unemployment insurance, and other social programs.

One of the men arrested in Regina was J.S. Woodsworth, leader of the Co-operative Commonwealth Federation (CCF). At the founding meeting of the CCF in 1933, the Regina Manifesto acknowledged the real causes of poverty:

> The present order is marked by glaring inequalities of wealth and opportunity ... and in an age of plenty it condemns the great mass of people to poverty and insecurity. Power has become more and more concentrated into the hands of a small irresponsible minority of financiers and industrialists and to their predatory interests the majority are habitually sacrificed.

The CCF soon became the official opposition in B.C. and Saskatchewan and won seats in Manitoba, Alberta, and Ontario.

By 1931, people of non-French or English origins made up about 20 per cent of the non-Aboriginal population. A letter to Bennett from "a Nanaimoite" shows how some people thought their British origins entitled them to the few jobs that existed during the Depression:

> Before we are much older there is going to be trouble in Nanaimo & Cumberland owing to the foreigners having jobs while the men & boys who are borne British subjects & who rightfully belong to these jobs have to go without jobs, therefore they have to go without sufficient food & clothing, in Cumberland you have Japanese & Chinese working in & about the mines also other foreigners from other countrys who can neither read write or speak English.

The new awareness about the economic and social causes of poverty missed a lot of people in another way, as another Depression letter to R.B. Bennett from New Brunswick shows: "Getting relief has come such a habit that the majority think only of how to get it regularly instead of trying to do without once in a while. Nearly all of them have dogs too which are fed by the country and are of no practical use."

While some people were still blaming the poor for poverty, and many were blaming people from other countries, workers were organizing for jobs and decent wages in relief camps, the CCF was calling for a change to the capitalist system, and public support for the unemployed was high. Business got scared. In 1934, Carniol reports, Sir Charles Gordon, president of the Bank of Montreal, wrote to the prime minister about unemployment insurance: "May I suggest to you that for our general self-preservation some such arrangement will have to be worked out in Canada, and that if it can be done soon so much the better." Bennett agreed that social programs were necessary to "save the fabric of the capitalist system." This time, the elite weren't hiding in a monastery like they had in Lyons some four hundred years earlier, but they were still talking about creating social programs to keep the poor from changing the system that had created so much wealth and poverty.

Charlotte Whitton's poor-bashing continued even during the Depression, according to James Struthers. Prime Minister Bennett asked her to investigate unemployment relief in Western Canada. Whitton reported that loose administration was letting thousands of people with intermittent work "swarm ... into relief on a year-round basis," raising their living standards "beyond anything that they have ever known." To make sure the unemployed took jobs as fast as they appeared, she wanted the federal government to guarantee that work would be "more attractive" than the relief. Whitton's recommendations look very much like welfare rules today. She wanted a "running record of earnings" of those on relief to "facilitate the acceptance of casual employment" through quick cancellation of aid. She also wanted continual "investigation into the circumstances of individual relief recipients."

By 1936 many of Whitton's recommendations were in place. Her poor-bashing ideas about relief were not shared by all social workers, but they did justify a system in which social workers got jobs to control the unemployed and ensure that they took low-wage and casual jobs.

The postwar years

By 1940 Canada had an unemployment insurance system that was a mix of the old poor-bashing principles and a recognition that unemployment was caused by the economic system, not immoral individuals. Benefits were set at about half the earner's previous wage, with a 15 per cent supplement for married people. Guest writes that this was a 1940s version of the old principle that relief payments had to be below what the lowest-paid worker could earn. It was designed to ensure that unemployment insurance didn't keep its recipients from applying for low-paying jobs with poor working conditions. On the other hand, people could appeal if they felt they were unfairly treated. This emphasized that UI was a right to which the unemployed were entitled.

The Second World War ended the Depression. But how would the country provide for the 800,000 returning armed forces personnel and 900,000 people who worked in war production?

In 1943 the federal government appointed Leonard Marsh, who had researched social programs and unemployment at McGill University, to plan for the post-wartime economy. Marsh presented his social security plan to the Canadian House of Commons the same year, introducing a comprehensive set of programs to deal with unemployment, sickness, disabilities, old age, births, deaths, accidents, major illness, the size of a worker's family, and job creation. There seemed to be a recognition at the top levels of government that individuals were not to blame for poverty, and that government action could at least substantially reduce it.

It was a recognition helped along by workers and the CCF, who were getting stronger. During the war years, CCF membership grew from 20,000 in 1942 to 100,000 in 1944; union membership doubled to 700,000.

The business class wasn't unanimous on the desirability of social programs. Some feared that Canadians were so determined to have decent jobs and wages that they might experiment with socialism or communism, and agreed to some social security to ward off the more radical threat. Guest says others joined the chorus of those who equated social programs with "totalitarian" governments. Maude Barlow and Bruce Campbell recount that the practical Liberal prime minister Mackenzie King, fearing that he would lose votes to the CCF, campaigned on the theme of "building a new social order" and promised jobs, homes, better labour conditions, collective bargaining rights, guaranteed farm prices, social security, veterans' benefits and family allowances.

While the Marsh report was not adopted, it had some influence and by 1945 Canada had a family allowance for children. Because the family allowance was a universal program, poor people could receive it without being stigmatized or bashed.

For a while, in the period between 1945 and the early 1970s, the idea that some groups of people were better than others was restrained by a more democratic view. A new consciousness about poverty and the atrocities that some humans could inflict on others had come out of the experiences of World War II and the Depression. And the presence of a Communist government in the world, while it was being condemned in the capitalist world, kept alive the idea that there was a different way to organize economies and thinking, and kept up pressure on capitalist governments to at least pretend to care for people who were poor.

The new way of thinking was reflected in the United Nations Declaration of Universal Human Rights signed in 1948 by most countries of the world, including Canada. At last people of all colours, genders, and classes were being officially recognized, on paper at least, as equal human beings. Its Preamble said, "Recognition of the inherent dignity and of the equal and inalienable rights of all members of the human family is the foundation of freedom, justice and peace in the world." Article 25 of the Declaration said:

> Everyone has the right to a standard of living adequate for the health and well-being of himself and of his family, including food, clothing, housing, and medical care and necessary social services, and the right to security in the event of unemployment, sickness, disability, widowhood, old age or other lack of livelihood in circumstances beyond his control.

Everyone was supposed to be entitled to all the rights and freedoms in the Declaration, regardless of any distinctions like "race, colour, sex, language, religion, political or other opinion, national or social origin, property, birth or other status."

But there was no way to enforce the Universal Declaration. And while poverty issues had a low profile in the 1950s, the big companies were keeping the poor-bashing myths alive. "Within relatively few years, welfarism has changed our ideas of how to get ahead in life. In place of hard work and the seeking of opportunity we now look for security and leisure without wanting to earn them," wrote P.M. Fox, president of the St. Lawrence Corporation at its annual meeting in 1959 (quoted by Porter). It's unlikely that Fox had the rich in mind when he spoke about not *wanting to earn* leisure or security. The editors at *The Globe and Mail* liked Fox's speech so much they reprinted it. John Porter says that the Chambers of Commerce and Canadian Manufacturers' Association had an "intense passion of ideology" that they stated often. "All measures toward welfarism are seen as the road to ruin," a former Chamber of Commerce president told a 1960 conference in Edmonton as he urged member groups "to study the impact, both economically and morally, of the extension of welfare benefits so that ... socialism cannot take over from free enterprise." In 1960, twelve years after the Universal Declaration, the rich were still claiming that poverty was a moral problem of the poor, not of society as a whole.

While business was keeping the morals of the poor in public debate, Canadians still elected politicians who brought in more social programs. Between 1944 and 1970 the family allowance, a better old-age pension system, expanded unemployment insurance, health care, and a national welfare program were put in place.

The 1960s and 1970s

The later part of the 1960s, say Barlow and Campbell, was a time when advocacy groups for tenants, the poor, seniors, Aboriginal people, consumers, and other groups sprang up everywhere. Government encouraged these groups to some extent with funding through various programs designed to create jobs for the young and the unemployed. By the 1960s and 1970s even the most privileged had discovered that about one in five Canadians was living in poverty. And people were finally noticing that poverty for women, people with disabilities, and Aboriginal people was much worse.

In 1966 The Canada Assistance Plan (CAP) made welfare a right for people in need, but didn't include an effective way of making provinces enforce its regulations. CAP was the federal government's recognition of the basic human right to an adequate standard of living, but the lack of enforcement allowed poor-blaming to infiltrate the provincial welfare bureaucracies that implemented welfare programs. (More on CAP in Chapter 7.)

So much attention was paid to poverty that the government gave the Senate a million dollars to study it in 1968. The Senate's report, issued in 1971, is an interesting example of what happens when you mix relatively kindly attitudes towards people who are poor with acceptance of an economic system based on competition, with winners and losers. "The poor themselves should have a right to participate, to be heard, and indeed, to share in the organization and administration of programs created for them," said the Senators in their report. "The economic system in which most Canadians prosper is the same system which creates poverty," they acknowledged. But, at the same time, they assumed that the economic system was okay; it was just that poor people needed a little help to compete in it. "[The poor] are the losers in the race for material sufficiency," said the Senators, taking it for granted that we have to depend for life-sustaining necessities on a race. We just have to give the poor better track shoes or a little more food or a little more coaching for this race and everything should be okay, the Senators seemed to be saying. But the Senators forgot, or neglected to mention, that in a competitive economic system, just as in a race, there are always losers. Workers compete with each other for jobs and wages; countries compete for corporate job creation; and corporations compete to make the most profit. Even though there is plenty for all, the system sets up a race with big winners and lots of individuals, countries, and companies who lose.

While he wasn't writing specifically about the Senate, Glenn Drover explains the way of looking at poverty at that time as merely a "kindlier version" of the old view that blamed poverty on character flaws. Instead of sobriety, religion, and discipline, the poor needed to acquire training, social services, and a little more money from government. "The essence of a new program must be to help [the poor] help themselves," said the Senate.

But if some people who are poor get educated and become air traffic controllers, or teachers, or computer programmers, for example, who will take their place cleaning washrooms, sewing clothes, serving food in restaurants, taking care of children, and picking fruit? These jobs are crucial for our society, too. And people who do them shouldn't have to be poor. But in this system, the owners of business, who make most of the decisions about employment, keep wages down so profits will be higher.

The recommendation that the Senate stressed most was for a Negative Income Tax (NIT). Everyone would fill out a tax return and people whose incomes fell below a certain level would get money paid to them, instead of having to pay.

The Senate wanted its NIT to be set at 70 per cent of the poverty line and exclude single people under forty years of age. This would have maintained, not ended, poverty for families. The old Principle of Less Eligibility was governing the Senate, even though they wrote nice things about the poor. And the old attitude about the able-bodied poor, that is, single people under forty, was foisting them onto provincial welfare rolls where they'd be even poorer than the people who got the NIT.

Families who got the NIT should be encouraged to take work, said the Senate, meaning low-wage jobs. Although the Senate also called for

increases in minimum wage, this version of the NIT was a sort of Son of
Speenhamland, the old British plan from the turn of the nineteenth century. It would use tax money to subsidize below-poverty wages and
undermine union organizing.

The Senate's proposal and a Guaranteed Annual Income (GAI) promoted in the 1970s by U.S. economist Milton Friedman have a lot of similarities. They are both attractive in some ways to people who are poor.
Some versions of the GAI and NIT would be universal, providing income to
everyone, even the rich, ending the stigma of receiving government help. At
first glance it seems that a NIT/GAI might end the intrusive, judgmental
process in which the poor have to declare and prove their poverty in front
of a welfare worker. Poverty groups that have advocated for a GAI or NIT
have always wanted payments to be high enough to provide a decent standard of living. But corporate lobby groups, as well as the Senate, wanted the
amount to be set so low that people would have to take paid work to supplement it. The NIT/GAI that the Senate and corporations wanted was a
seemingly caring way of transferring the corporate wage bill from the corporation to the taxpayers. But there's a hidden assumption behind the
Senate and corporate versions of the NIT/GAI: it's okay for businesses to
make profits by keeping people in poverty.

As we'll see in the next chapter, the Macdonald Commission of 1985
expanded this idea to justify slashing most social programs and replacing
them with a NIT/GAI that would be used to lower corporate wage bills
rather than to support low-income people at a decent standard of living.
I explored this issue at greater length in an article in *Canadian Dimension*
in 1994, and another in the December 2000 *Long Haul*.

Four staff working on the Senate report became angry when "any
attempt to discuss *the actual production of poverty* in Canada, the roles
played by competition, the tax system, corporate autonomy, collective
bargaining and the rest—was systematically eliminated from the drafts of
the report" (my italics). They quit and wrote their own book, *The Real
Poverty Report*. They exposed the role of systematic oppression in creating
poverty for women, Aboriginal people, and French Canadians. Social programs or not, by 1961, they pointed out, only 15.9 per cent of employable
Aboriginal and Métis people were working and only 13 per cent had running water.

If simply allowing poverty to exist is a form of poor-bashing, and I
believe it is, then it must also be poor-bashing to support a system that
requires it: a system in which business owners decide where jobs are to be

created or destroyed and what wages will be, based on how much profit they can make; a system in which there aren't enough jobs for everyone and people have to compete to see who will get work; a system in which racism, sexism, and poor-bashing are used to justify paying some groups of people less than they need; a system in which Aboriginal people still have high poverty rates and have not been compensated fairly for land taken away from them.

The Senate's rhetoric was about as positive as official views about people who were poor have ever been in Canada. As we'll see in the next chapter, however, Canadians who believed the poor were responsible for their own poverty were to take the upper hand in public policy for the next two decades. Economic theories that justified the rich getting even richer were pushed relentlessly by corporate think-tanks, and poor-bashing took on a new intensity.

Chapter 4

History: Justifying the race to the bottom

For people of colour around the world, there's always been a low-wage strategy. I think what's happening in Canada is that the numbers of people who fall into that morally justifiable group you can treat like shit is actually expanding.

Nandita Sharma

What the corporations and their political servants are grappling with is how they go about abandoning a whole section of the population from any form of social provision whatsoever.

John Clarke

I remember a woman trying to look after seven children in an area that was covered with polluted water. And a sixty-nine cent can of tuna. I was in Reynosa, Mexico, a city close to the Texas border, with lots of factories owned by companies such as Zenith, General Motors, Sony, and Converse. It was 1992 and Canada had signed the free trade deal with the United States and was planning to expand the agreement to Mexico. I was supposed to be at a conference on free trade but skipped most of it. Some delegates from Tennessee had already met some of the workers in the local factories on a previous trip when they had come with Tennessee women whose former jobs had been moved to Mexico. They knew a local union organizer. We North Americans pooled our money, hopped in a cab, and toured around with the organizer to see the factories and meet a few people who worked in them. Our guide worked at a

Converse shoe factory making about five dollars a day. She couldn't believe it when we told her that the shoes she stitched sold for around a hundred dollars in Canada.

We visited some people who lived in a little village of shacks in an area that flooded often. The residents used outhouses. They had dug huge trenches to carry the flood waters away, but they didn't always work and often the outhouses were flooded. Then the water ran through the village, where only a few of the homes were up on stilts. One of the women we met cared for her own three children and her two sisters' four children all day so her husband and her sisters could make their five dollars a day in the factory. She was the one who had to try to keep the children from playing in the polluted, disease-ridden flood water. Some of the children had sandals. Some had only bare feet. The parents couldn't begin to afford the shoes that they themselves were making in the factory. I knew that a huge percentage of children in Mexico die from diseases associated with polluted water. The houses didn't have sinks or running water. In one yard there was a chunk of wood with toothbrushes laid neatly side by side on it, the way my family puts them when we go camping.

The can of tuna was in a Reynosa supermarket. The price was in pesos but I did the calculations and figured out it would be sixty-nine cents Canadian. I had been thinking, if people make only five dollars a day, their expenses must be cheaper than mine. But sixty-nine cents was what I paid for tuna at home when it was on sale. I started looking in the produce markets. Fruits and vegetables, for the most part, cost about the same as I paid for them in Canada. I was discovering that I had been programmed with another lie, that people in poor countries don't need as much money as we do.

The next day I read in one of the Reynosa newspapers about a factory where the workers had gone on strike, demanding that government work standards be enforced. The owners announced they would be closing. Some of the people at the conference thought they would move the business to Honduras, one of the poorest countries in Latin America. Other companies were doing that. People in other parts of Latin America had to work for even less than people in Mexico. I kept thinking of the horrible living conditions that five dollars a day sustained, of how hard it would be, as a mother and aunt, just to keep those children from getting sick from the polluted water. What would conditions be like if wages were even less than five dollars?

I was learning about the race to the bottom that the free trade deals encourage. Corporations were moving jobs from Tennessee to Reynosa to Honduras, and each time the workers were getting less. But people in the poorer countries had to pay about the same price for food, and other necessities like fuel and clothing, and even more for water.

For decades Canadian workers had been at least partially protected from this race with people in poor countries. Welfare, minimum wage laws, and unemployment insurance had guaranteed a minimum standard of living, for some people anyway. Canada has always had its share of farm workers, domestic workers, and migrant workers, mostly people of colour, who fall through the well-thought-out cracks in our social programs, minimum-wage, and immigration laws. Farm workers, for example, have historically been paid piece rates that were below the minimum wage. Domestic workers have been exempted from minimum-wage laws until recently and are still sometimes expected to work extra hours for free, and tens of thousands of migrant workers have no choice of employer and can't use social programs like unemployment insurance or welfare.

Seventeen years before I was in Reynosa, only four years after the Senators produced *Poverty in Canada*, the corporations began organizing to weaken and destroy the social programs and laws that protected many people in Canada from that race to the bottom. In 1975 the elites of the world, members of an international group called the Trilateral Commission, published a report called the *Crisis of Democracy* (see Westbrook). The masses were participating too much in democracies, said the report. This was threatening the ability of the elites to maintain the international capitalist order. A crisis was imminent if the elites' members did not regain control, said the Commission.

Canadian corporations develop their lobby groups

Linda McQuaig reports that public opinion about business in Canada in the early 1970s was decidedly negative. David Lewis had run the successful 1972 NDP election campaign on the issue of "corporate welfare bums." In 1966 the Carter report on taxation had pointed out that the rich were getting far too many tax breaks. There was a new consciousness about the environment, and an oil crisis helped consumers see that the increased gas prices they paid were going into big company profits. The Canadian corporate elite decided they had to use their clout in a more planned and systematic way.

In 1975 Canadian corporate rulers began meeting with each other to design ways to twist public consciousness and government policy towards policies that gave them more power and profits. Tony Clarke recounts that by 1977 they had formed the Business Council on National Issues (BCNI), which included the presidents or chief executive officers of eight banks, ten top insurance companies, and eighteen oil and pipeline corporations, as well as of gas companies, big manufacturing firms like Ford, Kodak, and CIL, transnational corporations like Inco, Alcoa, IBM, Zerox, and IT&T, and companies from the media. Although the BCNI was obviously an organization for the corporate elite, it pretended to represent the interests of the country as a whole, rather than the huge corporations that it really stood for.

On the west coast, corporate executives led by Pat Doyle of MacMillan Bloedel met to form a propaganda think-tank to combat the "socialist" NDP government that had been in power in British Columbia since 1972. They imported Michael Walker from Newfoundland to head up the Fraser Institute and become another corporate voice supported by large companies, including media corporations.

In the same decade Milton Friedman of the University of Chicago began advocating neo-classical economic policies. Friedman wanted a return to the economics of the late eighteenth and early nineteenth centuries, the kind of thinking that was developing when Malthus was poor-bashing the unemployed. Friedman had great faith in markets and competition. He opposed state regulation of the economy and wanted an end to corporate income taxes. He wanted a flat tax on individuals (the poor would pay the same rate as the rich) and a Negative Income Tax for low-income people so the minimum wage could be abolished. He favoured free trade and wanted most welfare abolished.

At this time C.D. Howe Institute president Carl Beigie began promoting Friedman's theories. In *Shooting the Hippo,* McQuaig explains that the Howe Institute was an influential corporate think-tank named after C.D. Howe, who had helped organize Canada's war-production program in World War II. The Howe is also funded mostly by corporations, although both Howe and the Fraser Institute are registered as charities so their operations are at least partially funded by the public through tax refunds for donors.

The BCNI, Fraser Institute, and C.D. Howe Institute, representing their corporate directors and funders, went into action along with individual corporations, especially the banks, and other industry lobby groups like the Canadian Manufacturers' Association (CMA). Over the next few years they wrote briefs, gave speeches, put out reports and news releases, met with politicians, and spoke to the media, always supporting policies that would make corporations richer and weaken government's ability to control them.

Canada's social programs hadn't ended poverty. In fact, the National Council of Welfare showed that the poverty rate had climbed to 18.2 per cent in 1983. The official unemployment rate went from 7.5 per cent in 1980 to 11.3 per cent in 1984. By 1982 the country was in the biggest recession since the Depression. The corporations had ideas about what should be done. So did women's, labour, anti-poverty, and environmental groups. The Liberal government decided to set up a royal commission. In the past, commissions had been useful in creating the appearance of a public consensus on divisive issues.

The Royal Commission: mouthpiece for corporate thinking

The Royal Commission on the Economic Union and Development Prospects for Canada summarized the corporate thinking of the day in its 1985 three-volume report. For me, understanding what the report said about jobs, free trade, and social policy has been crucial to understanding what's going on with social policy in Canada. Poor-bashing is subtly embedded throughout the report, starting with the process the Commission used to gather information.

The $20-million Royal Commission was appointed by the Liberal government in 1982 and reported to the Tory government in 1985. A Toronto corporate lawyer and former Liberal finance minister, Donald Macdonald, was paid $800 a day to chair the commission. Welfare at the time paid $19 a day for a family of four in Newfoundland. In *The Other Macdonald Report*, Duncan Cameron and Daniel Drache say that Macdonald adopted an "elite model of inquiry" that kept low-income people and their organizations away from his commission, his private consultations, and his research, just like the Royal Commission on the Poor Laws had done in England in the 1830s. While groups speaking for low-income people did submit briefs to the Royal Commission, you would never know it by reading the final report because their views were virtually ignored. That's poor-bashing by exclusion.

Macdonald made several recommendations that affect people who are poor and people who will be poor. First, the report called for what it and most other people called "free trade" with the United States, as well as ongoing free trade negotiations with other countries. But these free trade deals are more about corporate rights than trade. They prevent governments from trying to make transnational corporations do things that will benefit their country's residents, like create jobs, or buy local products. They give corporations expanded rights to move to whichever country has the lowest wages and taxes.

Instead of suggesting a system that would raise the wages of people living in poverty around the world, Macdonald recommended a system that would force people to race to the bottom in fierce competition for the inadequate number of available jobs.

What had been keeping Canadians from being forced to work at extremely low wages, like people in the southern U.S. states or Mexico? Those pesky unemployment insurance and welfare programs. Macdonald recommended big changes to them. But how could a person who was raking in $800 a day believe it was acceptable to design a plan that would force people who are unemployed to live on less than the meagre cheque they were already getting, especially when unemployment was so high? Macdonald claimed that the hardship that comes from being unemployed had declined over the years, and that unemployment insurance "provides too generous a subsidy to Canadians whose labour force behaviour is characterized by repeated unstable employment." If Macdonald could make it seem like being unemployed wasn't such a bad thing and those unemployed were simply people with "unstable" behaviour, then it would be easier for people to accept his plan to cut people off UI and drastically cut the benefits for those who could stay on.

Macdonald also wanted to replace welfare with his own version of the Guaranteed Annual Income, this time called the Universal Income Supplement Program (UISP). This scheme was proposed to the Commission by the Canadian Manufacturers' Association. The UISP would destroy social programs like the family allowance, guaranteed income supplement (the program which had come closest to taking seniors out of poverty), social housing, and federal contributions to provinces for welfare. It would replace them with the UISP. We'll have a guaranteed income, said the Commission, but it won't be enough to live on. The old Principle of Less Eligibility was rearing its ancient, poor-bashing, labour-cheapening head.

The value of the UISP, said Macdonald, is that "it becomes less important, in dealing with poverty, to maintain high levels of minimum wages, since the UISP will provide a wage subsidy for very low-wage workers. This allows governments to de-emphasize minimum wages as a policy device." It sounds quite kindly. But it wasn't—unless you were an employer. How do you get Canadian workers to compete with low-wage workers in a free trade world? "De-emphasize" (my translation: abolish) the minimum wage; and get people to accept its end by promising that they can have a sort of guaranteed income to top up the low wages. These recommendations weren't calling the poor nasty names, but they were cheapening their labour and setting up a system where it was perfectly acceptable for the rich to get richer by paying below poverty wages—the old British Speenhamland Plan. And because existing social programs would be abolished, people would have to work at these low-wage jobs in order to survive.

Macdonald didn't think governments should create jobs either. This was a change from the 1970s. "The problem is not that ... jobs are unavailable but that they are often unattractive. Much of the unemployment ... occurs among individuals who find that the available jobs are neither appealing in themselves nor rewarding as pathways to better jobs in the future," he wrote. Macdonald was being a bit more subtle than Rev. Townsend was in 1785. He didn't say that the poor should "fulfill the most servile, the most sordid, and the most ignoble offices in the community" so that the delicate rich could be "relieved from drudgery." But he was justifying policies that would make poor people poorer These people weren't taking jobs simply because the jobs weren't "appealing," like a certain style of clothes; it was their own fault that they weren't employed.

The Commission was clear that the little bit of choice that UI and welfare had given people about the type of jobs they could take should end, and people should be forced to take low-wage jobs with poor conditions, just like the workers in the countries Canada would be trading with in the new free trade world.

The Commission quoted approvingly a recommendation from the Economic Council of Canada: "The appropriate measures to reduce unemployment should focus on facilitating rapid job search and increased job holding rather than on increasing the number of available jobs." In other words, unemployed people should be forced to compete fiercely for jobs as soon as they were laid off, and pressured to take the first available job, even if it didn't meet their needs and was totally unsuited to their goals in life.

In 1985, the same year that the Macdonald Commission reported, the C.D. Howe Institute began pushing for government to reduce the deficit by $15 to $20 billion, reduce wages, and start negotiating free trade with the United States. Deficit hysteria was to become an effective weapon in the corporate drive to mangle social programs, especially the social programs used by the poor. To deal with the debt, said the Institute, government should cut pensions and income security programs, slash UI, and reduce funding for health, education, and welfare. In fact, as economists and others, including Statistics Canada, pointed out later, the deficit was caused almost entirely by high interest rates and low taxes on the rich, not by social program spending. A Canadian Union of Public Employees magazine pointed out in 1983 that the 1981 federal budget reduced the top tax rate on the highest income earners from 62 to 50 per cent, saving $5,600 a year for people who earned over $100,000.

Corporate lobby groups joined Macdonald in an obsessive concern that unemployment insurance would keep people from working at low wages. That old Poor Law Principle of Less Eligibility cropped up again and again in corporate pronouncements: "There should always be an incentive for the unemployed to accept a job ... rather than remaining on unemployment insurance," said the Howe. Social programs should be redesigned to improve "incentives to work," said the BCNI in a 1985 paper.

The BCNI was also supporting the Bank of Canada's high interest rate policy, which kept unemployment high, and campaigning for free trade, which was about to cost Canada at least half a million jobs. These two policies were making millions of people poorer, regardless of what they did as individuals, despite this talk about incentive and disincentive.

The first free trade deal was passed in 1988. By 1990 the Tories were starting to implement Macdonald's other recommendations, meeting corporate demands to cut social programs. Federal payments to three provinces for welfare were limited. UI was slashed. Government stopped increasing family allowances and pensions to meet the cost of living.

U.S. corporations push poor-bashing "researchers"

While Canadian corporate lobby groups were busy pushing policies that increased poverty, blaming individuals for their own poverty, and providing cheap labour, corporate funded "researchers" in the United States were reviving the old stereotypes about poor people and adding elements of racism and sexism. Their "studies" provided a bogus "scientific" basis for poor-bashers in the United States and Canada.

George Gilder's book *Wealth and Poverty* was on the U.S. best-seller list in 1981. "Without monogamous, patriarchal family models, young men have little motivation to work, save and believe in the future," he wrote, sounding like a three-hundred-year-old Puritan. Sheila Collins pointed out how Gilder used biology to explain poverty: "Men's innate aggressive sexual drives motivate them to work hard, only if they are channeled through monogamous patriarchal marriage."

Gilder's book, according to Sally Covington, was sponsored and heavily promoted by the right-wing Manhattan Institute, a U.S. equivalent of Canada's Fraser Institute. Gilder's solution to the welfare "problem" was based on the familiar double standard: he said the rich should have more through reduced taxes, while the poor should have less through cuts to benefits, to improve their "incentive" to work at low-wage jobs.

Collins says George Murray's 1984 book *Losing Ground* was "often cited as the Reagan administration bible." Another U.S. writer, Michael Katz, reports that the Manhattan Institute also supported Murray while he wrote the book, spent thousands of dollars to send free copies of it to politicians, academics, and journalists, and paid a media relations person to manage "the Murray campaign." Murray went on TV, did lectures, and met with editors and academics. The book says (sounding like old Protestant myths) that social programs cause poverty, that people who are poor won't work unless they are forced to, that there should be private charity for the "deserving" poor and nothing for the rest. Murray said bluntly, "Some people are better than others. They deserve more of society's rewards."

In the next decade Murray's best-selling book, *The Bell Curve*, again repeated the biological ideas about poverty that were fashionable among the rich in the nineteenth century. Murray and his co-writer, Richard Herrnstein, claimed there is a scientific relationship between class, genes, and intelligence. Murray added racism to his poor-bashing, by claiming that the average African-American had an IQ fifteen points less than that for whites, ignoring the class and culture bias of IQ tests, which have been thoroughly discredited as a means of measuring intelligence.

In 1986 Lawrence Mead, a New York University political scientist, released *Beyond Entitlement: The Social Obligations of Citizenship,* also backed by right-wing think-tanks. Mead emphasized what he called the "obligation" of the poor to work at low-paid jobs. Government should enforce this "obligation," he said, like a military draft, Collins reports. Needless to say, Mead didn't talk about any "obligations" of the rich.

"Non-work is a political act" that underlines the "need for authority," said Mead, who assumed that anyone who wants a job can find one. Child care is not a problem, said Mead blithely, because "most prefer to arrange care with friends or relatives."

This U.S. attack on the poor was different in one way from that of previous generations. This time the corporate-funded think-tanks used the media to get the poor-bashing, racist, and sexist messages out. The right wing in the United States thought these so-called researchers had proved that social programs made the poor worse off, and that this justified cutting benefits and forcing people into workfare jobs. People like Gilder, Murray, and Mead laid the groundwork for Clinton's welfare changes, which took effect in 1996, abolishing welfare as a right for families in need, forcing people to work for their welfare, and telling states to limit the time people can spend on welfare to two years.

How government poor-bashing changed between 1970 and 1994

In Canada, two federal government papers on social policy clearly show the change in thinking largely brought about by corporate and government propaganda during the 1980s. A 1970 white paper was called *Income Security for Canadians*. A 1994 green paper was called *Improving Social Security in Canada*.

The two papers had totally different ideas about what the goals of an economy and social policy should be. The 1970 white paper said that "an adequate income on which to live" was an important goal for Canadians. It also said that the country's economy should be "enlisted in support of social objectives."

The 1994 green paper had abandoned the goal of an adequate income for all and said nothing about using the economy for social objectives. Instead, it wanted individuals to change themselves to serve the economy. It said programs should help unemployed individuals "retool" themselves, as though they were machines. Social programs were no longer aimed at human well-being but at promoting "independence, self confidence and initiative" (my translation: getting off welfare or UI and into low-wage jobs). Only children's poverty was considered worthy of mentioning, along with "waste and abuse," two words that didn't appear in the 1970 report.

In 1970, the federal government acknowledged criticisms of the social assistance system by anti-poverty groups, saying, "The stigma of poor relief and the dole still lingers and is often reinforced by humiliating procedures and policies, the insufficiency of assistance available, and the fear of arbitrary denial of benefits." It recognized that "many people genuinely in need do not get enough."

The 1994 paper, on the other hand, acknowledged criticisms of the system by employers and corporate interests and ignored criticisms by the poor: "Today's social security system doesn't adequately foster self-sufficiency, promote independence, and help people prepare for work."

What should government do about unemployment? The 1970 white paper included a long list of actions it could take, including fiscal and monetary policies to stabilize employment and prices; manpower, education, and economic expansion policies; and taxation. By 1994, the possibilities were reduced to "helping people to get and keep jobs." And the way to do this was not by having government create jobs itself, but by having lots of "employment development services." In keeping with the new focus on changing individuals to meet the needs of the market, employment development services provide needs assessments, counselling, literacy training, basic skills training, information about job vacancies, and subsidies to employers who hire people who are unemployed—but they don't create jobs.

What causes poverty? The white paper clearly saw that economic conditions were at the root of poverty: "Group poverty may arise from a downturn in the business cycle, from massive unemployment, or from a shortage of economic opportunities in depressed areas." The green paper, twenty-four years later, admitted that the economy was wreaking havoc with people's jobs:

> Plant closures, layoffs and wage freezes have eroded our standard of living, and created a new and insidious insecurity for many people. As hundreds of thousands of these individuals have prematurely lost their livelihoods, swapping unionized, secure factory jobs for the unemployment rolls or part-time, low-paying jobs in the services industry, whole towns have been hurt.

But, incredibly, it then proposed the 1994 corporate answer to poverty: individuals need "counseling, training, work experience, and wage supplements," not more jobs at decent wages. The 1994 paper, like so many

other documents we have looked at, shifted the blame for poverty off the
economy and onto individual unemployed people:

> People may need help for diverse reasons. Some may have
> work-related problems that are symptoms of deeply-
> rooted social problems—often arising in childhood, and
> then passed on through failure in school and early job
> experiences. Some may be highly skilled, but need infor-
> mation on how and where to market those skills. Some
> may live in communities with few job opportunities and
> need to explore alternatives such as self employment or
> mobility.

Who should be able to get welfare or UI? In 1970 the white paper writers agreed that people in need were *entitled* to welfare as a right:

> A fundamental weakness in the administration of social
> assistance in Canada is the failure to recognize that per-
> sons unable to support themselves have a right to assis-
> tance...The sole limitation on this right should be a
> requirement that he show willingness to accept suitable
> employment, training or rehabilitation where age, health
> and family responsibilities permit.

By 1994 the U.S. corporate-sanctioned theories about the obligation to
work were obvious in Canadian government philosophy. "[For] those
with the potential to help themselves, improved government support
must be targeted at those who demonstrate a willingness and a commitment to self help." The public relations strategy developed for the 1994
paper was even bolder, saying that new social programs must show "an
indication that the system will encourage participation and contribution
(work for government cheques for those who are able)."

What is the impact of income security measures? In 1970, the
writers acknowledged that "expenditures on income security affect
human beings and human relationships. They alleviate suffering and
hardship and improve the level of living of people at a time of crisis or
continuing need ... support at the right time may avoid individual or
family breakdown." The paper also observed that income assistance
payments to people who spend all the money meeting their needs helps
keep the economy stable.

By 1994 the Canadian government had adopted the U.S. theories that said the welfare state causes poverty. The green paper suggested that the UI system, not lack of jobs, encourages "repeat users"; that the welfare system, not its inadequate benefits, the lack of jobs and decent wages, or stereotyping of people on welfare, "traps people"; that unemployment insurance "discourages adjustment"; and that social programs in general don't "foster self-sufficiency."

The 1994 green paper showed that, like the Macdonald Commission and the corporations, the federal government wanted to get rid of the programs and laws that shielded most Canadians somewhat from that global race to the bottom. This is a crucial concept for understanding modern poor-bashing and linking it to racism and sexism. For the corporate propagandists, it's important to expand the numbers of people that they and the public feel morally right in treating shoddily. Then they can say, "Any job should be good enough for you." That's what the Macdonald Commission was doing when it blamed the unemployed for not taking jobs that they didn't find "appealing." That's what Gilder did when he said the poor had to be forced to work in bad jobs just as some people have to be drafted into the army.

Building up a poor-bashing mythology is part of enlarging the group of people who should have to take any terrible job, stretching it to include not only people of colour, Aboriginal people, and women, but also more white people than it has in the past, and people in North America as well as in poorer, mostly southern countries.

"We cannot allow a world to exist where we see poor people as the enemy, as subhuman. We cannot allow poor-bashing to get to a level that racism has gotten to," Nandita Sharma told me. Sharma had been studying racism and migrant workers, working on her doctoral degree, and volunteering in the fight against racism when I talked to her in 1997. But the Canadian corporate think-tanks didn't agree. They spent a good part of the 1980s and early 1990s perfecting a language that couldn't be used without bashing the poor, and making it seem acceptable that the poor should be forced into low-wage jobs with bad conditions.

Chapter 5

Using language to corrupt thought

"Those cheaters [on welfare] are useless,"
the young man says. "The best thing
to do is set up a machine gun
at Hastings and Main
and open fire.
They're gonna die anyway, so it
might as well be sooner as later."

From a poem by Sandy Cameron about
a conversation he overheard

A Party member called upon to make a political or ethical
judgment should be able to spray forth the correct opinions
as automatically as a machine gun spraying forth bullets.

George Orwell, *Nineteen Eighty-Four*

How is it that government policy-makers and politicians can get away with cutting welfare and UI below the minimum necessary to live on when unemployment rates are high? How can corporate executives justify paying wages that aren't enough to live on? How is it that people who are probably nice people in many ways end up implementing policies that make other human beings suffer? One way is by asking the wrong questions about poverty. In the 1970s the Senate asked, "How can we create more opportunity for the poor?" instead of "How do we end poverty?" By the 1990s politicians and corporate lobbyists had reverted to the question of the late eighteenth century: "How can we change the behaviour of the poor?"

Over the last twenty years, poverty has increased because federal and provincial governments have implemented the policies of the corporate funded think-tanks like the C.D. Howe and Fraser institutes. In 1992 the two institutes went into action to ensure that people didn't ask the right questions about the poverty their policies were helping to create. The Howe Institute began publishing books in a series called The Social Policy Challenge. The Fraser Institute released *Poverty in Canada* by Christopher Sarlo in 1992.

The C.D. Howe Institute is not modest about its influence on government. Its goal is to "help define the agenda for policy makers." It claims in its 1995 annual report, probably accurately, that the first eleven books of the Social Policy Challenge series "have had a profound impact in policy circles and among business and social services leaders," resulting in provincial and federal government policies that reflect the Howe's thinking.

The Fraser Institute argues that poverty "is simply not a major problem in Canada." Far from asking questions about the huge gap in wealth and income between the rich and poor and how we can make Canada a more equitable society, the Fraser Institute's Christopher Sarlo says he has "no problems with large variations in income and wealth." In 1997 the C.D. Howe's John Richards summarized several years of Howe social policy theory in *Retooling the Welfare State*, in which he says the "primary goal for social policy for the able-bodied ... is to change behaviour." Needless to say, Richards wasn't referring to the behaviour of the able-bodied rich.

The corporate think-tanks write books and reports, send them to politicians, hold briefing sessions with politicians and civil servants, run conferences, and see to it that their ideas are pushed in the media. This isn't hard. Media corporations such as Maclean Hunter, Rogers Cable, Southam, Standard Broadcasting, Sterling Newspapers, and Thomson Newspapers are members of the C.D. Howe or Fraser Institute or both. In asking the wrong questions about poverty, the think-tanks have revived or invented a vocabulary about poverty which they pump into government bureaucracy, the media, and politicians' mouths. The problem is, you can't use this vocabulary without blaming the poor for poverty. You can't use this vocabulary without supporting policies that force more people to work cheaply. And you can't use it without diverting attention from the people who have most of the real power and wealth. By 1994 the Brussels-based Organization for

Economic Co-operation and Development (OECD) was lending international sanction to the poor-bashing vocabulary, and provincial and federal government policy papers were using it too.

A glossary of poor-bashing words and phrases

The idea of a "social policy newspeak," or poor-bashing words, was developed at a board meeting of End Legislated Poverty in 1994. This glossary builds on some of the thinking that flowed from that meeting and includes input from other anti-poverty activists since then.

Transfer dependency or, simply, dependency: *These words imply that people use welfare or unemployment insurance ("transfers" of government money to the unemployed) because they are lazy or childlike or personally flawed in some way.*

This has become one of the phrases most frequently used to blame and demean people who are poor. "As the growth of Ontario's welfare caseload illustrates, transfer dependency may no longer be a problem exclusive to the Atlantic region," Thomas Kierans wrote in the Foreword to *Helping the Poor*, the patronizing title of a book in the Howe's Social Policy Challenge series. "Dependency is rife" said a heading in *The Case for Change*, another book in the series, above a poor-bashing anecdote about a man on welfare with a "live-in" girlfriend. "In some parts of the country, dependency rates are extremely high," the book said, adding judgmentally, "Increasingly numbers of the dependent do not seem especially worried by their dependency."

"In spite of various euphemisms, recipients are dependent on the state, on society, on fellow citizens for survival," asserted Christopher Sarlo in the Fraser Institute book *Poverty in Canada*, claiming that this so-called dependence automatically stigmatizes and shames people who need to collect welfare.

We live in an interdependent world. All people are dependent on other people for a livable environment and income. The wealthy owners of the Nike shoe corporation depend for their profits on women who work for very low wages in poor countries. In my value system, I think being dependent on profits creamed from paying extremely low wages should be more harmful to a person's self-esteem than needing welfare to survive. Yet the Fraser Institute doesn't make generalizations about the self-esteem or dependency of people who depend on exploiting others for their profits.

By 1995 the word dependency was cropping up in provincial social policy papers like the B.C. Premier's Forum report (see Chapter 1). "Young people need to become attached to the labour force early, and their dependence on income security programs should be minimized," it said. In Nova Scotia a joint federal and provincial project evaluated whether or not a training and employment program assisted "individuals at risk of long-term dependency on social assistance." A Newfoundland government report on a provincial economic plan wanted to "reduce dependency on income security."

The word "dependency" promotes the stereotype that people on welfare or UI are like children dependent on parents, unable to care for themselves. Then it seems appropriate for others to tell them what to do, without consulting them—even to make them do things, the way we make children go to school or to bed on time. If these dependent people can't take care of themselves, the logic goes, it must be acceptable to force them to work at workfare jobs where they get either their welfare benefits or very low wages.

But do the C.D. Howe and Fraser institutes really want people who use welfare and unemployment insurance to be independent? No way. They want government to redesign social programs, denying welfare to able-bodied people and forcing them to work at low-wage jobs and be dependent on low-wage employers. In fact, according to Tom Courchene of the Howe Institute, they want to abolish the minimum wage.

It's interesting that the word dependent is only applied to poor people who get government money. What about richer people or corporations who get government transfers? In October 1997 a headline in *The Vancouver Sun* read, "Fight over tax break adds to *X-Files* woes." Two Hollywood companies that made films in Canada were lobbying to keep the tax break that allowed them to sell shares of their productions to Canadians who paid $45,000 in cash and received a tax benefit equal to about $50,000. This was a profit of $5,000, "an immediate and guaranteed 10 per cent return," according to *The Vancouver Sun*. A person in British Columbia in dire need would have to be on welfare for ten months to get that much. The film companies were admitting that they were dependent on government money. But the headline didn't say "U.S. mega-corporations dependent on government transfers."

Reward effort or reward work: *These words suggest that if you have paid work, you should get more money than if you are on welfare or unemployment insurance.*

The 1995 B.C. Premier's Forum report said that income security programs should be changed to "encourage and reward work." When he was
introducing his federal review of social security programs, Human
Resources Minister Lloyd Axworthy said that social programs should be
radically overhauled to "reward effort" by the jobless and welfare recipients.

For Dave Ross, a Vancouver anti-poverty volunteer, "the first thing
that comes up is fear" when he hears the phrase "reward work." When I
talked to Ross at the end of 1998 he explained that it's more socially acceptable for governments to say they are rewarding work than to say they are
"threatening you with starvation." Ross says the phrase comes from a value
system that respects only one kind of work, the kind that "helps the rich get
richer." Volunteer work with a charity or a social justice organization is discouraged by welfare officials, he points out, because they want you to be
spending all your time looking for paid work.

Many people on welfare and employment insurance work hard in
their communities, or raising their children, or caring for others. It takes
a lot of work and effort to get by on what welfare pays—standing in
soup lines, washing clothes by hand, going to rummage sales instead of
stores, walking instead of driving or even taking the bus. Many put huge
effort into searching for work; provincial welfare regulations and
employment insurance rules require this. Hidden in the "rewarding
effort" phrase is the idea that paid jobs are available for people to take if
only they would make an effort to find them, which is another way of
blaming people who are unemployed for their lack of a job.

What are the policies that politicians enact, supposedly, to "reward"
effort or work? They chop welfare and UI, and invent workfare programs
that make destitution the only alternative to low-paid, crummy jobs.
They change welfare rules to force single parents to work in the paid
labour force even if they and their children might be better off with the
parent staying home to work raising their children.

Incentive and disincentive to work: *These words suggest that welfare
and unemployment insurance payments are so comfortable and generous that
recipients won't look for paid jobs.*

Whenever you see or hear the phrase "incentive to work" in welfare
or social policy talk, you know that the topic has been changed from
poverty or reducing poverty to making people work at low-wage, poor-
quality jobs. This phrase changes the important question from "should
we be reducing poverty?" to "how do we force people into working
poverty instead of welfare poverty?"

Incentive and disincentive language is related to the old Principle of Less Eligibility that we met in Chapter 2. Heaven forbid that anyone on welfare or UI will get more in benefits than the lowest-paid worker can get by working, even if the worker is starving.

Incentive language has been used a lot by the Howe and Fraser institutes, starting with Tom Courchene's 1987 book, which said that one of the most important social policy questions was, "Is there sufficient incentive for UI or welfare recipients to re-enter the workforce?" It crops up more than once in *Helping the Poor*. For example, Thomas Kierans, Howe president and CEO, writes in the Foreword, "Policies that were introduced for very good short-term reasons have created harmful long-term disincentives."

In *Family Matters*, another book in the Social Policy Challenge series, the authors abhor the fact that welfare benefits are higher for families than for singles, and therefore are an "employment disincentive" for adults in families to take minimum wage jobs. This book wants government to bring in a child benefit so parents on welfare can be forced to take minimum-wage jobs.

Whenever the phrase "incentive to work" is used, it should really include "at low-wage, often part-time, casual, and temporary jobs with poor conditions."

By 1994 federal government officials were using the incentive language. A *Globe and Mail* article reported Lloyd Axworthy saying that UI is "killing and destroying the incentive to work," when announcing his intention to gut the program. "I'm concerned about the values inherent in a system that creates a certain expectation that you don't have to be involved in the workplace and it simply becomes a way of life," he added, poor-bashing people who turn to UI when no jobs are available.

The language of incentive and disincentive avoids issues of power and equality. It focuses on the behaviour of poor people, creating the impression that they are to blame for poverty, not lack of jobs or low wages. It ignores the work of women in the home raising children. The policies it makes acceptable are the usual list: UI and welfare cutbacks, rules that force the unemployed to compete even more fiercely for jobs, employer or wage subsidy programs that push more people into a labour force that doesn't have enough jobs for all who need them, and provincial welfare laws forcing single parents to work when their children are younger and younger.

"What they mean by incentive is punishment," Bev Brown told me. Dave Ross used the same word in a different interview: "There's a taboo about talking about what this really means," he said. "Incentive is a code word for punishment."

Social policy experiments: *These are programs designed to change the behaviour of individual poor people so they won't use welfare or employment insurance.*

When I think of the word "experiment" I think of something that is scientific and objective. That's what the corporate think-tanks and government want us to think about their social policy experiments. By 1994 the C.D. Howe Institute was advocating experimenting with social policies that were supposed to benefit people who were poor. John Richards writes in *Helping the Poor*, "Uncertainty [about the cause of poverty] does not justify inaction; it is a rationale for carefully evaluated experiments to find out what works and what does not." In 1997 Kenneth Boessenkool of the Howe Institute said, "Policy experimentation is a great asset of Canadian federalism." He then lauded Alberta's welfare "experiment," which shoved tens of thousands of people off welfare, reducing the provincial caseload from 98,000 in 1992 to about 40,000 in 1997.

In the summer of 1994, NAPO board members held a workshop on social policy experiments that the federal government was urging on the provinces. They reported on forced job searches in Prince Edward Island; a plan to replace welfare and UI with a guaranteed income of $3,000 a year in Newfoundland; Ontario's $10,000 gift to employers to hire people on welfare; welfare cuts and just plain kicking people off welfare in Alberta; the so-called self-sufficiency projects in British Columbia and New Brunswick, where single parents were given wage top-ups of up to $10,000 a year and expected to get raises amounting to that amount so they could go off the project in three years. At the workshop, board members from every province and territory summed up what the experiments had in common: they subsidized wages; they didn't create jobs; they assumed that not having a job was the individual's fault; they emphasized that the only way to participate in society is with a paid job; they devalued unpaid community and family work; they promoted conflict among low-income people; and they didn't reduce poverty.

What's more, they treated the poor as objects, not subjects, a dehumanizing, poor-bashing process. Poor people have as much control over government experiments or think-tank theorizing about their future as lab rats have in a cancer experiment. They have no role in deciding what question the experiment is designed to answer. Will it help figure out what it takes to reduce poverty? Are the questions the experiments are designed to answer based on poor-bashing stereotypes? Are they based on other false assumptions such as a plentiful supply of jobs?

Anti-poverty activist Linda Moreau describes how the experiments really work: "It's like how many portions of food can you take from people who are poor before they will have the incentive to take a really bad job or leave their children with someone they don't even know because they can't afford good child care?"

Central to these experiments is the idea that people who are poor have to change themselves to be more competitive. One Nova Scotia experiment was devised to figure out, among other things, if participating in subsidized work changed the attitudes of people on welfare about keeping a job or being on social assistance. It didn't, and, according to a *Vancouver Sun* story, "did almost nothing to end the longer-term dependency of participants." An experiment designed to measure attitude changes in jobless people did not create jobs.

Chronic users: *This phrase implies that unemployment insurance and welfare are like illegal drugs and that people who use them have the same type of "chronic" problem as drug users.*

By 1994, corporate lobbyists and government officials had stooped to using the language of drug addiction to stigmatize people who have to use welfare and unemployment insurance. In its 1995 annual report, the Howe Institute bragged that the federal government had adopted some of its recommendations on "chronic users" (of unemployment insurance). Bev Brown told me that in Newfoundland the phrase "UI syringe" is quite common. In Atlantic Canada, says Brown, "you can't work all year if you work in a seasonal resource industry. If you're laid off, you're not lazy. That's just the way industry works here. 'Chronic users' means all the people who work in resource industries. They want us to think of all these workers as addicts."

(Of course, if drug users weren't stereotyped and bashed so intensely, it would be a lot easier for governments to set up programs that actually help them too.)

Welfare and UI fraud and abuse: *These words imply that merely needing welfare or UI is abuse and/or that many people claim them illegally.*

By 1994, federal government polling showed that 81 per cent of people thought social programs were "too easy to abuse." A leaked Human Resources Development communications document said, "The public's definition of abuse includes legitimate and recognized use of programs which the public sees as too lenient. They disagree with program criteria and it is this definition of 'abuse' that must be addressed."

The same year, the Fraser Institute joined those accusing people on welfare of fraud. Christopher Sarlo complained in a supplement to *The Fraser Forum* that welfare fraud in unspecified "local offices" was "between 15 and 20 per cent." C.D. Howe bragged in its 1994 annual report that its Social Policy Challenge series had introduced "UI abuse" as an important topic for governments to deal with.

Abuse is a powerful word. Not only is it associated with drug abuse, but also with sex and child abuse. To consider people who are forced to use social programs, people who are using the programs legally, as "abusers" was pretty strong poor-bashing. Not only that, the federal government's own communications advisors were saying that government should go along with this poor-bashing definition of abuse.

The real fraud lay in how media and government officials exaggerated the situation. In 1996 I did some calculations based on what B.C . Minister of Human Resources Dennis Streifel told a committee of the B.C. legislature on June 23. With about 371,000 people per month on welfare in the previous year, Streifel said the Ministry did 14,000 fraud investigations. From those they laid 365 charges, which led to 188 convictions and 6,105 repayment agreements. Repayment agreements happen when the Ministry confronts a welfare recipient with a problem that might involve fraud. The Ministry can threaten to withhold further monthly cheques if the person does not sign the agreement. So some of these people are guilty, and some probably just need next month's cheque. In any event, the number of people who were either convicted of fraud or signed a repayment agreement that year in British Columbia was far less than 1.7 per cent (6,105 + 188 = 6,293 divided by 371,000). It's less than 1.7 per cent because each month some people go off welfare and others go on so the number of people who received welfare that year was higher than 371,000. The Ministry could not give me the number.

The emphasis on fraud criminalized, in the public's mind, the act of legally claiming welfare when you are in need. With welfare fraud so allegedly rampant, cutting back on the program and forcing people to work for the shoddiest employers seem almost reasonable. Meanwhile, no one is looking at fraud by the rich, or at our economic and political system with its unequal distribution of income and power.

Delay gratification: *This phrase blames the poor for not being able to delay gratifying their immediate wants, allegedly for sex, booze, or simply a leisurely life on welfare.*

In 1994 Christopher Sarlo wrote a poor-bashing update on his *Poverty in Canada* for *The Fraser Forum.* Sarlo picked up on the concept of delayed gratification, proposed at the end of the eighteenth century by Thomas Malthus and revived by right-wing U.S. academics. "It is characteristic of the immature and of those who lack self-esteem to focus on the short term," Sarlo asserted.

If he had asked a low-income person about focusing on the short term, he might have learned that poverty does limit your ability to plan for the future. "When you have income that is very minimal, you can't plan, you can't look ahead, you don't know what's going to happen to you next month; you don't know if you're gonna still be in the same place two months from now," Jo Grey told me. "Your security goes as far as a law that protects you from being evicted. That's a defining difference between the middle class and the rest of us. We have no security ... it's very hard to have any hope under that circumstance."

But to say that low-income people focus only on the short term is gross poor-bashing that ignores the fact that in all income groups, some people do and some don't; it's just harder when you don't have a house, a savings account, or an RRSP.

Poverty, UI, or welfare trap: *These phrases suggest that people receiving welfare or unemployment insurance are "trapped in dependency" because if they took a low-wage job, they would lose their social benefits, like welfare and UI income, or health, or child benefits. "Trap" language also implies that welfare and UI themselves, not the lack of jobs or low pay, keep people from getting jobs.*

"Poor are escaping trap of welfare dependency" said a *Vancouver Sun* headline. The article reports that B.C. cabinet minister Streifel said that welfare cuts "are transforming welfare from a system that traps people in dependency and poverty to one that is actively supporting the move from welfare to employment." The subtitle of another C. D. Howe book is *Atlantic Canada and the UI Trap.*

"Trap" language has spread around the globe. The OECD gave a section of its *Jobs Study* (1994) to a discussion of the poverty trap. So did the International Monetary Fund (IMF) in a 1999 paper on Canada. For government officials and corporate think-tanks, welfare and UI are "traps" because benefits are so generous that people on welfare and UI don't want jobs that pay less.

Part of the corporate globalization strategy, explains Australian Bruce Bradbury, is to "increase the demand for labour by lowering wages." So the trap language is one more tool in the job of making people who receive social benefits such as UI, welfare, or child benefits do low-wage work that makes a profit for an employer even if it's not enough to sustain the worker. If jobs with decent wages were available, there'd be no theorizing about the poverty "trap."

Of course, the OECD and IMF don't quote people who are poor about trap theory and its accompanying assumption about generous benefits. Debbie Ellison had been a single mother on welfare for years. When I talked to her she was running a successful house-cleaning business. For her, welfare trap has a different meaning: "[Welfare] is a trap in that all the crises come up, the life situations, like your landlord won't fix anything and you have to move. [The trap] is from not having enough money to solve the problem or from the depression of being in that situation." If it does get passed on to children, says Ellison, it's because of lack of money. "When kids don't have what they need, they get depressed. School is not a good experience for them because they have no money for clothes or food or field trips."

If welfare and UI are traps, then people would be better off if they were ended. That's what the corporate language about traps suggests. I asked Ellison if people would be better off if welfare were abolished. "If you have a big influx of people into the job market," she said simply, "not all are going to get a job. Some will die. Labour codes and safety will be out the window," she added, "because people will grab what they can get. They wouldn't be able to afford to care about these things. No one wants to be on welfare. It's not something that people intentionally get into."

How do you change welfare and UI so they aren't traps? This is the question that comes from the corporate version of the trap theory. The corporate lobbyists' answers are to cut welfare and UI benefits; to provide more benefits to working low-income parents but not to parents on welfare. So the trap theory, once more, justifies policies that push more workers into the economy that doesn't have enough jobs for people as it

is and diverts the discussion away from policies that would help redis-
tribute income and power to the poor.

Obligation to work: *This phrase says that people on welfare have a moral obligation to work in return for their welfare cheques.*

The C.D. Howe's John Richards advocated forced labour or training
for people on welfare (workfare). Reviving Puritan values from the seventeenth century, ideas more recently reinvigorated by U.S. corporate
think-tank authors like Lawrence Meade, Richards's 1995 book claimed
that poverty would be reduced if *"the obligation* of social assistance recipients to work or train in exchange for benefits was *enforced"* (my italics).

It is interesting that the corporate think-tanks promote the idea
that people on welfare have an obligation to work but don't talk about a
corresponding obligation of the corporations to provide decent jobs or
life-supporting wages. When companies don't meet their obligation to
supply jobs, where workfare programs are in place, workfare workers are
forced to displace ordinary workers at much lower wages. As a result,
labour is cheapened for all workers at the lower end of the scale, and
poverty increases.

Anti-poverty activist Jo Grey exploded with indignation at the idea
that people have an "obligation to work." The obligation theory "assumes
that paid work always benefits society and always brings virtue to the
workers." Grey was talking about the kind of paid work that people in
her Toronto neighbourhood are likely to get: low-paid, part-time, irregular jobs. "I can't understand how a person can be obligated to be exploited," she said.

Grey believes the idea that any kind of paid job is better than
unpaid work in families and communities is directly responsible for
increased violence and gang and drug activity in her "working poor"
neighbourhood. In most families, she said, both parents work. "Six thousand unsupervised teenagers roam the neighbourhood. The older the kids
get, the more they cost and the more time they need. There's a direct connection between the amount of time parents have to waste earning
money to feed them and the amount of violence, gang, and drug activity. In my neighbourhood the impact is beyond tragedy."

Grey told me about a woman she had known for years: "She raised
her four kids while I raised mine. She was a safe home for a lot of kids.
Fed them. Helped start a food bank. I credit this woman with keeping my
sanity. She's the person I could run to in the middle of the night. She

saved my life. She tried various ways of becoming, quote, productive, unquote. But in the meantime she was keeping her community together. With welfare cuts she had to work under the table to keep her housing. She got caught and was cut off welfare. She lost her housing and now lives in a one-bedroom apartment with her boyfriend, and her children are on their own or with their father. Now she's off welfare and does phone sex. She's 'productively' employed. That's how she survives. She wasn't able to complete raising her children. She had her family torn away because she couldn't find a place in the workforce.

"This is an example of the difference between productive employment and the philosophy that any job is better than no job," Grey explained.

Psychology of poverty: *This phrase implies that the fact of being on welfare, in itself, shames and erodes the self-confidence of people who need benefits.*

Christopher Sarlo again: "The welfare system has a tendency to trap people in a sort of 'psychology of poverty' from which it is difficult to escape. It affects the lifestyle, attitudes, health and outlook of recipients ... The stigma and shame of being dependent on the state further separates them from the rest of society." Being on welfare results in "a loss of self-esteem, loss of pride and a loss of confidence," he writes.

I talked to anti-poverty worker Bev Brown about this in June 1998. At the time she was living on social assistance in Newfoundland, the province with fewer jobs per person than any other. She pointed out that people on welfare are discriminated against in "most of their social contacts." She said they "don't have access to banks like other people. Families are unkind to them and isolate them. People are turned down for jobs because they are on welfare."

Brown says there is a lot of systemic discrimination that fuels people's attitudes about themselves. Sarlo's claim that people are shamed merely because they are on welfare is part of that systemic discrimination. Sarlo blames individuals, says Brown, when the real problem is lack of decent jobs. If people who are poor feel stigmatized and shamed, it comes from continually having to get by with inadequate resources and from relentless poor-bashing experienced in nearly every daily interaction with people who aren't poor (and sometimes with people who are poor).

It's often true that being on welfare affects people's attitudes, lifestyle, outlook, and/or health. For example, you can't have a lifestyle that requires spending a lot of money if you're on welfare. And you are more likely to be depressed and sick, according to health statistics. But this is not because getting money from the state is intrinsically shameful, as Sarlo theorizes. Billionaires get money from the state in the form of tax loopholes, grants for their companies, and interest-free loans. Again, I've never heard of any studies investigating their loss of self-esteem or confidence.

In 1994 I asked a young man who worked as a dishwasher in a Vancouver restaurant, the only job he could get, if working at his job contributed to his self-esteem. He didn't want me to use his name because he felt it could jeopardize his job. He lived in a rooming house and ate at his job, because he couldn't afford food on his six-dollar an hour part-time income. "It's almost like I'm a slave," he said. "I just go through the motions. I don't see how it's building my self-esteem or confidence."

"One thing I find very frustrating about my work," he added, "is that all my money goes to rent and other necessary expenses. I can't save for anything of value. So it's very hard to keep up my interest and motivation in going to work." The young man thought that if the minimum wage was raised to nine dollars or ten dollars an hour and university was affordable, his situation would be a lot better.

Again, the phrase "the psychology of poverty" suggests that poverty can be explained by the behaviour of individual poor people and should be reduced by changing these individuals—usually changing them so they take a low-wage job. They will still be poor, but the corporate-funded experts can stop being concerned about their psychology, self-esteem, or confidence.

Generous and unconditional benefits: *This phrase claims that welfare and unemployment insurance benefits are high and anyone can get them easily.*

In *Retooling the Welfare State*, Richards asserts that "generous income transfers" over the last twenty years have been a mistake. "Long-term unconditional aid to the able-bodied poor inevitably disrupts communities." Of course, welfare and UI are not unconditional. For welfare, people must meet stringent criteria about income and assets and search for work if they are deemed "employable." For unemployment insurance, people must have the required number of weeks of work and must search for work while they receive UI, which will run out within less than a year unless they get enough weeks of work to extend the benefits.

Sarlo reinforced the idea that welfare rates, which ranged from a low of 24 to a high of 80 per cent of the poverty line in 1994, provided adequate funds for people. "There are a great many problems with our welfare system," he said, "but inadequacy is not one of them."

"That's nonsense," Jo Grey told me in 1999. "It's outrageous duplicity. Where did they decide they could lie?"

When these lies are repeated by the media, the general public starts believing them. This fuels hatred of people who use these social programs and undermines support for them.

Training: *In social policy-speak this phrase means information on how to apply and search fiercely for jobs. The word is associated with the belief that enough decent jobs are available for all who need them.*

"It is, of course, not the purpose of government to create jobs," wrote William J. Milne in Howe's *Helping the Poor*. "Concern over job creation should not be allowed to interfere with the introduction of training programs." Training seems like an innocent word. Most people agree that training helps people get jobs. But the Howe Institute and the Liberal government advocate training as an alternative to job creation.

The beauty of training, if you're a corporate think-tank, is that it focuses on changing individuals, not the economy. We won't have to tax the rich or increase the minimum wage or create any jobs if people are unemployed because they have neglected their duty to become trained. The Liberal government's 1994 paper on social security reform was enthusiastic about training. "The best form of social security comes from having a job," asserted the paper. Did it then propose how the government would create jobs for people? No way. "The answer lies," said the paper, in "more focused training," among other things. I've heard Newfoundlanders quip about how many hairdressers one small community can use. People have taken many so-called training programs and still can't get jobs because they don't exist.

A lot of these training programs don't teach any specific skill but teach people to compete more fiercely for the few jobs that are there. Writing in *The Long Haul*, British Columbia's anti-poverty newspaper, a young unemployed person who had taken two of these courses described a typical program:

> There were four smiling counsellors and aspects of the class were reminiscent of kindergarten, with games and singing and arts and crafts sessions. This was all designed to boost the self-esteem of the participants ... reflecting the philosophy that the individual is somehow defective when

unable to get a job. There were endless personality tests. Several people quit in disgust a few days into the program, refusing to be patronized and treated like defects.

There were, of course, the obligatory resume and cover letter writing sessions, complete with videotaped interviews. Some participants, who ranged from "unskilled" workers to people who had been downsized from their jobs, complained that they already had the skills and the training to find a job and that the only problem was that no one was hiring. These issues were never really discussed by the counsellors.

"Unjustly blaming the unemployed," concluded the unemployed worker, who didn't want his name used because he was still looking for work, "takes the focus away from business and government who put so many people out of work in the first place. It is cowardly and unfair to the many people trying desperately to find a job."

The wealth policy challenge

What would happen if we applied to the rich the same language that the think-tanks and others use to attack the poor? Let's assume that an anti-poverty group wrote a series of studies called The Wealth Policy Challenge.

Study 1: *Helping the Rich*. This will examine the dependency of the rich on tax loopholes and inheritances. What government policies would end this dependency and help the rich to become *productive citizens*? What kinds of wealth policy experiments should provinces undertake to change the behaviour of millionaires so they would be more likely to share? Is the new "Dare to Share" life skills course for millionaires effective?

Study 2: *Delaying Gratification*. This study would include theories by a selection of non-rich people about why the rich keep taking foreign holidays, buying expensive clothes and cars, and living in mansions. Is it because they are *immature, lack self-esteem, and cannot delay immediate gratification*? What government policies could give them an incentive to delay gratification? Would higher taxes on profits work? Or wealth taxes?

Study 3: *Loophole Abuse*. This study would examine the *chronic abuse* of tax loopholes by wealthy users. Would counselling and information about job vacancies help them get back on the right track?

Can Canadians afford to lose the tax dollars of people who invest in foreign tax shelters to avoid paying Canadian taxes? How many billions are we losing because of this *rampant fraud*?

Study 4: *Incentives to Be Responsible.* Why are corporations polluting the environment, laying off more and more people, and threatening to move to countries where they don't have to pay taxes and decent wages? The study would recommend ways of enforcing their *obligation to engage in responsible behaviour.* Could the owners of companies that get government assistance be *required to work for their handouts*? Could executives of forest companies be told to plant trees, for example, if they are getting subsidies, or care for the children of their laid-off workers while the parents look for new jobs?

Study 5: *The Wealth Trap.* Is it wealth that keeps its victims from seeking *productive employment,* knowing they can rely on its *generous* and *unconditional benefits*?

Are the problems of the wealthy passed on to the children of the wealthy, generation after generation? To what extent do family trusts (tax shelters that allow the rich to avoid taxes for a generation) contribute to generational wealth?

The study would ask a group of people on welfare to develop theories as well as graphs and mathematical equations about hypothetical and anecdotal rich people. The opinions of wealthy people would not be sought.

Study 6: *The Psychology of Wealth.* Does the experience of wealth have an unhealthy effect on the wealthy? Does it prevent them from getting productive skills; give them undeserved self-confidence; or create inappropriate attitudes? Would the wealthy have more *self-esteem* if they worked for their money instead of inheriting it?

Study 7: *Rewarding Effort.* Does the Canadian economic system *reward effort* or do too many wealthy people get money while they sleep? Is wealth an *attractive alternative to work* for some people? Does it provide a *comfortable fall-back* situation for people who would prefer not to work, and does it *reduce the intensity of their job search*?

Study 8: *Improving Productivity.* Should the rich be forced to *train for productive employment* so they wouldn't spend so much time speculating and wheeling and dealing?

After the studies were completed, people who were poor would present options for policies that give the wealthy *a hand down, not a hand up*.

The B vocabulary

George Orwell's famous book *Nineteen Eighty-Four* introduced the term "newspeak." Newspeak had an A vocabulary for everyday use and a C vocabulary for scientific and technical material. The B vocabulary "consisted of words which had been deliberately constructed for political purposes; words ... which not only had in every case a political implication, but were intended to impose a desirable mental attitude upon the person using them." The vocabulary pushed by the corporate think-tanks about people who are poor is the B vocabulary. It imposes a mental attitude that the poor are to blame for poverty, and not an economic system that creates wealth alongside poverty. The political implications of the words are that it's acceptable for people to be denied welfare or forced into workfare jobs; therefore policies that promote cheap labour, trash social programs, and (incidentally, of course) increase corporate profits are fine.

Orwell's newspeak was also designed "to diminish the range of thought." If the corporate think-tanks can limit the language of discussion to their newspeak vocabulary, questions about inequality, the distribution of wealth, and whether we even want this type of economic system cannot be asked. The range of thought about these issues will be limited to blaming the poor.

Another purpose of newspeak was "to make speech, and especially speech on any subject not ideologically neutral, as nearly as possible independent of consciousness." Let's not think before we talk about why people are unemployed, or whether it is ethical for there to be colossally rich people while others sleep in parks. Our mouths can just blurt out phrases about dependent people with no incentive to work because we've heard them a lot. "A Party member called upon to make a political or ethical judgment," the book explains, "should be able to spray forth the correct opinions as automatically as a machine gun spraying forth bullets."

What words would we use if we wanted to end poverty? *Distribution* would be one. How can we change the distribution of wealth and income so the poor get more and the rich get less? *Equality* would be another. What policies will promote more equality in power, income, and wealth? *Ethical*: is it ethical that some people make money in their sleep while others slave at minimum-wage jobs or unpaid work and don't even reach the poverty line? *Class*: which class is benefiting from government polices and which ones are being hurt? *Racism and sexism*: how does discrimination based on skin colour or gender hurt some and help others? *Power*: how can we change our system so that corporations and the rich have less power and the rest of us have more?

But these aren't the questions being asked or the words being used in recent years. Instead, armed by the so-called research of the corporate think-tanks, with their poor-bashing vocabulary and focus on changing the behaviour of people who are poor, the media and politicians launched a lengthy campaign of fierce poor-bashing, followed by policies that slashed welfare and unemployment insurance and increased poverty in one of the richest countries in the world.

Chapter 6

The media and politicians: Poor-bashing today

Question: *What do these quotations have in common?*

1. *Under everyone's nose, seemingly innocuous Bob Rae, following the lead of Liberal incompetent David Peterson, is paying pogey equivalent to $24 an hour or $865 a week.*

2. *Millions of dollars in welfare money collected fraudulently by Somali refugees across Canada are being used to buy arms for Somali warlords.*

3. *In Canada, welfare ... carries no responsibility to be honest or seek independence.*

Answer: *They are lies printed in prominent Canadian papers in three series of articles that poor-bashed people on welfare in the early 1990s.*

About ten years ago the Canadian media launched a vicious attack on people who were poor. Two-inch headlines made criminals of people on welfare, without offering solid evidence. Gossip and lies in stories and columns reinforced false stereotypes and blamed people on welfare and unemployment insurance for the deficit. When the media did deign to give people who were poor a voice, it was often in "poornographic" articles as experts on suffering, while their understanding and analysis of social programs and the economy were ignored. The media onslaught made it acceptable for poor-bashing politicians to pass poor-bashing laws, chop welfare and UI even more, and force people to accept sub-poverty level jobs to survive.

The first blast came from a newspaper for people who own and manage wealth. The *Financial Post* (now a section of The *National Post* but then owned by the Sun Media group, noted for its sensational tabloid dailies in several major Canadian cities) called itself "Canada's business voice" and was full of ads for luxurious vacations and mutual funds, with articles on business ventures and corporate takeovers. In April 1991, columnist Diane Francis began a sustained attack on people on welfare. Francis's columns also ran in the *Sun* papers, exposing non-rich people to her poor-bashing columns.

Francis wrongly claimed in one of her first poor-bashing columns that for a working family in Ontario to make as much as a couple with two kids on welfare, they would have to earn $45,000 a year or $865 a week. To a monthly welfare payment of $1,800, she inaccurately added clothing allowances, back to school allowances, the child tax credit, and "freebies such as eyeglasses for junior, a gum job for mom at the dentist and prescription drugs." Her calculations were off by about $20,000 a year, but the article revealed the real point of her concern with welfare rates: "Just who will work for $4, $5, or even $12 an hour when staying at home is so lucrative?" The old English Principle of Less Eligibility was still in effect for *The Financial Post* in 1991.

A few days later, Francis claimed that the Ontario NDP government had "hiked welfare across the board in January by 17 per cent," again not true, and called on the federal government to halt payment of welfare money to Ontario. She repeated her claims about a hypothetical couple with two children on welfare getting $45,000 a year, this time saying how unfair it was to "Canada's 12 million workers who pay taxes."

Anti-poverty activists pointed out quickly that Francis's statement that "anyone making less than $45,000 a year should go on welfare in Ontario" was wrong on two counts. First, a family of four would need a gross income of only $25,000 to equal what people on social assistance were getting. Second, single people and smaller families got a much lower amount, yet the article left the impression that anyone could get $45,000. The Social Assistance Review Committee Network pointed out that a single person on welfare in Ontario could get about $9,300 a year. The poverty line at the time was $14,951. Further, Ontario had increased welfare by a maximum of 8.5 per cent, not 17 per cent.

On April 29, Francis was bashing refugees for claiming welfare, as well as unnamed women on welfare who allegedly refused to change their behaviour by learning to use blenders and to sew.

On December 5, 1992, a *Financial Post* editorial was headlined "Taxpayers won't support cheats." Did the *Financial Post* mean corporate cheats who hid profits in hard-to-trace foreign investments so they wouldn't have to pay taxes? Was it concerned about cheats who dined in luxury restaurants with relatives and friends, then wrote it off as a business expense? Was it concerned about business cheats who were bilking billions from taxpayers by taking advantage of the Scientific Research Tax Credit? No way.

The editorial, plus a poor-bashing cartoon of a person with a top hat leaping out of his chauffeur-driven limo to get his welfare cheque, with an ad for "top ski resorts" also in plain view, took up most of the page. It ranted against "countless Canadians ... ripping off this country's welfare and unemployment insurance systems for years." It said that government budgets "groan under the unnecessary added weight of fraudulent payments," and recommended a crackdown on welfare and UI fraud so that taxes wouldn't be "feathering the nest of criminally inclined opportunists."

While the *Post* was poor-bashing with fraud anecdotes, some business people were using a tax credit to fraudulently feather their nests. The Scientific Research Tax Credit had been introduced in the early 1980s. By 1996 April Lindgren of the *Ottawa Citizen* was reporting that the credit had cost the government $4.2 billion and Revenue Canada was saying that $2 billion of that amount was fraudulently claimed and would probably never be collected from "firms that never lived up to their research promises." Where were the *Financial Post* columns condemning businessmen who preferred fraud to $4 and $5 an hour jobs? Was anyone telling them to use blenders and learn to sew so they could live within their means without defrauding us?

It's always easiest to incite contempt for people who don't have much power. Take, for example, refugees from Somalia struggling to get started in this country. In 1993, sixty to seventy thousand Somalis living in Canada were maligned by a series of articles in *The Vancouver Sun* and other papers claiming that welfare fraud was rampant in the Canadian Somali community.

"Welfare scam 'buying arms for Somalia'" was the headline of the front-page story by Moira Farrow in the *Vancouver Sun* (then owned by

Southam) for October 20, 1993. In a series of eleven articles, the *Sun* claimed to be exposing massive welfare fraud by Somali refugees. I can't find any facts that confirm the allegation of the first sentence of that story: "Millions of dollars in welfare money collected fraudulently by Somali refugees across Canada are being used to buy arms for Somali war- lords." The next day the language was modified: a front-page story head- lined "Mounties probe Somali welfare 'scam'" began, "RCMP have begun an investigation into *allegations* that millions of dollars in welfare money collected fraudulently by Somali refugees across Canada are being used to buy arms for Somali warlords" (my italics). But, allegation or fact, the damage to the Somali community and to people on welfare continued.

As the stories by Farrow continued over the next year or so, the B.C. government said it was aware of the allegations, had investigated them, and found no problems. Federal Immigration Minister Sergio Marchi said the allegations were based on a report that contained mis- takes and represented only the opinion of the author. Three Toronto res- idents from Somalia were charged with welfare fraud totalling $26,733, not "millions." On March 4, 1994, under the huge front-page headline "Warlord's welfare scam confirmed," Farrow wrote: "Another immigra- tion report states that eleven cases of refugee welfare fraud have cost Canadian taxpayers over $1,000,000." It's not until the fourth-from-last paragraph on the second page of the story that she admits that the figure "refers to the *cost of investigating* 11 cases of refugee welfare fraud and probably includes the amount of fraud involved. It is not known if charges were laid" (my italics). In other words, the *Sun's* articles didn't show that "millions of dollars" were collected fraudulently—only that it cost a lot to investigate allegations, gossip, and innuendo tarring people from Somalia as welfare fraud artists. Out of all the Somalis in Canada, the *Sun* series found only three charged with welfare fraud and eleven who may or may not have been charged, hardly a massive number. In fact it's about 0.02 per cent, assuming the eleven were charged. Of course many Somalis were not on welfare.

But the general public was influenced by the poor-bashing they saw in the papers, heard on the radio, and watched on TV. Later that year, I talked to some members of Vancouver's Somali community about the *Sun's* poor and immigrant-bashing articles. Abdi Warsame told me that it was difficult for Somalis to get jobs because there is lots of competition. But after the *Sun* articles, he said, "Everybody suspects Somalis, every- where you go."

Cab driver Abdullahi Barre added, "[The employers] say 'oh, you're the guys in the welfare scam.'" One of his customers asked him, "How come you make an extra $2,500 on welfare and still drive a cab?" "I feel the shame," said Barre. "I told him this is not true, but he didn't believe it because he believes the news."

Barre told me that children from Somalia were being hurt by the *Sun* articles. "The insults are coming into everyone's living room," he said. "In some families children tell their parents, 'I don't want to go to school. I'm ashamed.' When the children go to school, the others say, 'You live on welfare. You take our money.'"

Abdirahlan Egal Hasson told me that one day after the first *Sun* article, his boss asked him, "How can you take welfare when you work?" Hasson wasn't taking welfare. "The newspaper has tried Somalis before the court did. The media found us guilty and this is unacceptable. Even if the *Sun* says it's sorry, it won't help. The damage will stay for a long time," explained Hasson. "I'm a Canadian but [the articles] make it seem to me that I don't belong here."

Ismail Warsame, another person from Somalia, tried to explain why the *Sun* would feature such articles. He thought "the media is trying to mobilize public opinion to curtail Canadian policy on immigration, multiculturalism, and universal social programs. The media is creating an atmosphere where legislation on these issues will happen."

On August 1, 1995, Sandy Cameron was drinking a coffee at a restaurant just east of Main and Hastings in Vancouver. The previous day's Vancouver *Province* lay open on the table in front of two young men who were having breakfast. One of them was expounding on a column by Kathy Tait. "If I had my way, I'd get rid of those welfare bums fast," one of the young men said. "I'd kick everybody off welfare who could walk. There's jobs out there.

"Those cheaters are useless," he continued. "The best thing to do is set up a machine gun at Hastings and Main and open fire. They're gonna die anyway , so it might as well be sooner as later. They're good for nothing."

Cameron was horrified by what he heard and later wrote an article and a poem about it. Apparently, said Cameron, the young man didn't know that unemployment was close to 10 per cent, more like 20 if you counted the hidden unemployed. Here was a series of articles that made it seem legitimate for a reader to "spew forth bullets" of hate while having breakfast with a fellow worker. Media poor-bashing had amounted to an incitement to violence.

Cameron's article explains that Tait's column had "triggered this unthinking tirade of frustrated hatred." Its welfare fraud accusations were based on unnamed studies and the unsupported opinion of a woman who wanted to work for the government as a welfare cop. The *Sun*'s owner at that time was a member of both the Fraser and C.D. Howe institutes. Most of the articles even had their own little logo: a hand, a one-dollar coin, and the words WELFARE WASTE.

On June 19, Tait claimed, inaccurately, "In Canada welfare ... carries no responsibility to be honest or seek independence." In fact people who apply for welfare have to prove their need with rent receipts, pay stubs, and information from banks and numerous other institutions. If they receive welfare based on lies about about their financial or personal situation they can be jailed. Employable people must look for work as a condition of getting welfare. Another article on the same page was titled "Fraud police pay off," giving the impression that welfare fraud is high. The WELFARE WASTE logo was there, along with a dark box encouraging readers to call their nearest social assistance office if they suspect fraud, and telling them where to find the phone number.

On June 26 the headlines were "Pirates plunder safety net," "They skim the cream," and "Ask any cabbie: it's monthly mayhem." Tait invited readers, who may or may not have been poor-bashers, to write or fax her with ideas on "how to stop waste and preserve this social safety net." The July 9 headlines on Tait's columns also reinforced poor-bashing stereotypes: "A druggie's tale" and "Alcohol, drug abuse shoots up welfare costs."

The stories in the *Financial Post*, and the Vancouver *Province* and *Sun* are only three examples of media whipping up hatred against people on welfare. Throughout Canada in the last decade, numerous articles, radio, and TV shows poor-bashed people on welfare and unemployment insurance, and, later, panhandlers and squeegee kids.

Poor-bashers in the media have many techniques besides lying. Using ignorant and/or poor-bashing informants is one. Sometimes reporters interview members of the public about alleged welfare cheating, but often these people don't know what the welfare rules are. Reed Eurchuk wrote about a story on CKVU television in Vancouver in which the reporter interviewed a bank teller who claimed that a person dressed as a construction worker cashed a welfare cheque with another small cheque that the teller assumed was for wages. This incident was portrayed as fraud when, in fact, it is perfectly legal to work while on welfare. In fact, welfare officials encourage it because it reduces the amount of welfare that people are eligible for.

Another problem is that reporters and columnists rely on claims by informants who assume people are on welfare when they aren't. On July 17, 1995, in *The Province*, Tait quoted unsubstantiated claims of readers that young able-bodied males on welfare have gold chains, beepers, and cellular phones; that others go to Reno twice a year; and that some even buy shrimp! Here was another column that relied on biased, poor-bashing informants whose stories may well not be true.

May McIntyre, a welfare advocate in Salmon Arm, B.C., told me about a conversation she had with the welfare manager in her area: "He was laughing and shaking his head and saying to me 'You'd be surprised how many times people are reported [for fraud] and you look on the computer and the names aren't there.' They may have other means, be on disability, on Canada Pension or whatever."

In Winnipeg, welfare officials had to throw out 117 complaints from the first three weeks of their welfare fraud tip line because the alleged fraudsters weren't even on welfare. The *Winnipeg Free Press*, in a story by Gordon Sinclair, said that "as many as 97 per cent of the accusations could be groundless" based on statistics from previous years. If 97 per cent of alleged "tips" to fraud hotlines are false, imagine what percentage of calls to poor-bashing reporters and columnists might include false information.

Police officers, social workers, and people who write government reports may be considered reliable sources, but they can still have poor-bashing attitudes that colour the so-called facts they give to reporters or write in their own reports.

Francis and others often use as proof of fraud an informant's assumption that people on welfare work for money if they are not home during the day. Of course there are a million good reasons for people to be out of the house during the day, whether they are on welfare or not. They could be looking for work, which they are supposed to do if they are employable. They could be working in the community for no pay. They could even be working for pay, which is perfectly legal if you are on welfare, so long as you declare what you make.

Ottawa anti-poverty activist Linda Lalonde told me that she was once cut off welfare because her worker assumed she was working when she phoned three times one afternoon and Linda wasn't home. Her cheque was stopped and she had to go to the office to explain herself, even though her file included the information that Lalonde was in school. Once she explained this, again, to the worker, she got her cheque.

There's another type of media poor-bashing that angers anti-poverty activists. They call it "poornography"—a word invented by Pat Chauncey when she worked at End Legislated Poverty in Vancouver. Poornography happens when poor people are portrayed as sufferers, to titillate the audience, perhaps to evoke sympathy, or donations, or good-will towards a media outlet that is collecting donations. Poornography often happens just before Christmas. A paper—or radio or TV station—picks a poor family as deserving sufferers so readers will send in money, clothing, or toys and the paper will get good publicity. The story won't mention that the family is poor because they were denied welfare or because welfare rates are intolerably low. It won't include an interview with the relevant politician demanding to know why the government is causing this hardship. By January 1st, the paper will be back to stereo-typing people on welfare as lazy rip-off artists.

Jo Grey has a lot of experience with poornography. When reporters need a comment from people who are poor, they often call her at Low Income Families Together (LIFT), a Toronto anti-poverty group. "What poor people are allowed to put out is only our sob stories. It's only how much we suffer," she told me. "LIFT is like the poverty casting agency sometimes. [The media] call us every two weeks looking for somebody who is in this situation or that situation. I always end up arguing with them, saying people don't particularly want cameras in their homes. People's kids resent it ... so the only way you're gonna get to interview someone from our organization is if you let us talk about what needs to be done. After that there's probably about 20 per cent who will continue but even then, [our opinions are] cut. Sometimes we get to slip in a line or two." Grey gave the example of the time that the media were covering the federal Child Benefit. "They came to see me and I said 'Okay, you can take a picture of my kids, fine, but this is on the understanding that you give me some solid print on this issue because I help design policy. I want to be treated as an expert.' So they promised and promised." Grey was angry about the article that resulted because the picture made her family look "pathetic." "My reason for being involved in that article was because of my expertise on the issue, not because of my hunger," she explained to me.

"Whenever I explain to a media person about not going into the house and exposing the children and allowing people to have some dignity," Grey went on, "they'll always say 'You have to put a face on the problem.' I get so tired of hearing that 'put a face on the problem' bullshit. Can't we put an analysis on the problem? Can't we have a discussion about the problem? It's not sympathy that we need here," she continued, "it's a general outrage that the system is so screwed up that it creates so much poverty." Grey says that some media people now know her views on this and will still approach her and give her the chance to add her group's point of view, but these relationships have taken years to build up.

Sometimes, well-meaning reporters, because they believe in the "put a human face on the story" technique, will create poornographic media stories unwittingly. Marie Wadden was a thoughtful CBC-TV reporter in St. John's, Newfoundland, when I talked to her in 1997. She wanted to get out a message that poverty is "a very big problem in this province, that the segregation of poor youth is wrong." So she produced a series of six stories about a poor family in rural Newfoundland, focusing on the family's teenage daughter, Joanne Sinnick. The programs were a stunning success with viewers. "We got all these phone calls [saying] what a good story," Wadden told me. As a result of the programs, the Sinnick family received—literally—truckloads of donated clothing and other articles. Some people were angry that all the donations were directed to one family at a time when many were in need. Soon the community opened a thrift store with the donations.

Wadden told me that she was "conflicted" about the programs "because the message that I wanted to send out, which was the depth of poverty in the province, the long-term effects, got lost in the particular story of Joanne." Joanne Sinnick, meanwhile, had a good answer for the problem of poverty in her community: "If they had jobs in Hawks Bay, it would be perfect," she said in the TV story. But that would take political action, not charity.

In the spring of 1998, Bev Brown reluctantly gave in to a reporter's request for names of people on welfare to talk to. Ryan Cleary wrote a series of articles on welfare for the St. John's *Evening Telegram*. In some ways the articles were respectful. They seemed to agree that welfare rates were too low. They portrayed enough of the individuals' stories to show they were not to blame. But the stories appeared in the Lifestyle section of the paper, implying that poverty is a choice, like certain fashions or food. And the articles promoted the stereotype of the welfare cycle—once a person is on welfare, the whole family is on it for the next umpteen generations. For example, one person Cleary interviewed had been raised as a child on welfare before going on to obtain a university education. She hadn't been on welfare or UI as an adult and still was portrayed as part of the "welfare cycle." She objected with a letter to the editor. Another woman was shown as being quite deserving, and donations immediately flooded in for her and her children. This woman was quick to point out, however, that people needed to speak out to the politicians because "poverty is all around us." So even though the reporter intended his story to be "objective," even to help poor people, the impact of his poverty-cycle thinking and his focus on individuals and not the economic situation didn't help readers to make judgments about poverty that would help to reduce or end it.

Many media show a double standard when covering fraud stories. Mere allegations of welfare fraud will be given prominent coverage with huge headlines, while stories about business people who are actually convicted of defrauding the public are ignored or buried deep inside the paper or news program. In one instance, for example, the Vancouver *Province* had a two-inch headline "Stop the scam" on the front page, alerting readers to the page five article with a one-inch headline: "'We're legitimizing fraud,' police say." The article was an attack on people on welfare who allegedly falsely claimed that they lost their welfare cheques and got them replaced. "Armed with a file number from the police," said the poor-bashing article, "the cheat returns to his welfare office—-and gets a new cheque." Nowhere in the article was there any evidence of even one proven case of someone who did this. The article intimated that between $2.35 million and $3.76 million was lost to taxpayers due to lost-cheque fraud. This could only be true if everyone who reported a lost or stolen welfare cheque was doing it fraudulently.

The next month, a small article with a half-inch headline was buried at the bottom of page A16: "Four convicted in $17.5 million fraud free pending appeal." A lawyer, businessman, accountant, and an engineer had been investigated for five years by Revenue Canada, which told the court that the four took $73 million, although they didn't have enough evidence to prove the full amount was stolen. Here we had government investigators who proved to a jury that these four men stole $17.5 million from taxpayers. This was over four times the amount of the completely inflated and unproved estimate of welfare fraud in the previous month. Where was the two-inch headline on page one? Where were the calls to change the system to prevent this kind of fraud? Why were the fraudsters not called "cheats," or "accountant cheats," or "engineer cheats?" Why was there no estimate of the total amount of business fraud?

While it is true that poor-bashing was around before the media assault of the 1990s, I believe, along with many anti-poverty advocates, that media coverage made poor-bashing acceptable to many Canadians who then did it themselves. Todd Cunningham was organizing low-income people at the Somerset West Health Centre in Ottawa when I talked to him in 1997. Cunningham said he thought the middle class was justified in its anger at the economic system, but that the anger "is being manipulated and being focused towards the poor people when it really should go at people who are exploiting us, the corporate structure and very wealthy. It seems to me that comments like 'That lazy mother on welfare should go get a job' are more tolerated now than a couple of years ago. Before, people might think that, but they wouldn't be as comfortable saying it out loud."

As the media, on purpose or unconsciously, poor-bashed with lies and poornography, it also poor-bashed by virtually ignoring the most important Canadian social policy change in thirty years—the abolition of the Canada Assistance Plan (CAP), which set out five rights for people in need. At the time, in 1996, the anti-poverty movement was desperate to waken Canadians to what was happening. Hundreds of people across the country were involved in occupations, fasts, demonstrations, presenting briefs to politicians and various government committees, writing news releases, holding news conferences, writing opinion pieces for local papers, and spending countless hours phoning and faxing reporters and columnists to urge them to cover the story. Still I suspect that hardly any Canadians knew what ending CAP would mean for poor Canadians because the media, with a few small exceptions, refused to give the issue the coverage it deserved.

Politicians have been quick to follow the media with their own poor-bashing. Members of the NDP, who in the past had stuck up for the poor, were no exception. B.C. Premier Mike Harcourt told the press on September 21, 1993, "We want to clear the cheats and deadbeats off welfare rolls. We're not going to allow people who could and should be in the work force to sit there and do nothing." Harcourt's comments—reported in an End Legislated Poverty flyer—followed months of what he called "relentless" media coverage of welfare fraud. He told me in an interview, "It was the scrum of the earth, as I call the press gallery in Victoria and here in Vancouver, in full stride. Particularly odious. Every day, a camera in your face about this welfare case or that welfare case."

Shortly afterwards Harcourt fired Joan Smallwood, Minister of

Social Services, who had made some small improvements to the welfare system and argued publicly that welfare fraud was no more prevalent than other types of fraud.

When low-income delegates from ELP met with Harcourt on December 3, they demanded and got a sort of apology for his name calling. Mickey Smeele told Harcourt, "Your comments validated exploitative, negative, damaging hot air about single welfare moms." Joanne Shaw explained, "Maybe it's unfair that your comments affect people so much, but it goes along with the power you have." ELP's newsletter, *Actionline,* wrote that Harcourt responded with, "I heard what you have to say. It's a very powerful message .... I acknowledge the criticism ... that's the last time I use the 'c and d' words. But he refused to apologize publicly, telling the ELP delegation: "The problem is, when you deal through the media, you risk problems."

While it was the last time Harcourt used the "c and d" (cheat and deadbeat) words, it wasn't the last of his poor-bashing. Soon after came a host of poor-bashing government policies, as we'll see in the next chapter.

In April 1994, the official Canadian unemployment rate averaged 10.4 per cent and the government was getting ready to slash UI benefits. How better to justify the cuts than to bash UI users? Prime Minister Jean Chrétien, Geoffrey York reported, gave a speech to a black-tie dinner in Toronto, a nice place to say it was better for unemployed people to be "at 50 per cent productivity than to be sitting home drinking beer at zero per cent productivity."

Mike Harris used poor-bashing to get elected as Ontario's premier in 1995. While Harris has made numerous blatant name-calling poor-bashing remarks, his pre-election Common Sense Revolution leaflet included more subtle poor-bashing. The leaflet was an effective mix of poor-bashing jargon and innuendo, scare tactics about the cost of welfare, and more kindly phrases that sounded helpful on the surface but actually reinforced poor-bashing myths.

The leaflet said the Harris Tories wanted to "open up new opportunities and restore hope" (kindly phrase) by "breaking the cycle of dependency" (think-tank jargon implying inferiority and blaming and labelling people on welfare). It talked about investing half a billion dollars in programs to help those most in need, implying that many on welfare aren't in need. It repeated the "hand up not hand out" phrase, reinforcing the false concept that people have to go on welfare because of their individual problems, not because of lack of jobs or decent wages or because they are already working raising their children. The leaflet said Harris's welfare police will demand "responsible behaviour" from people on welfare, implying that their behaviour is not responsible now. People on welfare had been required to accept any kind of paid work they were physically capable of before Harris. But Harris's leaflet promised that people on welfare would have to work or train in order to get their benefits, evading the problem that not enough jobs exist for all who want them and reinforcing the stereotype that people on welfare have to be forced to take jobs or that they can't get jobs because they are untrained, rather than because the jobs don't exist. The Common Sense leaflet also promised to save over half a billion dollars by reducing fraud and tightening eligibility, supporting myths that there are vast amounts of welfare fraud, and that people who don't really need welfare are in the system.

But welfare only took up about one page in the twenty-one-page leaflet under the heading "Less government spending." It was only after the election had been called that Harris shifted his main focus to welfare and started going up in the polls.

On May 25, Harris announced that if he were elected, all able-bodied people on welfare would be ordered to work at jobs such as hall and yard monitors at schools, as crossing guards, or planting trees or doing farm labour. People with children could look after more children. Welfare would be cut by about 25 per cent. The front page of *The Toronto Star* reported that Harris said that workfare programs will "get them up in the morning, get them out of the house," adding his personal support to the false stereotype that people on welfare are too lazy to get up by themselves.

The anti-welfare theme was so popular that the Tories' opponents stole it. Liberal leader Lyn McLeod promised that her party would reduce welfare costs by over $1 billion over the coming three years—$300 million of this to come from cracking down on alleged welfare fraud.

Toronto Star columnist Tom Walkom noticed that Harris began rising in the polls when he switched from promising tax cuts to promising tax cuts plus welfare cuts and workfare. Promises to "make the poor hurt" seemed to increase his popularity. Walkom noted that the Liberals were also being tough on welfare, but that Harris was blunter and more dramatic.

"Workfare is the policy issue that has really made it okay to bash people who are poor," Susan Learoyd told me in her office at the Ottawa Social Planning Council in March 1997. Learoyd did research on social issues and was a strong advocate for the rights of low-income people. "It's done it by saying that poor people have to be forced to work. They're not gonna do it of their own free will. They're interested most in feeding off the system and collecting that wonderful welfare cheque and won't do anything more if they aren't forced …. Now that they are hearing government say it, people are saying, 'Oh yeah well that's what we always believed and now we can be more boisterous with what we felt all along.' All of a sudden all the anger about high taxes and increased social spending is getting focused entirely on people on welfare."

After he was elected, Harris continued to bash people on welfare. In 1998 he abolished a $37-a-month allowance for pregnant mothers on welfare, saying "What we're making sure is that those dollars don't go to beer, don't go to something else," according to Robert Vipond's report in *The Globe and Mail*. While Harris was worrying that pregnant mothers on welfare might spend their meagre cheques on beer, I saw no mention in the report that he worried about rich Ontarians who might spend the thousands they saved from his tax cuts on Scotch. By July 2000, the Harris government was considering two more poor-bashing policies: forcing expectant couples to take parenting courses before they could get welfare and deducting fines for criminal offences from welfare cheques.

Harris, Harcourt, and Chrétien were just three of numerous Canadian politicians who poor-bashed their way through the 1990s. In 1994 New Brunswick's Premier Frank McKenna told single moms they would have to name the father of their child in order to get welfare. This implied that single parents didn't know the names of the fathers, reinforcing the stereotype that mothers on welfare are promiscuous. New Brunswick anti-poverty groups responded by distributing buttons that said, "Frank's the father." Anti-poverty activists even had to challenge Ontario's NDP government, which announced that it would hire hundreds of new welfare police in 1994, pandering to the public view that welfare fraud was rampant. Other provinces also claimed to be mounting a new attack on welfare fraud.

While the *Financial Post* and the prime minister felt okay about openly poor-bashing to their upper-income audiences, several premiers who were busy reducing taxes for the rich, and cutting services for middle- and low-income people, bashed people on welfare while pretending they were really sticking up for the working poor. For example, in 1993, Alberta Premier Ralph Klein told the *Calgary Herald*: "There is a public mood that we have to get really tough on those who abuse the [welfare] system.

There are hard-working people out there who prefer not to go on welfare
—taking jobs that really don't pay an exceptionally high salary—and see
somebody down the street who is doing no work whatsoever and taking
home more money than the person who wants to be employed."

Klein's front-page statement promoted the myth that the welfare
system is full of "abuse," that emotionally charged word. He intimated
that people go on welfare because they "prefer" it, not because it is a
dreaded necessity. His statement suggested that "hard-working" people
who take low-wage jobs are morally superior to those on welfare. His corporate backers would probably rather extol the morality of their workers
than pay them fairly.

What is the connection between media and politicians who poor-
bash, and what could be the ultimate consequence of their use of power
against the poor? In an article about the role of government in creating
communal hatred, Jonathan Power criticizes media coverage of modern
mass murders that happened in Rwanda and Yugoslavia. Power says that
these atrocities were not the result of "deep-seated hatreds" or "ancient
animosities," as the media often claim. In fact, he writes:

> The present-day outbursts of communal hatred are due
> more to government manipulation than ancient ani-
> mosities. Time after time, governments play on existing
> ethnic, racial and religious tensions to entrench their
> own power or advance a political agenda. Discrimination
> and violence against targeted groups, denial of equal
> political rights and tolerance for private attacks upon
> minorities can be traced too often to official policies.

Some poor-bashing is, as Orwell would say, "independent of consciousness." But I believe some poor-bashing by the elite-owned media
and politicians is explained by Power's comments on the promotion of
communal hatred. Poor-bashing media and politicians play on classism,
as well as racism and sexism, to advance a political agenda.

The poor in Canada are not yet being murdered by government bullets, although some of them are being murdered when they try to supplement inadequate welfare rates with prostitution. And because of society's neglect they are dying earlier in life than richer people, as the loss
of control and hope for decent job or living standard leads to depression
and poor health. But the contempt, the lies, the innuendo, and the stereotypes of the media and the politicians are the first manipulating steps to

the hatred that must be necessary before killing seems acceptable. Already thoughts and talk about killing the poor are creeping into people's minds, as I've shown in the Introduction and Chapter 1.

Piven and Cloward wrote about the English workhouses in the nineteenth century:

> The workhouse was designed to spur men to contrive ways of supporting themselves by their own industry, to offer themselves to any employer on any terms. It did this by making pariahs of those who could not support themselves; they served as an object lesson, a means of celebrating the virtues of work by the terrible example of their agony.

In 1990s Canada, it was writers like Francis and politicians like Klein who made pariahs of people who used welfare in order to "celebrate the virtues" of low-wage work.

The lying, vicious, and distorted media stories made receiving welfare or UI seem like a crime. The put-a-human-face-on-poverty stories may not have intended to denigrate people who were poor, but they did help to make poverty an individual, not a societal issue, and kept the public from seeing the laws that caused poverty and the people who benefited from those laws.

When all this helped make the general public's thinking about people on welfare and UI "independent of consciousness," and when their "range of thought" about poverty issues was "diminished" to bashing the poor, then welfare and UI could be slashed without the public outcry one would have expected in a country with a forty-five-year history of pride in its social programs.

Chapter 7

The new poor laws: Helping employers and cheapening labour

Why pay people if Mr. Harris will give you slaves?

**Ontario Coalition Against Poverty,
Northumberland**

Members of the Walton family, owners of Wal-Mart department stores, are tenth to fourteenth on *Forbes Magazine*'s list of the richest people in the world. The Waltons have over $100 billion between them. They aren't dependent on welfare; they aren't even dependent on work. The Waltons, an article in *The Nation* reports, inherited their wealth.

Warren Smith wasn't born so lucky. When I talked to him in 1997 he depended on work and welfare to survive and support his family. He didn't want me to use his real name, he said, because his poor-bashing experience "brings back too many bad memories." On the same night in 1995 that Mike Harris was elected Premier of Ontario, someone painted huge red letters on the outside of the house where Smith lived with his wife and two children: "Get a job welfare."

"It was degrading and humiliating," Smith said about the graffiti. "In a small town everyone knows everyone. The kids get teased."

Smith had worked in a factory at $11-12 an hour, then got laid off and had medical problems. He was on welfare and going to school when the poor-basher painted on his house.

Two years later, Smith was working seventy hours a month at his local Wal-Mart store for $7.50 an hour, or $525 a month. He was also on welfare because the Wal-Mart job didn't pay nearly enough to support his family. Even on full-time hours, his pay would have been too little to live on—less than $1,300 a month—and would have had to be topped up by welfare. Smith didn't mind Wal-Mart, but he hated Harris.

What are the connections between the billionaire Waltons, their poor-bashed employee, Ontario's Premier Harris, and other people who may not be on welfare but have to take low-wage jobs? Harris used poor-bashing to get elected, then brought in welfare policies that hurt people who are poor but also helped the Waltons get employees without having to pay them a living wage, adding to those billions they inherited. Harris's policies also meant workers who aren't on welfare have to compete with people who are and take wages that are as low as Smith's. In other words, the Ontario government's welfare system is designed so that public money, funnelled through the very poor, subsidizes the incredibly rich, and helps pull down the wages of the working poor.

We haven't heard yet that Wal-Mart has fired workers who weren't on welfare to hire workers who were, but that's what was happening in Speenhamland by 1834. As we saw in Chapter 2, English historian E.P. Thompson noted that this way of combining welfare and work "had a single tendency: to destroy the last vestige of control by the labourer over his own wage or working life." In Ontario today, and in other provinces, the welfare system is organized so workers who aren't on welfare have to compete with those who are. The new welfare rules also provide that any person on welfare who quit or was fired from a job like Smith's would be cut off welfare for three months, or six months if it was the second time.

Smith understood the political and economic situation that put him in poverty: "Lack of jobs is the main reason people go on welfare," he explained. "I'm not putting Wal-Mart down or anything. You have to do what you gotta do. It's work. It's honest. There's nothing wrong with it. A lot of people say 'Get another job.' Well, where? Boeing hired three hundred and had thirty thousand applications. They hired the ones with experience."

The Harris government, like other provincial governments and the federal government, was changing welfare rules to force the poor to fit into the new part-time, casual, temporary, and low-paid work of the 1990s and beyond. By 1997 more than half of part-time workers in Canada didn't work a regular day shift and more than one-third worked an irregular or on-call schedule. Part-time workers earned an average of 26 per cent less per hour than full-time workers and had far fewer benefits. According to the Canadian Labour Congress, "Employers have replaced full-time with part-time jobs to cut costs and to foster competition between workers for access to hours as part of a deliberate anti-union strategy." George Pedersson, a Vancouver business economist, explained that the pressure on business to cut costs caused the growth in part-time work. "The biggest cost is labour cost," he told a *Vancouver Sun* reporter. "Part-time workers allow employers more flexibility—they can be scheduled to work only during peak business periods—combined with no fringe benefits." Modern corporations, like the Speenhamland landowners, want to pay workers a pittance and discard them the instant they are not needed. Across Canada the new poor laws of the 1990s were accommodating them.

Smith's story is just one of hundreds of thousands about people whose lives were affected by Canada's new poor laws of the 1990s. In this chapter, I'm going to examine some of these poor laws, passed by Liberal, Conservative, and New Democrat provincial governments, and the Liberal federal government. In each case these laws were "justified" with poor-bashing rhetoric; they undermined the wages and working conditions of other workers who weren't on welfare; and they pushed people who didn't have jobs into deeper poverty. Some of the laws are very similar to the old British Poor Laws that were put in place as the capitalist system developed.

Federal poor-bashing laws

The mother of Canada's new poor laws was the Canada Health and Social Transfer (CHST), which replaced the Canada Assistance Plan (CAP). It was announced in the 1995 federal budget and became law on April 1, 1996. The government prepared for the CHST with its poor-bashing green paper *Improving Social Security in Canada*. CAP put into law five economic rights:

- the right to welfare when in need
- the right to an amount of welfare that meets basic requirements
- the right to appeal welfare decisions you disagree with
- the right not to have to work or train for welfare
- the right not to be denied welfare because you're from another province.

The CHST abolished the first four of these rights and cut billions of dollars from federal grants to provinces for health, education, and welfare.

The only CAP right that employers liked was the right not to be denied welfare because of the province you're from. This was kept. It helps workers move from province to province seeking jobs.

CAP had been guaranteeing standards for poor people for thirty years. The federal government was supposed to give provinces half their welfare costs only if they met the CAP standards. It's true that the standards were often ignored. For example, welfare rates were never enough to meet recipients' basic requirements, as CAP required. In addition, several provinces brought in workfare programs during CAP's last years even though CAP forbade them.

All the same, CAP provided a national standard of rights that was useful for the poor. I can remember being at a meeting of ELP members and the B.C. minister of social services, Claude Richmond, a Social Crediter, in the late 1980s. Richmond told our delegation that if it weren't for CAP, his government would have brought workfare to British Columbia. So CAP was protecting province's low-income people then.

The CHST was a poor-bashing law. It destroyed the legal rights of low-income people to adequate welfare and freely chosen work; it allowed provinces to drastically undermine the standard of living for people who needed welfare and those who worked at low-wage jobs. The changes actually started before 1996 because the provinces knew the federal government had no interest in enforcing CAP. A NAPO study released in 1997 showed how the CHST affected provincial and territorial laws about welfare:

- Welfare rates were cut in British Columbia, Alberta, Saskatchewan (for "employable" people sharing rent), Manitoba, Ontario, Quebec, Nova Scotia, Prince Edward Island, and Newfoundland.

- Single parents were forced to look for paid work when their children were at younger ages in the Yukon, British Columbia, and Manitoba.

- More stringent requirements to search for work, or workfare, were imposed in the Northwest Territories, British Columbia, Alberta, Manitoba, Ontario, and Quebec; failure to meet provincial requirements led to welfare cut-offs.

- People were forced to apply for the Canada Pension at age sixty, the pension amount was deducted dollar for dollar from welfare (New Brunswick, British Columbia, Saskatchewan). Nova Scotia began deducting children's CPP survivor benefits from welfare.

- In some provinces supplementary grants for extra food, shelter, clothing, or crises were revoked. Dental assistance was reduced in other provinces and health user fees imposed.

- In Manitoba and British Columbia, welfare laws were changed so that the provinces were no longer required to provide assistance to people in need.

With CAP gone, the welfare guarantees that had been a sort of lowest minimum wage, below which no worker would have to fall, were also lost.

Another federal poor-bashing program is the Child Benefit, sometimes called the Canada Child Tax Benefit. Sue Bruce and Michelle Forrest tipped me off to the poor-bashing nature of the Child Benefit before it had been officially announced. Bruce was a single mother on welfare and Forrest a welfare advocate. We were talking in Bruce's Winnipeg home in December 1996 with Deborah Graham, also a single mother on welfare. They were angry. Bruce had been telling us how she tried to make ends meet for herself and her two children. One child had been injured in a car accident and had only one kidney; the other had schizophrenia. "You're always taking from your food budget to buy what they need, vitamins or special fat pencils," Bruce told me. "The kids eat but I only eat about once a day cause there's just not enough to go around."

Parents on welfare eating once a day was old news for this group. Their disgust was prompted by what Forrest had heard on the news. "The first ministers say they're going to help children by putting money into food programs, not money for parents."

The Canada Child Tax Benefit was to be announced as part of Paul Martin's February 1997 federal budget. The details we were just learning about that December are complex, but Forrest's analysis proved to be correct.

Before that budget, low-income parents in Canada, including parents on welfare, were eligible to receive a Child Tax Benefit of $1,020 per year, paid monthly, for their first child; $2,040 for two children; and $3,105 for three children. If they had a paid job, parents with incomes under $20,921 could also get up to $500 from the Working Income Supplement.

The gist of the new plan, as explained by a Human Resources Development Canada (HRDC) pamphlet, was that by July 1998 families with incomes under $20,921 with paid work would get a Child Benefit Supplement of a bit more money than was available in 1996: $105 more, per year if they had one child, $510 a year if they had two children, and $840 if they had three children.

What enraged Bruce, Forrest, and Graham was that families on welfare, which included about 60 per cent of the poor children in the country, would not see a penny of the new money. That's because the two levels of government conspired to allow provinces to deduct the increase in the benefit from the welfare received by families with children. (As it turned out, only two provinces, Newfoundland and New Brunswick, passed the Child Benefit increase announced by Martin in 1997 to families on welfare.) Theoretically provinces would be encouraged to put some of the money they saved into services for poor children, such as school breakfast programs. That's what Forrest had heard on the news.

"This is poor-bashing," she pointed out. "Many mothers [on welfare] are suffering from low grade malnutrition. It sends the message to kids that their parents are failures, that they aren't parenting.... It teaches children to have a real target for their anger, the failing parent," Forrest went on. "I think it's obscene."

"It creates a class system of good rich and shitty poor parents," added Bruce in anger.

Why would a government concerned about child poverty design a program that left out the poorest 60 per cent of poor children?

Martin's 1997 budget speech tried to sound concerned. "Let us never come to believe that there is such a thing as a tolerable level of child poverty," he orated, "or that a growing gap between the rich and the poor is ever acceptable," implying that he was concerned about poor adults too. "It is a time to say that this will not be a good country for any of us until it is a good country for all of us." The privileged minister, whose own personal worth is estimated to be around $30 million, even said, "We must be able to speak for those whose voices are drowned out by the winds of change and the forces of privilege." I guess he didn't consider letting these people speak for themselves or listening to what they said.

Human Resources Development Canada paid Ekos Research over $45,000 to hold focus groups in major Canadian cities to figure out how to design and "spin" their Child Benefit proposal. Ekos concluded in its report, "Welfare recipients are seen in unremittingly negative terms by the economically secure." They added that focus group participants held vivid stereotypes of people on welfare that included "bingo" and "booze." As well, people on welfare were considered to be lazy and abusers of the system.

Ekos classified members of their focus groups as "secure" or "insecure" based on what they said about their chance of losing their job, control over their economic future, and difficulties making ends meet. While many, especially in the insecure group, said that more full-time jobs paying more than minimum wage are needed to reduce child poverty, many also based their views on "stereotypical images," said the report. "The working poor were esteemed and sometimes lionized" while "welfare recipients are ascribed a number of emotional, moral and intellectual deficiencies." One focus group member said, "I'm sorry, but you've got a lot of people out there who don't give a damn about their kids. As long as they can go to bingo and buy their beer and cigarettes, they're happy."

While Sue Bruce and other parents on welfare live on one meal a day so they can afford what their children need, the Ekos report said "there was a great deal of scepticism expressed about the ability and/or willingness of parents to transfer assistance to their children."

The Ekos report admitted what the government was doing. The rationale for the Child Benefit proposal "reinforces the growing moral interpretation of poverty." Ekos also observed that there was a contradiction between the focus group participants' stereotypes of people on welfare and their own understanding that unemployment "will be a fixed feature of the new economy."

By October 1997, *Globe and Mail* writer Edward Greenspon exposed what anti-poverty groups had been trying to get heard for over a year: "As details of the national child benefit come into sharper focus, it is emerging as far more of a work-incentive program than an anti-poverty one." In other words, the Child Benefit is a program that forces parents to work at poverty and below poverty level jobs. Greenspon gave examples of provinces planning to use their savings from the federal benefit for programs that would help only families with paid jobs. For example, Ontario was considering a day-care tax credit for working families with incomes under $40,000 a year and health benefits for children of working parents.

In Bruce's Winnipeg living room that December, Deborah Graham explained that the provincial government was "trying to dump single mothers with kids over six into the garment industry and call centres," industries notorious for low wages and low opportunity. Graham talked about a woman she had met who worked for twenty-five years in the garment industry. At the end she made $8.50 an hour. "This is what they are training women for. They are entrapping women in poverty and their kids in poverty."

Writing in the C.D. Howe Institute publication *Family Matters*, Nancy Naylor said a child benefit program "would make welfare less appealing" to families with children whose prospects for jobs were at or near minimum wage. I think I knew what Bruce, Graham, and Forrest would say about welfare being "appealing." And I wondered if single parents working at a Manitoba call centre at minimum wage would think their job was "appealing" even if the government kicked in Child Benefit money.

Naylor revealed why corporations like the Child Benefit: "It would ensure that parents of dependent children could ... move into the labour force on the same basis as adults without dependents." In other words, the parents can afford to compete with single people for minimum-wage jobs; the corporations have more people competing for low-wage jobs. In Manitoba and most other provinces, single parents on welfare are forced to accept any "suitable" job available if their children are over a certain age. The federal Child Benefit, combined with the provincial rule that forces single parents to look for work when their children are over six, meant that Bruce and other single parents on welfare could be cut off welfare regardless of the needs of their families, if they don't take minimum-wage jobs.

The Child Benefit and the work-when-your-child-is-six welfare rules had nothing to do with getting people out of poverty. After all, you could only get the full benefit if your income was below $20,921, less than the poverty line for a family of two by 1995. They just meant that government, not the employer, would support the children in poverty. Meanwhile, the children would lose the work and nurturing that the parent was able to do at home before she had to work full-time.

Just before I left Bruce's house, her children delighted in giving me some Christmas candles they had made. I've kept them to remind me of the meals Bruce didn't eat so her children could buy the wax, and the time she spent helping her children learn to be generous so they could have the pleasure of giving in the Christmas season. Would she have been able to do that if she had been chained to a minimum-wage call-centre job taking home (with the Child Benefit) about the same amount of money as welfare paid?

Some groups in Canada thought the Child Benefit was a good idea because it provided extra money to working families, just as many groups liked the mothers' pension in the 1920s. In the 1920s people of colour and Aboriginal people were excluded from the pension. Since the 1990s, people on welfare have been excluded from increases in the Child Benefit. In both cases the idea that one group is more deserving than another was firmly in place, and people suffered because of it.

The Child Benefit is a component of another policy we need to watch out for. The C.D. Howe Institute's Thomas Courchene, in *Social Canada in the Millennium*, suggested in 1994 that a good project for the next century would be for provinces to experiment with ending the minimum wage. This could be done, he said, if the government was supporting children with the Child Benefit and if workfare and trainfare policies were in place for all employable people, including single parents. In other words, the Child Benefit is part of a corporate strategy to justify ending the minimum wage.

Will the Canada Child Tax Benefit make a dent in child poverty? I don't think so. In the minds of a lot of powerful people, really ending child poverty would "destroy the incentive" of the child's parents to work at low wages. The public stereotypes about lazy, drunk, single parents help justify a plan that really serves employers who want low-wage workers. The Child Benefit is the federal government's part of a network of policies that use the public's concern for poor children to force poor parents to flood a cheap labour market that doesn't have work for everyone who wants a job.

British Columbia's new poor laws

By 1995, British Columbia's NDP government, which had a history of sticking up for low-income people when in opposition, was preparing new laws that would hurt people on welfare and undermine wages for low-paid workers. My best guess is that NDP politicians had lived through the poor-bashing campaigns described in chapters 5 and 6. As well, government social policy people and spin doctors convinced them that their welfare changes were a new, made-in-B.C. policy, not a modern version of the old Poor Laws. The B.C. experience is a warning about depending on a social-democratic government to treat the poor humanely and to reduce poverty. When its welfare policies were attacked, the NDP government bashed the poor to save itself.

All this was preceded by the traditional report, in June 1995, establishing the language, the "spin," and making policy suggestions. It was called the *Premier's Forum Report*. As we saw in Chapter 1, the thirty-person Forum included only one representative of poor people. The report used the poor-bashing language of dependency, incentive, and rewarding work. It said young people should be "streamed into training, treatment, or work," implying that any young person not working or training needed "treatment," presumably for alcohol or drug addiction. The poor-bashing vocabulary accompanied labour-cheapening policy recommendations. Single parents on welfare with children over three should be forced into the labour force even though the official unemployment rate was 9 per cent. Young adults, the report said, should be required to work for their cheques; welfare should be reduced for people who refused government so-called "training"; and some jobs would be subsidized, meaning employers would get a windfall and people who weren't on welfare would have to compete with those who came equipped with a welfare subsidy. The report also said that federal government rules should be changed to allow workfare.

In November 1995 the B.C. government followed up on the Premier's Forum report and announced the B.C. Benefits Acts to replace the old program that had been called Guaranteed Available Income for Need. Details of the new welfare rules were set out in a pamphlet called *BC Benefits: Renewing Our Social Safety Net*. Welfare for single people was cut from $546 to $500, lower even than under the Conservatives in Ontario ($520). The support portion of the B.C. welfare cheque, $175 a month for everything except rent, was lower in actual dollars than the $191 it had been in 1980 when the right-wing Social Credit Party was in power. And the cost of living had doubled since then. Couples without children were cut by $92 a month, from $903 to $811.

Youth were to be denied any kind of training for the first seven months on welfare. Government statistics showed that most of them would be off welfare by then without being pushed. But after seven months they would be forced to jump through Ministry job clubs, and/or career planning hoops or be cut off. Job clubs are programs in which people learn about writing their resumés, and how to be interviewed, and they often force people to apply for a certain number of jobs per day. While youth don't have to enter a workhouse, as the poor did in England in the nineteenth century, or break 650 pounds of rock, as they did in Toronto in 1915, youth now had to endure being "patronized and treated like defects," as one youth described two job clubs he attended. Even though the job clubs resulted in "flashy, competitive resumés, and new interview skills," there still were not enough jobs to go around. Failure to do what the Ministry told you to do, however, meant that you could be denied welfare.

The province's 1995 poor laws included subsidized jobs for youth on welfare. Like the poor boys in Lyons in the sixteenth century, B.C. youth were to be attached to employers who could get up to $8,000 a year for hiring and supposedly training them while paying minimum wage.

In earlier days welfare rules recognized motherhood as a legitimate calling if the children were under twelve. Now, single parents on welfare were forced to look for full-time low-wage jobs as soon as their youngest child turned seven. The government said it was helping these mothers find work with its new B.C. Family Bonus, a forerunner of the federal Child Benefit. The Family Bonus provided up to $103 per month per child to low-income families *with paid work*. Although people on welfare would get the $103, it was deducted dollar for dollar from their welfare cheque. This revived the old deserving/undeserving judgments: a child in a family where the parents were not on welfare was deserving and got to keep the $103 a month. A child in a family on welfare was undeserving and couldn't keep the $103.

Like the federal Child Benefit that followed it, the Family Bonus, while it did provide a bit more money to some working families, was also part of a cheap labour strategy, really a workfare or forced labour program in disguise. The welfare rule forcing single parents on welfare to accept "suitable" employment when their youngest child was seven, in some provinces younger, is a crucial aspect of the Family Bonus and similar federal Child Benefit schemes.

In British Columbia it didn't matter how many children were in the family. It didn't matter if the "suitable" employment paid far less than the poverty line. It didn't matter if mothers were needed at home by their children, unless the government agreed that a child was disabled. The government's B.C. Benefits brochure pointed out proudly that a single mom with two children could work full-time at minimum wage and get $43 a month more than she could on welfare, because of the new family bonus. The brochure didn't point out that $43 could go pretty fast in extra day-care, transportation, and clothes expenses, leaving the family still thousands of dollars below the poverty line. It didn't say that it takes time and work to survive while living in poverty; that mom would be too worn out at the end of her paid workday to still cook from scratch, shop at rummage sales, and walk instead of drive.

The corporate-funded C.D. Howe Institute approved. John Thompson of the Institute said that the B.C. government plan had "to some extent accepted the logic of workfare."

The same month B.C. Benefits was announced, The Kamloops Active Support Against Poverty Society demanded that Dan Miller, then Minister of Skills, Labour, and Training, resign or be fired. "I've never helped my kids by simply giving them everything they've ever asked for," Miller said. "I've helped them by giving them some direction. Sometimes a little tough love. I think that's the way we should approach these kinds of questions." His remarks fuelled the poor-bashing public perception that people on welfare were to be treated like undisciplined children. "Miller is talking about adults who are desperately looking for work in a shrinking labour market with wages that are not keeping up to the cost of living," Charlene LaCombe of the Kamloops group pointed out.

Like the federal CHST, B.C. Benefits took away the right to welfare of any person in need. Only the "deserving" were entitled now. People from other provinces were definitely not deserving. B.C. Benefits made them wait three months before they qualified. Advocacy groups heard of hundreds of people who were affected by this. One man, for example, came to the province for a job, took the job for a few days, got sick, and ended up on the street panhandling to pay for his colostomy bags because he had not lived in British Columbia for three months. People with AIDS were denied benefits. Although the waiting period was later rescinded, it was a shock to the people who needed benefits.

Welfare was also denied to people who had outstanding arrest warrants from other provinces. These were people who had moved to British Columbia before their charges were dealt with. They hadn't been proven guilty, and in many cases they tried to get the police bureaucracies to obtain and process the warrants, which could take months. In November 1997, *The Long Haul* reported that Vancouver's Downtown Eastside Residents' Association tried to help a person who was forced to plead guilty to a ten-year-old charge that would have been dropped if he had had the resources to deal with it. The man pleaded guilty so he could get welfare to feed his children. In another case, a man with HIV and a warrant did everything government wanted him to do about the warrant, but was still told he would have to wait months before the charges against him could be removed from the police computer. It wasn't until June 2000 that anti-poverty activists were able to win a court decision that said the government could not deny welfare to people because of outstanding warrants.

The old B.C. welfare act had said the purpose of income assistance was to "relieve poverty, neglect and suffering." The B.C. Benefits Acts replaced that phrase with a preamble that talked about self-sufficiency, individual responsibility, training, and financial accountability.

In April 1996 the new premier, Glen Clark, shortly to face an election, proudly released a study by the accounting firm KPMG. It said that changing the "management culture" at the social services ministry could reduce welfare caseloads by 5 to 10 per cent. Just what is "management culture?" According to KPMG, the welfare system should change from seeing itself as a program where financial assistance employees "are expected to pay [welfare] cheques based on the regulations" to a system where workers are "expected to assist and encourage claimants to pursue all alternatives."

"Changing management culture" was the 1996 newspeak version of the 1834 Poor Law commissioners' "work, confinement, and discipline" and "surrender of free agency." It was government policy that tried to change financial aid workers from helpers to harassers. There were new rules about lost cheques, having to pick up your cheque at welfare offices, not being able to keep what you earn, and more red tape for verifying that you were eligible for benefits. New rules also made it harder to get extra benefits like crisis grants. Leslie Campbell, a welfare advocate at First United Church in Vancouver, was outraged by a new policy that required people who needed winter coats to go to at least three charities that dispensed free clothing first. If none of them had a coat that would do, the person had to get each charity to write a letter confirming it. "I think it's evil," Campbell told me. "It's a way of saying to people, 'You're not worth anything. We only believe someone else.'"

In June 1996 B.C. had a new minister in charge of welfare and a significant change in the name of the Ministry from Social Services to Human Resources. The new name suggested that humans on welfare are "resources" for employers, not human beings with inherent dignity, reason, and conscience, as the United Nations' Universal Declaration on Human Rights defines us. And (low-paid) work was the focus of B.C. Benefits. Youth Works was the title of one program; Welfare to Work of another. Instead of a safety net for people in need, welfare was becoming a program to help employers get cheap labour, a "labour market readiness program" in social policy jargon.

ELP developed a questionnaire about the impact of B.C. Benefits and circulated it through anti-poverty groups in the province in early 1997. Some answers to the questions were reprinted in the February 1997 *Long Haul*: "The attitude of welfare workers has changed," wrote one respondent. "They now try to discourage and intimidate you from asking for help. I leave the office feeling useless, helpless, desperate and demeaned."

"I am being constantly harassed; treated like a worm," wrote another. "I would work if I could find a job."

The ELP questionnaire asked, "What welfare changes have helped you?" One person responded, "The changes aren't meant to help me. They're meant to punish and to be seen to punish." Another wrote, "They keep my ex out of the province." Most simply wrote "None," "Zilch," "Zero."

The last sentence of the B.C. government news release announcing the KPMG study said that the government wanted to "make work a better deal than welfare." Here was the old English Principle of Less Eligibility cropping up again. While the government did raise the minimum wage occasionally, even full-time work at minimum wage in 1996 paid only 90 per cent of the poverty line for a single person in a city. According to a report from the Social Planning Council of Metro Toronto, the B.C. minimum wage had paid 122 per cent of the poverty line in 1975.

Instead of making work a better deal, the B.C. government made welfare a worse deal. One financial aid worker, writing in the February 1997 *Long Haul*, said, "I have never experienced such punitive measures as have been instituted by this government." He had to deny welfare to young people "who've quit their telemarketing jobs because they couldn't face another day of pressure and insults; to middle-aged women who've quit apartment managing jobs because they couldn't tolerate the 24-hour demands of the job which allowed them free rent and a pittance for their work." This worker also had to deny benefits to young men who came from Newfoundland looking for work and encountered British Columbia's residency requirement for welfare (now repealed). "They sleep where they can, beg food where they can. They frequent job sites, willing to undercut hard-fought wages and benefits," wrote the worker.

When ELP asked people getting B.C. Benefits what was needed to make things better, their comments reflected the poor-bashing they had received under the "management culture" of the province's new poor laws: "Not to be harassed, or treated like a criminal because I ended up on welfare," wrote one respondent. "Having my word taken as being truthful, not being considered guilty until it is proven," wrote another. "I want to be treated as who I am, an educated, literate person who cannot find work, instead of a no-account useless and shiftless bum, which I am not," said a third.

In January 2000 *The Long Haul* revealed that agencies hired by the Chamber of Commerce and Tourism BC were setting up shop inside or next to welfare offices to funnel desperate people into jobs with members of these associations. The Chamber had been lobbying the government to allow scab labour and not to increase the minimum wage. The employment agency would get nearly $5,000 if a person who applied for welfare took one of the jobs and stayed with it for nineteen months. If people on welfare, or applying for welfare, turned down jobs, they could be cut off. What incentive would an employer have to pay a decent wage, knowing this? What impact would this program have on other workers in small businesses across the province and in the tourism industry, already notorious for low wages? It was actually the Chamber of Commerce and Tourism B.C. that approached the government asking for this program and its fresh supply of potential employees who had to take any job offered.

The B.C. Ministry wasn't auctioning off families to textile factories, as the old English poorhouses did, but it was serving them up to the tourism industry for chambermaid jobs that couldn't be refused, and offering desperate young workers to employers with an $8,000 "training" allowance. The Ministry wasn't forcing people into workhouses to get food, but it was forcing them to surrender their freedom by taking any job offered or Ministry job and employment programs, even when they already knew about resumés and interviews. And people who quit jobs couldn't collect welfare unless they could prove they had reasons that the Ministry approved.

People on welfare in the province were especially angered by the infamous consent form. In January 1998 the Ministry sent out 75,000 letters to people on welfare telling them they had to sign a form or their benefits would stop. The form allowed anyone in the Ministry to ask "any person" for "relevant" information about a person on welfare. It listed examples of who "any person" might be: the Workers' Compensation Board, the Insurance Corporation of B.C., Human Resources Development Canada, foreign countries, banks, cheque-cashing services, landlords, and (the one that upset people the most) "past, present or future employers of myself or my family members." Outraged people swamped the phones at anti-poverty groups using words like "blackmail," "suicide," "nazi," "coercion," and "poor-bashing." "Could concen-tration camps and microwave ovens that seat hundreds follow?" Bernie Boyd asked, in a letter to the editor of the March 1997 *Long Haul*. Tom Anderson wrote, "The issue is not just privacy, it's also human dignity." People on welfare had to consent to their privacy being invaded if they wanted to feed their children or themselves.

People on welfare gathered and burned the forms in public places, while carrying signs saying "We are human too." They badgered their politicians and designed their own forms revoking consent. The govern-ment temporarily withdrew the form, redesigned it with minor improve-ments, and then forced people to sign or lose their benefits.

Why did the government bring in such a form? Was it really because they needed the information to prevent fraud? Or was it to send a message that if you apply for welfare, your privacy ends—a message that any job would be better than welfare no matter how low the wage, or how insecure or bad the working conditions are?

Shortly before people on welfare were protesting the consent form, another group of much better-off people, with Premier Clark's support, was protesting an income tax form that required them to provide personal information about their foreign assets. Under Canadian law they were supposed to pay taxes on money they received from these assets. The federal auditor general was concerned that this income was not being reported, so the 1995 federal budget announced a new rule requiring all Canadians to report foreign assets over $100,000 to Revenue Canada.

By January 1999 the B.C. government was still after Ottawa to "change their position on the federal asset disclosure legislation." If it was okay with Premier Clark for the rich to avoid giving information on their assets, why was it not okay for the poor do to the same? "Our govern-ments expect low-income people to disclose all their assets in order to get welfare, but they don't expect high-income people to disclose their assets," tax expert Neil Brooks explained to me over the phone.

Anti-poverty activists, including me, found the NDP's betrayal of the poor hard to take because the party had taken good positions on poverty in the past. I wasn't expecting a lot from the NDP, but I certain-ly wasn't expecting it to cut rates, deny welfare to people in need, pur-posefully devise a harsh "management culture," and call poor people names.

Mike Harcourt was still premier when B.C. Benefits was announced in 1995. When I interviewed him in 1997 after he had retired from government, he was clearly aware of his blatant poor-bashing and wanted to distance himself from it. "I made some dumb remarks that I felt bad about and I apologized for it publicly, and was beat up for it by caucus and party members, for months on end. We had to deal with the focus on welfare fraud, the focus on the welfare system, funds going into the welfare system, the level of spending. It was a large issue with the B.C. public. I think we attempted to address it reasonably well."

But Harcourt didn't seem to know that B.C. had cut the rate for single employable people below Ontario's rate. He seemed not to understand how the B.C. Benefits policies were forcing people to take low-wage jobs. He acted as if B.C. Benefits was a new, not a centuries-old, program for people who were poor. He admitted that most people who are considered to be employable are on welfare for a short period only, about three months, he said, but then added that "a lot of them have alcohol and drug dependency problems, they have low skills or low self-esteem or all of the above"—a huge poor-bashing stereotype.

"We set out to change the whole structure dramatically; to treat people more in an individual way, or with encouragement either to seek employment or to be left alone and just lead as dignified a life as possible," he told me, as though B.C. Benefits policies were actually helpful to people who were poor.

"I don't know how anybody can live on $500 or $550 a month," he admitted. "It's very tough. But you can start to at $1,200-1,400 plus the other benefits and then move on up the employment scale to better jobs," he added cheerily, as though those jobs were sitting around ready to be claimed.

B.C. Benefits—low rates, management culture, and outright denial of benefits to some—was about harassing and degrading people on welfare. It was about making them into pariahs, like the people who had to enter workhouses in the nineteenth century. It was about making sure that no worker would want to endure what a person on welfare had to endure, so the worker would accept any job, no matter how low the pay and how demeaning.

More of Ontario's poor-bashing laws

In Ontario, workfare, or forced labour for people on welfare, was at the top of the Harris political agenda. Not only did the Conservative government reduce welfare rates by almost 22 per cent for everyone, but it was in Ontario that people on welfare were also forced most directly into workfare jobs. By 1996 it was announced that virtually all able-bodied people on welfare "will be required to accept offers of community place-ment, and/or employment support or employment placement as a con-dition of eligibility." A government summary of its new "Ontario Works" (welfare) programs said municipalities were to be the "service delivery agents" for workfare. Workfare, euphemistically called "community par-ticipation," would be mandatory for able-bodied people who had been on welfare for four months or longer. These people would work for seventy hours a month at the minimum wage of $6.85. They would be required to look for real jobs at the same time.

Workfare Watch, a joint project of the Community Social Planning Council of Toronto and the Ontario Social Safety Network, was set up in 1996 to monitor workfare policies and their impact. Its newsletter, also called *Workfare Watch,* reported on a huge outcry against workfare and an organizing effort from social justice groups across the province. As a result many municipalities, including Toronto and community groups like the Elizabeth Fry Society and Children's Aid Society of Metropolitan Toronto, initially refused to find workfare placements for people on welfare.

The province responded by ordering all municipalities to prepare "business plans" for workfare by September 30, 1997, to be approved by the welfare ministry. While government guidelines said that workfare jobs couldn't displace paid employees, the requirement was virtually impossible to enforce, according to *Workfare Watch*. A survey of towns with workfare plans revealed that people on welfare were to do clerical work, paint municipal offices, and install wheelchair entrances. They were to work in day cares, nursing homes, school breakfast programs, and tourism centres, in order to get their welfare cheques.

Harris's 1998 throne speech outrageously bashed the poor, saying, "Neither the people nor the government of Ontario will tolerate those who enjoy welfare benefits paid for by the Ontario taxpayer while they defy our laws and threaten the safety of hardworking citizens." Four paragraphs later Harris gave notice that the government "must and will overcome" the atrocious possibility (in the government's thinking, anyway) that people in workfare jobs would unionize and collect vacation pay or go on strike for higher welfare benefits. Soon the government passed the Prevention of Unionization Act. This made joining a union, bargaining collectively, or going on strike illegal for people in workfare projects.

That year Ontario government ministers talked openly about forc-ing people on welfare to do their workfare with private-sector employers.

In July Social Services Minister Janet Ecker promised to provide workfare workers to the private sector for free, with some restrictions. One possibility, according to a July 9, 1998, *Globe and Mail* article, would be to give employers the welfare cheque.

A government news release in November 1999 announced an insidious plan that would encourage municipalities who didn't agree with workfare to enforce it anyway. If municipalities didn't place enough people in workfare jobs, the province would hold back some of its municipal grants. Municipalities that exceeded their quota would get $1,000 per extra person they placed in a workfare job. In addition the government promised to put workfare placements in the Ontario public service, eroding yet another source of real jobs for workers who needed them. Real jobs didn't count towards a municipality's workfare quota, the Ottawa-Carleton region discovered in late 1999. The *Ottawa Citizen* reported that this region placed about eight hundred people a month in real jobs, while placing only about five hundred in workfare jobs. The provincial government wanted Ottawa-Carleton to find seven thousand workfare placements over two years.

By 1999, non-profit agencies and government departments were posting workfare jobs they called "community placement orders," like these from Northumberland County on May 18:.

- **Office Manager.** Essential to manage tourism office. Person should have excellent communication skills with ability to promote, supervise, maintain records and liaise with other organizations. Person would have understanding of the area tourism and [be] able to handle inquiries. Computer skills are an asset.

- **Labourer.** Duties would include moving materials and equipment, general building maintenance and light carpentry. Person should enjoy working outdoors and doing physical work.

- **Seniors recreational volunteer.** Involves dealing with the elderly in a long term facility, providing recreational activities such as playing cards and reading. Desire and ability to deal with the elderly in a long term residential setting.

- **Library helper.** Dealing with the patrons of a public library. Internet instruction for a rural community.

Good communication skills, desire to deal with the public, dependable, friendly and outgoing.

- **Receptionist**. Provide reception skills in a public government centre. Assist clients with photocopying, internet logging, faxing. Answer incoming phone calls and take messages. Book appointments and keep the centre's resources tidy and up to date.

- **Janitorial maintenance**. Cleaning and maintaining offices and program areas, involves lifting. Reliable, can use janitorial equipment and have an understanding of cleaning products.

In June 2000 Community and Social Services Minister John Baird announced that the provincial government would give over $7 million to municipalities for reaching workfare participation rates above the provincial target. Toronto, after first refusing to implement the program, got $622,000.

"The government's sole purpose is to ensure that ordinary people will work at any price and under any conditions," wrote *Workfare Watch* in August 1996:

> Many measures introduced in the past year have had exactly that effect: slashing welfare rates to starvation levels, repealing anti-scab labour laws, reversing changes in collective bargaining laws, gutting employment standards protections, workers' compensation and occupational health and safety standards. This is why it is more important than ever that we remember that workfare is not just a welfare issue. It is a fundamentally important issue for all working people and all those who care about the meaning of human dignity in society.

Eliminating adults from the discussion of poverty

As poor-bashing continued through the 1990s and new federal and provincial poor laws created deeper poverty, all across Canada adults were disappearing from public discussions about poverty. There was some talk about child poverty and the Child Benefit, and some outrage that child poverty had increased even though federal politicians had voted to eliminate it by the year 2000. But there wasn't even a pretence that the new poor laws would alleviate poverty for adults, only that they could get them working in paid jobs or workfare jobs. Welfare polices should be designed to provide "income support for those in need, while fostering independence, self-confidence and initiative, and starting to tackle child poverty," said the 1994 federal green paper on social policy. Tackling adult poverty wasn't on the federal agenda.

It's poor-bashing for governments and think-tanks to want to tackle only child poverty and exclude adult poverty. "What are the parents of these kids?" asked Rick Salutin in his *Globe and Mail* column "Debris?" For the most part the poor children that we're talking about are not orphans. They have parents who have been laid off from public- or private-sector jobs, or single parents working hard to care for them, or parents who have been cut off unemployment insurance, parents who are seeking jobs but can't find one—or maybe they have a job but the pay is so low that they need a welfare top-up. And what about adults who don't have kids? They are human beings with "inherent dignity, reason and conscience," and they need jobs and decent wages or a decent income too.

How the new poor laws hurt people with paid jobs

In virtually every province, poor-bashing in the 1990s paved the way for new welfare rules that forced both people who were on welfare and people who weren't to compete even more fiercely for low-wage jobs, and helped employers get even cheaper labour.

Eric Shragge describes how the poor-bashing stage was set in Quebec in 1986 when welfare officials dubbed "Bou-Bou Macoutes" were given power to visit the homes of people on welfare and interrogate their neighbours, ostensibly to root out fraud. By 1990 the province had a workfare program in which the government paid two-thirds of the wages of former welfare recipients who worked at places like Zellers, Canadian Tire, and Pizza Hut. Over half the employers surveyed said they would have hired people anyway.

In 1996 Manitoba's Social Services Minister Bonnie Mitchelson announced new poor laws for her province too: welfare rates would be cut, and single parents with children over six and everyone else except people with disabilities and women in crisis shelters would be expected to find work. She added that new jobs in the garment industry and in telephone call centres were opening up. That same year, *The Globe and*

Mail reported that a call centre of the Canadian Liver Foundation, lured to Manitoba with government training money in 1995, had shut down after six months, throwing about 140 people out of work, including 40 single parents who "exchanged welfare cheques for $7.50 an hour tele-marketing jobs."

The new unemployment insurance laws, renamed employment insurance, were even harsher than the new welfare laws of the 1990s. UI rules were changed so that fewer than half of unemployed people were eligible, and those eligible received a lower level of benefits—only 55 per cent of previous earnings, or less, compared to 60 per cent before the changes.

A report from the Canadian Centre for Policy Alternatives (CCPA) examines the impact of welfare cuts in the mid-1990s on the low-wage workforce in Quebec, Ontario, Alberta, and British Columbia. For the study, the authors Seth Klein and Barbara Montgomery use an economic model that assumes there were no other changes in the broader economy. Although the study is technical, it comes to a dramatic conclusion about how welfare cuts hurt low-wage workers: the only way the labour market could absorb all the people forced off welfare in those provinces would be to reduce wages for the bottom 40 per cent of hourly paid workers by almost 12.5 per cent.

An earlier study in the United States, where cuts have also been brutal, had similar results. Vermont economist Elaine McCrate reports on a study by the Economic Policy Institute estimating that wages of the poorest 30 per cent of workers would be depressed by nearly 12 per cent because of the influx of low-paid workers into the economy. McCrate also reports on another study by the Russell Sage Foundation. It found that by 1998, thirty thousand workfare workers in New York City had displaced twenty thousand other workers and reduced wages for the bottom third of the New York labour force by 9 per cent.

A *New York Times* article on April 1, 1997, explained, "Normally [employers] raise wages to lure people who would not otherwise be willing to take [low-wage] jobs. But with the injection of so many welfare recipients as workers, the wage pressure is dulled." The article quotes Richard Reinhold, chair of SOS Staffing Services in Salt Lake City. This company had placed seventy thousand temporary workers, making $6 to $8 an hour, in factories, assembly lines, warehouses, offices, and telemarketing companies. Without the people from welfare, Reinhold said, "We cannot fill all our orders for temps. To get enough people without them, we would have had to raise the wage." Keith Wine, of Norrell Services in Richmond, Virginia, agreed: "Everyone has been raising wages to get people. [The influx of people on welfare seeking jobs] will make it possible to hold pay steady."

In an article about how welfare "reform" is pushing wages down, McCrate describes welfare as a wage protection policy. Welfare allows job seekers to refuse the worst jobs because they have an alternative source of income, she explains. Since millions of people wouldn't "compete for jobs at whatever rock-bottom terms employers were offering, the labour market was not flooded with every single, desperate parent of a young child, displacing workers and driving down the earnings of the working poor and near-poor."

There is no doubt that Canada's new poor laws are forcing or harassing hundreds of thousands of Canadians to undermine the wages and working conditions of other, primarily low-wage workers. Many workers don't know this. They don't know it because the corporate think-tanks, the media, and politicians have manipulated and inflamed the old animosities towards people who are poor. After all, the elites and their media wanted Canadian workers to believe that people on welfare got $45,000 a year, as *Financial Post* columnist Diane Francis claimed. They wanted Canadian workers to then ask, as Francis asked, is it fair to "Canada's 12 million workers who pay taxes" that people on welfare get $45,000 a year? They wanted working people to believe, as Ralph Klein said, that "somebody down the street ... is doing no work whatsoever and taking home more money than the person who wants to be employed."

Some workers may think that people on welfare are too stupid or lazy or undisciplined to compete for their jobs. But that's the stereotype, not the reality. Most people who use welfare have worked in their lives and will work again. Many *are* working raising children or in jobs with low pay. Some 11 per cent of the heads of households on welfare in 1997, according to the National Council of Welfare, have attended some form of post-secondary education.

I believe that welfare is an important program for workers to have in case they are laid off, or become single parents, or sick, or can't work or earn enough for any reason. But because of poor-bashing, welfare and the people who use it are so despised that many workers can't imagine themselves ever needing welfare or ever having to take part in a workfare program. In the short term, it's important for people with paid work to think about these things and ask themselves, could I survive and function on the welfare benefits and under welfare rules as they are now if I become disabled, or my spouse left, or I lost my job? Should welfare rules force me to put up with very low pay and poor working conditions? Should they force me to go through their job clubs or so-called training programs if I already know how to look for jobs or already am trained? Should they force me to take a workfare job or any kind of job I may hate? If you still can't imagine needing welfare, ask yourself this: "Could I afford to compete with someone on workfare?" Answering these questions can help us see that we need to change our system so that no one is forced to live in poverty for any reason.

But if the public's thinking about people on welfare is "independent of consciousness," and its range of thought about poverty issues is "diminished" to bashing poor people, then few will understand how Canada's new poor laws are pushing down the wages of other workers, or even their own wages.

Chapter 8

Substituting charity for justice

Charity is nice but power is better.

**Placard message written by a person
who uses charity**

*I thought that giving was supposed to be a pleasure. Why
does it get turned around? Why are we made to feel
humiliated because we're receiving? We're supposed to be
grateful. We're not supposed to be arrogant, but why does
the giver get to be arrogant?*

A woman who uses charities

*There is no problem, of course, with private charity to the
unemployed, or to the poor, at whatever level ... First of all,
since it is voluntary, it can be cut off if contributors feel it
is doing more harm than good.*

Walter Block, Fraser Institute

Stretch limos drove up to the luxurious Trade and Convention Centre in
Vancouver. Women in evening gowns, accompanied by men in elegant
suits, entered the Pan Pacific Hotel. They had each paid $62.95 for a
ticket to the Taste of the Nation feast, which was to raise money to buy
a truck that would take leftover food from hotels and restaurants and
deliver it to the poor.

Outside the hotel, about twenty activists from ELP and other local
anti-poverty groups were making a statement about charity. Sheila
Baxter, the author of several books on poverty and a woman on welfare,
was wearing a handmade button that said, "charity, not justice." She sat

at a card table decorated with a single rose in a vase. Because she was portraying a rich woman, Baxter wore the fanciest clothes she could
scrounge: a fur stole, a dripping necklace and bracelet, and a hat. And she
had a nice meal in front of her, although it was nothing like the banquet
inside the hotel. As the skit proceeded, members of the anti-poverty
groups portraying "grovellers" got down on their knees to approach
Baxter for a bite of her meal. A woman came on her knees with a couple
of children. "Here are two bites of Brussels sprouts for the children,"
Baxter said, chowing down her own chicken, and then to the mom, "but
nothing for you. Haven't you heard of birth control?" Baxter was having
a ball, mimicking the poor-bashing lines she had heard during her years
on welfare. "What you need are some good budgeting lessons," she added.

Over a thousand people dined in luxury on April 25, 1991, at that
event and raised about $70,000.

Taste of the Nation was organized by a U.S. group called Share Our
Strength (SOS), which has been sponsoring these feasts since 1988. By
1998, SOS said, Taste of the Nation events were being held in over a hundred North American cities and had raised a total of $45 million for
grants to over a thousand organizations that provide food, job training,
and mentoring, and promote economic self-sufficiency. During roughly
the same period, according to Marianne Means, the U.S. government cut
about one trillion dollars out of social programs. Canadian federal and
provincial governments slashed billions from social programs and unemployment insurance.

SOS has a number of corporate partners, including American
Express, which had profits of nearly $2 billion in 1997 and over $100 billion in assets. Its chairman, James D. Robinson III, "probably did more to
bring about the [free trade] deal than any other single person in Canada
or the U.S.," according to author Linda McQuaig. In Canada, David
Culver of Alcan also worked hard for the free trade deal. Alcan was
another Taste of the Nation supporter.

Anti-poverty groups had been concerned that if the free trade deal
went through, Canadian federal and provincial governments would
change unemployment insurance and welfare systems to be more like the
U.S. systems. That would mean drastic cuts and more jobless people with
less income, or no income at all. Soon after the agreement went into
effect, drastic unemployment insurance cuts increased poverty for over
400,000 unemployed Canadians. Nearly $3 billion of federal funding was

cut, and longer periods in work were necessary to qualify for benefits for a shorter period; people who quit a job waited longer for reduced benefits.

According to a 1989 Global Economics study, 247,000 recipients with incomes under $10,000 a year would lose as much as $1,800 a year just from the UI cuts. Tens of thousands more would lose a little bit less. According to my calculation, based on this study, twenty-four fundraisers just like Vancouver's 1991 Taste of Nations event would have to be held *every day, every year*, just to make up for that 1989 UI cut for people with incomes under $15,000 a year.

Two years later the Taste of Nations event had become a regular occurence in Vancouver and Toronto. Barrie Mowatt, co-chair of the 1993 Vancouver Taste of Nations organizing committee, told reporter Karen Gram he did not think social programs were the answer to hunger. "If we institutionalize hunger by making a social welfare system, you deaden the soul," he said.

In Toronto the ticket price was $95 in 1993 and included "lavish feasting" on "Grilled Spanish Mackerel Marinated in Sweet White Bean Paste; Marinated Salmon with Mascarpone; Portobello Mushrooms on Snow Pea Vine with White Truffle Vinaigrette, French Macaroons, and Chocolate Fruite Japonaise," according to columnist Marion Kane. That was the year Professor Marjorie Cohen tallied up federal government cuts: social housing slashed $660 million; student loan subsidy ended; universal family allowance converted to a targeted program for only the poor; more cuts to unemployment insurance, cutting off completely people who were fired or quit, and reducing benefits from 60 to 57 per cent of earnings.

"It is rare that a program can effectively meet both philanthropic and business objectives as well as our Taste of the Nation sponsorship does," said Lloyd M. Wirshba, of American Express on the SOS web site in 1998. Yes, American Express could look good, sponsoring an event to feed the hungry, and obscuring the fact that its head honcho had lobbied fiercely for the deal that had led to the layoffs and slashed social programs that caused the hunger in the first place. Meanwhile only a few were asking if the Taste of the Nation met the nutritional needs or contributed to the dignity of people who were poor.

What kind of charity poor-bashes?

Talking about charity and poor-bashing is dicey for people who want to end poverty. I discussed the issue with NAPO executive members in

1997. Deb O'Connor, the Cobourg Ontario anti-poverty worker we met in Chapter 1, explained it this way: "There are a substantial number of people who are donating to charity and volunteering with all the best intentions in the world. I think that we have to be careful how we approach this because what we really want to do is get them to join the fight for justice, and I always worry that if we come on too strong, and accuse them of poor-bashing, we're not gonna get where we want to go."

Many of the low-income people I interviewed volunteer and contribute to charities in many ways. Poor people are doing acts of charity for each other all the time, although they mostly don't call it that. Sheila Baxter told me that once a week the people in her low-cost housing building have a meal with food donated from the food bank. She said it is a good way to get people together, that people really need the food, and she's grateful to the food bank for providing it. Millions of people who donate to charities and volunteer with them are kind and generous people. Some individuals work their hearts out with no thought of blaming or judging the poor, and some charitable organizations work hard to treat people with respect and even risk their charitable tax numbers by advocating for change. And people who are poor need the help.

I'm not criticizing the dictionary definition of charity as "love," "lenient judgment of others," and "help for the needy," but I believe we must think more critically about the role of charity in the economic system we live in. During the 1990s, as corporations pushed for cuts and governments implemented them, the public did notice that hardship and suffering were increasing. Not wanting to appear totally heartless, governments changed laws to promote charitable giving, as though that would make up for what they had cut. Corporations became more concerned about appearing to be generous.

Many low-income people see the idea of using charity to meet people's basic needs as a poor-bashing concept that replaces the human right to jobs, decent wages, unemployment insurance, pensions, and welfare. Sandy Cameron fasted for a week to protest the Taste of the Nation's 1994 Vancouver feast. "Private charity can't be a foundation for the human right to an adequate standard of living because it is voluntary, unpredictable, unable to meet a national crisis, and contributors can cut charity off," he wrote in an unpublished letter.

There are other problems with charities. It's common for people who receive charity to be poor-bashed; charities aren't accountable to the people they serve or to the public; lots of well-meaning charitable ideas have bad effects on people who are poor; and the very corporations that push to cut government job creation, welfare, and unemployment insurance are using their charitable donations to manufacture a good corporate image they don't deserve.

What are charities?

Canada has about 74,000 registered charities. To be registered, they have to be non-profit groups set up to relieve poverty or advance religion or education, or for other purposes beneficial to the community as a whole. If the government agrees that the group meets its criteria for registration, the group is given a tax number. This means that people who donate to that charity can receive a tax credit for what they donate. This works only if a person's income is high enough to pay taxes, which is another form of discrimination against the poor. If your taxable income is between $29,590 and $55,866, for example, and you donate $1,000 to a registered charity, your taxes would be reduced by about $400, depending on the rate in your province. But if your taxable income were zero and you donated to charity, you would get nothing.

Many of the 74,000 groups that have charitable tax status are not what we ordinarily think of as charities. They are non-governmental organizations like Big Sisters, or agencies that serve people with AIDs. Even the Fraser and C.D. Howe institutes have charitable tax status. In 1995 only 17 per cent of Canada's registered charities were welfare-related. Of course people and groups can give charitable food, shelter, and clothing without tax numbers or being registered and receiving tax deductions.

Who gives and how much? Jeffrey Frank and Stephen Mihorean say that in 1995 all the charities together had $86.5 billion in revenue and 67 per cent of that came from government. Donations from individuals accounted for 7.6 per cent of charity revenues, while donations from corporations accounted for a mere 1 per cent. The poorest people are the most generous, according to another article. People whose income is under $20,000 a year donate almost 1.5 per cent of it to charity, while those who get over $80,000 donate less than half a per cent.

How charity poor–bashes

Can charity be a form of poor-bashing? That's a question I asked many of the low-income people and anti-poverty activists I interviewed. Most said that it usually is, although they noted that they themselves were often volunteers with groups that have charitable tax numbers or provide free services or goods for low-income people.

Continuing unequal power relationships

People think charity is a poor-bashing concept because of its power relations. Charity creates a relationship of power and dependence instead of equality and respect. An ELP research project asked about a hundred people who use charities for their opinions. The researchers asked a small group of these people, "What is charity?" The first answers were things like "sharing," "helping out those in need," "gifts," and "kindness." Then one person mentioned that all those definitions related to the giver of the charity and not the receiver: "To a lot of people who give to charity, or who have never needed it, charity is a good thing. It's sharing ... but when you don't have anything to eat for yourself, let alone donate, then you see things differently ... it's humiliating and degrading." This comment moved others to add to their comments about charity: "cold," "impersonal," "dependency," "tax-free," and "poorly distributed." One person in the study simply wrote on a placard, "Charity is nice but power is better." ELP's study was called *The Waste of a Nation*.

A couple of weeks before the first Vancouver Taste of the Nation dinner in 1991, I went to a food bank lineup to ask people what they thought of the event. "We shouldn't have to eat scraps, but it's better than climbing in bins," one person told me. Another said, "I think it's the government's responsibility, not charity's. They should raise the minimum wage. Do you want people to live like animals?"

The Fraser Institute, famous for saying that poverty is not a problem in Canada, for poor-bashing people on welfare, and for advocating policies that increase poverty, admits that it likes charity *because* it gives the donors power over the poor: "There is no problem, of course, with private charity to the unemployed, or to the poor, at whatever level.... First of all, since it is voluntary, it can be cut off if contributors feel it is doing more harm than good," wrote Walter Block of the Institute. For the Fraser Institute, it's perfectly acceptable that the "contributors" have the power to decide who should eat and who shouldn't. In fact, in the Fraser Institute's 1994 brief to the federal Social Security Review, senior policy analyst Owen Lippert says that welfare should be returned to the principles of "public charity to provide short-term assistance for individuals in dire need."

"Charity is a form of poor-bashing for sure because it is based on an unequal power relationship," Bev Brown told me, speaking of the Fraser Institute type of charity that judges and controls the poor. Brown herself spends hours each day volunteering her time to work on poverty and human rights issues. To Brown, "If you think you're better than the person you're being charitable to, then it's poor-bashing."

The idea that donors are somehow better than people who receive charity probably has deep psychological and sociological roots. In Canada it is also infused with over four hundred years of the Protestant and then Puritan ideas about work and morality described in Chapter 2. According to these beliefs, God was pleased by disciplined labour at any work, and the accumulation of wealth is a sign that God favours you. To be without work is a sign that God does not favour you. Along with these beliefs goes the usually false assumption that people who need charity for basic needs don't work, or refuse work.

Whatever their origins, feelings of superiority allow many donors to make all kinds of judgments about who "deserves" charity and who is "undeserving." Behind this thinking lurks the notion that some human beings deserve to have food and shelter but others don't, and the donor has the right to make these distinctions. In my thinking, people have a right to decide if they are going to donate money to, say, a Christian church or a Sikh Temple. But when the issue is food, clothing, and shelter, the necessities of life, I agree with the United Nations, that these are basic human rights that are too important to be left to the whim of potential donors.

In 1998 Vancouver radio station JRFM advertised a fund called Basics for Babies. The station solicited donations and participation in fundraising events like golf games by saying "Somewhere in Vancouver right now babies are going hungry." If that is true, and it probably is, it requires a much more intense effort by citizens and politicians than simply going to a golf game that raises funds for charity. The hungry babies shouldn't have to depend on your decision to play golf for their food. The donors have the power. If they decide to play in the special golf game, babies in need get food. If they don't, the babies stay hungry.

Babies are seen as the "deserving" poor. But if you're seen as the undeserving poor, it's more difficult to get charity. Have you ever heard of Basics for Unemployed Single Men or Basics for Hungry, Homeless Drug Addicts? These people need food, shelter, and "basics" too, but are less likely to get them because many people don't consider them "deserving."

"If we have a family who needs something; if they're a nice family; if mom was beaten by her ex-boyfriend or husband and she has three kids under five and they're all blond and blue-eyed and curly haired; if she is struggling through getting her Grade 12 and working in the evenings as a waitress at John's diner and doesn't smoke, drink or play bingo, I can get her anything." This has been Linda Lalonde's experience advocating for people who are poor in Ottawa. "If I have a woman who is drug addicted and just got her kids back from the [child protection authorities] because she's kept herself clean for a period of time and her abusive boyfriend is in and out of the picture and she drinks from time to time, and her kid needs special medication not covered by the medical plan, I'm gonna have to pull teeth to get that," Lalonde continued. "Charity encourages that kind of deserving, undeserving distinction, because the kind of charity that most Canadians are interested in is the kind where they see that they've given money that has specific results. Their gratification is not to advance the cause of mankind, it's that 'I have saved that cute little blond blue-eyed kid from being cold because while I was watching my soap operas I knitted toques and mitts for him. Damn, I'm a good person.' That model is the poor-bashing model."

Lalonde blames the "disease telethons" for giving donors the idea that they are "entitled to gratification" for whatever they give. Many people are really giving to their conscience, she says, not to the person in need. But "they want a picture to put in their conscience while they're giving to themselves" because that picture blocks the obvious self-gratification." Donors can say, "I'm not giving for the self-gratification, I'm giving for that picture that I can see."

Todd Cunningham, of the Somerset West Health Clinic in Ottawa, told me that charity "sets up ... the whole pity thing .... If you're pitying people, you're not really treating them with dignity. That's ... the charity model. It's, 'Oh you poor thing. You need help. We'll give it to you.' Or, 'You rotten jerk. We're not helping you at all cause you're an alcoholic or a drug addict.' But if you're pitying someone, you're not seeing them as an equal. If you're not seeing them as an equal, you're not respecting them. So many people in that area would probably think they're doing wonderful work, and in some ways they are, I suppose, but they're not seeing the bigger picture."

Aline Akeson had worked for decades on poverty issues at the Centre for Social Justice when I talked to her in Ottawa in 1997. She encountered a lot of people who made judgments about the poor when she started a food bank in Ottawa, a move she later saw as a mistake. People had been coming into her office who had been hungry for three or four days. Akeson put signs up saying which churches people could get food at on which days, and "all the churches started calling up saying, 'They can't come here. They're not Catholic or they're not Italian' or whatever. They were just hungry. So I decided to get them all together to open a place that would give food .... It was hilarious in a way. 'We can't give them food if they're not married. We can't give them food if they have children out of wedlock. We can't give them food if they're drinking. We can't give them food if they smoke.' We finally got the thing opened and we argued over what we gave them. It had nothing to do with what people needed, and they didn't [understand] it, even there, providing food to people. They don't understand why people have to come to the food bank."

Because charity is an unrelentingly positive concept in the media, its unequal power relationships are assumed and accepted. The idea that citizens should be equally powerful and respected, which is basic to democracy, is undermined.

Creating the illusion that needs get met
Another way that charity can poor-bash is by creating the illusion that charity meets the needs of people who are poor, and that, therefore, our economic system is more or less working well.

One person I talked to in the food bank lineup in 1991 told me that he thought fundraising events like the Taste of Nations would "alleviate 1 per cent of the problems for a short time." Alleviating 1 per cent of the problems for a short time is hardly dealing with the other 99 per cent over the long term. He said that accepting charity made him feel "downtrodden" and have negative feelings. "But you go with your needs and not your feelings," he explained.

When I talked to Susan Learoyd at the Ottawa Social Planning Council, she told me that charity "is a visible way of making people feel good about a problem, but not really addressing it in any depth. It doesn't address the issue of why the person is poor. It doesn't address jobs. It doesn't address income levels."

The Montreal *Gazette*'s Christmas charity fundraising stories in December 1995 are an example of what Learoyd was talking about. One was about a young couple. The man had cancer and lived on unemployment insurance that was about to run out, and the woman had part-time wages for day-care work. The couple was determined to find more work, and the man with cancer was determined to overcome it and lead an active life. The last sentence urged readers to donate to the Christmas fund so this couple could have happy holidays. These two people were poor because of illness, low wages, and lack of jobs. Yet nowhere did the story acknowledge these systemic issues. There was no interview with the federal politician in charge of unemployment insurance about why his cuts were hurting this couple; no interview with the provincial labour minister about wages for day-care workers. The system was working fine and with a little donation at Christmas these people would be all right, implied the article.

Another story was about a family on welfare. The wife had asthma and severe depression and the man fixed and repaired things he found in the garbage to sell and supplement his welfare income. One of their children wore running shoes with holes to school in the Montreal winter. Milk and food for the children were rationed to make them last the month. The man needed day care so he could go out and look for a job, but it was too expensive. *The Gazette* proposed to give this family something for Christmas. But what about the real problems revealed in their story? No affordable day care. No decent jobs. Welfare rates so inadequate that the family was rationing cereal. Housing costs so high that little money was left for food. The article ignored these problems.

"We can't rely on the government to take care of the poor, the sick and the disadvantaged," said *The Gazette* after Christmas that year. That was obviously true at the time, but shouldn't we be working to change this situation? Not if we follow *The Gazette,* which went on to praise the individuals and groups that donated to its fund. "Thankfully, more and more individuals, community organizations and businesses have picked up the slack and are taking on that responsibility themselves," continued the article. "They are examples to us all. We should all think of what each of us can do .... It could be as simple as asking your New Year's Eve party guests to bring along a can of food for your local food bank." Yes, that's all you privileged people have to do to deal with the suffering and hardship that poverty causes. Keep your tax loopholes but take a can of food to your New Year's Eve party. Feel good about it. Maybe even get praised in *The Gazette.* And don't even give it a thought that UI has been slashed, that wages are low, that welfare is too low to live on, that necessity forces people in poor countries to subsidize your luxuries with their cheap labour. The economic system is doing fine for me, and this can of food will suffice for those in need.

Substituting charity for justice
I believe charity becomes poor-bashing when it is a conscious or even an unconscious substitute for justice and equality, when it becomes a way of saying, "It's okay that we have very rich and very poor in our country because the poor can get free food or clothes or Christmas hampers from charities," or "Our economic system is working just fine, thank you. Poor people won't die of starvation because we have a truck that will take left-over food from banquets and distribute it to a small percentage of them once in a while."

Demeaning people who use charity
Charities can also poor-bash by invading people's privacy, treating them as stereotypes, demeaning them, and punishing them with useless rules and procedures.

I can remember being reduced to tears by a woman at the Salvation Army in Winnipeg in the early 1970s when I had gone seeking winter clothing for my two kids. After a forty-minute interview that I can't remember, except for my tears and fears that I wouldn't get anything for them, I got a voucher for $20 to get used clothing at the Salvation Army store. I went there, picked out the things with my kids, and took them to the cashier, who informed me that we couldn't have those clothes because I had a voucher, not cash. We had to go upstairs to get what we needed, she said. So, with the kids now crying because they had expected to get what they picked out, we trudged to the stairs, only to find a huge line-up of adults and children all the way up to the top of the stairs and down again and overflowing to the hall. The door at the top was closed for lunch. So we all waited, with the kids crying, sniffling, coughing. About an hour later the top half of the door opened up and a woman started doling out items. Behind her were huge shelves filled with blankets, coats, shoes, and all the things people needed. When our turn came I gave the woman the voucher, which listed each item my interviewer agreed that I could get: two pairs of children's boots, two coats, two scarves, a blanket, etc. The woman looked at the list, and passed me over two pair of boots that would have fit a ten-year-old. My children were three and four. I pointed this out to her and noted that there were some boots on the shelves that would probably fit, but she wouldn't change them. Nothing that I got came close to fitting my children except the scarf, which one of them could use if I wrapped it around several times. I did get a nice blanket that I used to make them coats. The same thing happened to everyone else. We traded a bit as we went out of the store, or gave away the things that were useless to us to others who needed them.

Why was I grilled to tears before I got the voucher? Why couldn't the very poor (the ones with vouchers) use the same store that the less poor used? Why were we forced to line up and wait? Why didn't the woman at the top of the stairs give people what they needed when she clearly had it? Was this a case of charity being used to punish people? To reinforce the idea that they were less than other people who had enough money to shop in regular stores?

Lynn Fabar wrote a letter to ELP's *Action Line*: "I was a recipient of the food bank for a few months. I have a very bad allergy to dairy products so my food costs are higher than usual. For example, I can only drink soy milk. When I go to the food bank I must make sure that I don't have milk products or by-products such as milk solids. Plus I can't have citrus, spices or brown beans.

"The other week I told the lady at the desk that I couldn't have creamed corn. My bag wasn't ready so they told me to come back. So later that day I came back and got yelled at for complaining that I couldn't have creamed corn. Well, believe me, that's the last thing anyone needs to hear. We feel humiliated standing in line just so we can eat, having cars driving by, but worst of all being treated like freaks.

"I have a mental illness which is hard enough to cope with. Being poor isn't a sin. One of the hardest things in most people's lives is to ask for help. When standing in a line at the food depot all your pride, self-esteem and dignity are taken away. You can't hold your head up high, *not because of asking for help, but because of the way we are treated*" (my italics).

People who used two Vancouver mission soup kitchens were interviewed for the ELP's *Waste of a Nation* study. Missions like the Salvation Army's Harbour Light and the Union Gospel Mission serve meals to hungry people who line up, then often listen to a sermon before getting any food. "It's better than going hungry," said one man about eating at a mission. "At night ... they give a sermon before we get to eat ... but, when you need to eat, you have to put up with that bull."

Another said, "I think it's ridiculous to have to listen to all the crap [the preacher] says, but sometimes there's no choice. When it's go hungry or come here, what choice do you have?"

By my standards, it's poor-bashing to force people to endure your particular religion in order to get their basic human right to food.

Karen Holton and a group of users of the Comox Valley food bank on

Vancouver Island formed a group to try to make the bank more accountable to the people who needed food. Food-bank users were being yelled at when they went to get food, and had questions about the safety of some of the food being distributed. They didn't know what species some of the frozen meat was; salad dressings had been opened; some food was over ten years old. The local social services group organized a mediation between the administrators and the users and came up with eighteen recommendations, which the food bank wouldn't consider. One local paper responded to the conflict with a poor-bashing cartoon of food-bank users looking a gift horse in the mouth. Janie Zammit wrote a letter to the editor responding that the paper was "making public spectacles of people who are less fortunate by typifying them as not worthy enough to be heard."

Some food-bank users interviewed in the *Waste of the Nation* study had faced similar treatment: "You know there's a lot of hostility here. They demean you, they yell at you; they treat you like children, and they have this attitude that they're better than you," she said. Said another, "If there was some other resource, we'd just say forget it. We wouldn't continue to come here and be put down. I think that people end up feeling very, very demeaned."

"Some folks come in here and expect to be given the world on a platter," David Tutton told me in late 1998. Tutton was the Salvation Army captain responsible for the Salmon Arm, B.C., food bank. Delegates to the annual meeting of the federated anti-poverty groups of British Columbia were concerned about the intrusive form that people had to fill out and sign before they could use his food bank. The form would force anyone who needed food to allow any "food bank associates" to verify information given to the food bank "as needed," and inform the food bank of all other organizations that were helping them out. The anti-poverty groups were also concerned that people in need could only get food six times in a lifetime from this food bank unless they had a letter and a phone call from a social worker giving a "satisfactory reason for the continuation of assistance." Tutton told me they used the form because "we've had a lot of abuse."

To me, it's hard to abuse food. To go to a food bank you have to admit you're in dire need, be grilled about your impoverished state, stand in humiliating lineups—all for the human right to eat. When I asked Tutton if welfare rates were high enough, his answer included the poor-bashing assumption that the reason people needed help from the food bank was because of poor budgeting, not low rates: "I know that [welfare officials] try their best to assist, paying directly to landlords, so it doesn't go through the client's hands. We issue them a budget book as well," he explained.

Good intentions, bad results

Antoinette Saleh was furious. She was making lunch and opened her cupboard to get a can of soup. The cupboard was "nice and clean," as she put it—totally bare. None of the cans that this mother on welfare had stocked up on during sales were there. Then she remembered. Her ten-year-old son had asked her for some cans to fill Christmas hampers that his school was making. Saleh gave him ten cans. "He wanted more," she wrote in *Action Line,* "because the teacher praises whoever brings the most cans." Saleh's son had cleaned out the cupboard to get praised by the teacher—even though, as a family on welfare, his family should have been on the receiving, not the giving, end of charity. "I went to the school and made a scene," she recalled. School officials responded by taking her to the library where the food was kept and asking her to take whatever she needed. "I didn't take any," said Saleh. "I was too mad to bother."

I can remember my children coming home from school, too, and asking, "Mom can we have some cans of food for the poor?" I would always say, "We *are* the poor," but they would take the cans anyway. I figured it was more important for their mental health to be able to donate than it was for their physical health to keep the food.

Deb Andrews, an Ottawa anti-poverty advocate, told me about a wonderful teacher she had in Grade 1. The teacher was concerned about Deb's wardrobe because she was a poor child and didn't have much. "So she did a clothing drive within the school. Best intentions. Best heart. Wonderful teacher. But of course as you're wearing the clothes that the kids have brought in you're teased and ridiculed even more. You're walking down the hall wearing someone else's shoes and that particular dude wants them back."

How many teachers realize that their good intentions and concern for people who don't have much can create traumatic embarrassment and shame for poor children and their parents?

When charities respect the poor

Not all food banks or charities are demeaning. Some work hard to treat people with respect and raise hunger as a social justice issue. The Code of Ethics of the Canadian Association of Food Banks states that everyone has "the right to their daily sustenance" and pledges that members will organize activities to "bring about the greatest degree of personal dignity possible." The Code also states that members should ensure that they do not "reduce the impetus of improvements to government social assistance programs" and that they will bring the "greatest attention possible to the problems of hunger and of food surplus."

I can remember eating free meals with my children in a church basement in Winnipeg in the early 1970s. The meals were nice, the atmosphere was like a cafeteria. The food was served by respectful people who gave me extra fruit for the children.

The Waste of a Nation summed up the differences between the poor-bashing charities and the ones that treated people with respect. In the poor-bashing charities people feel they are "treated like a number, given inadequate food, yelled at, demeaned, told to get a job, lectured, forced to endure sermons, forced to line up." The charities people felt best about were the ones that had advocates for welfare and other problems, respect for the people who used them, good food, no lineups, cleanliness, a chance to meet people in a social situation, and safety.

One person said that the good charities were the ones that low-income people were involved in. "In a good place you bring what you can and take what you need. No one stands there and says, 'You can have one pair of undies and one shoe. No, you got a swimming suit last month.' It's based on the honour system."

Another person said "[At a good charity] they're not telling you what you can have. They listen to what you need."

Using the poor for public relations

Ken Thomson controls more wealth than the poorest one-third of Canadians. Among his holdings is *The Globe and Mail* newspaper. On November 6, 1998, *The Globe and Mail* published a twelve-page advertising supplement about the Imagine program.

Imagine is a non-profit organization formed in 1988, just after Canada signed the free trade deal with the United States. The purpose of the organization is to try to get individuals and corporations to give more to charities. Imagine is funded by the government and foundations. Foundations are mostly funded by rich people or corporations. In January 1998, Imagine and the Business Council on National Issues (BCNI), held a Corporate Citizenship Forum.

By September 1999, *The Globe and Mail* reported, the BCNI represented companies with over $2 *trillion* worth of assets. The BCNI had been lobbying for free trade and cuts to social spending for years. For example, Eric Beauchesne wrote in 1995 that the BCNI sent a letter to the prime minister asking for even more unemployment insurance cuts. The letter used familiar poor-bashing words. The UI system is "prone to systemic *abuse*," claimed the BCNI letter. "Most tragic of all has been the cycle of *dependence* which the current system has induced among many Canadians" (my italics).

By 1998 the government had taken the BCNI's advice, and UI had been chopped so that a mere 27 to 40 per cent of unemployed people (depending on the month and the area) were eligible. Poverty had increased from 14 per cent in 1989 to almost 18 per cent in 1996. In a discussion paper on corporate charity, Imagine admitted that "governments, *often encouraged by business*, have significantly cut back on their program expenditures for social services" (my italics). Anthony Fell, the chairman and CEO of RBC Dominion Securities, explained that it was corporate lobbying that had convinced governments to "get out of certain fields," presumably UI and welfare.

What was the purpose of the Imagine-BCNI forum? Was it to plan how corporations could work for different policies that wouldn't create more poverty? No way. Was it to figure out how to increase corporate giving to charity so people wouldn't suffer so much from the cuts? No again. The purpose of the forum was to figure out what corporations could do to set or manage the public's expectations about their charitable giving. The corporations had seen a poll showing that the majority of Canadians thought companies gave a lot more to charity than they really do. In addition the poll showed that a lot more Canadians were feeling that corporations were acting irresponsibly when they laid people off. I guess they figured that if public expectations were low, then when those expectations were exceeded, the public would be more approving of those big corporations with, literally, *trillions* in assets.

Imagine's target was that corporations would donate 1 per cent of pre-tax profits to charity, far below the 13 per cent that polls said the public thought corporations should give, and half a per cent below what low-income Canadians gave. Donate a mere 1 per cent of your pre-tax profits to charity, and you could become one of Imagine's "Caring Companies."

One of Imagine's Caring Companies for 1998 was the Royal Bank, with $1.8 billion in profit that year, according to *Canadian Business* magazine. Media companies whose editorials have called for social program cuts were also Caring Companies, including *The Globe and Mail*, Southam, and Sun Media Corporation.

The Caring Corporations had no intention of increasing their donations enough to make up for the cuts. Most of their donations don't even go to people who are poor, and besides, the BCNI's David Stewart-Patterson said, "We need to weave a new web of relationships between individuals and organizations in all sectors of our communities." Stewart-Patterson went on to describe this new relationship in which charities, desperate for funding that government has cut, have to tailor their requests to meet corporate wishes for better public relations. A new relationship all right: a charitable relationship, an unequal relationship, in which corporations lobby for policies that increase poverty, then try to get a good image by becoming a 1 per cent "Caring Company." While homelessness and hunger grow in a very rich country, Imagine proposed a list of ways to get good public relations for their "Caring Companies," knowing that "to make up for every 1 per cent loss in government support," corporations would have to increase their donations by 49 per cent.

While the corporations were devising ways of getting the biggest public relations impact for each charitable dollar they spent, the federal government was changing laws to end basic economic human rights set out in the UN's Universal Declaration. In 1993, it cut all spending on new affordable housing, increasing the number of homeless people to about 200,000 in 1998. In 1996, as we saw in the last chapter, the federal government ended the basic human right to an adequate income when in need when it abolished the Canada Assistance Plan and replaced it with the Canada Health and Social Transfer. By 1998 the basic human right to unemployment insurance had been preserved for only about one-third of the unemployed, because of massive federal cuts to that program.

The 1990s was a decade when human rights were out of fashion and institutional charity was in. Focusing on charity gave government a chance to pretend it really did care about all those people its cuts were hurting. Not only did the federal government fund Imagine to promote more donations, but it was also changing tax rules to make it more profitable for rich people to donate to registered charities. By 1996 the government was allowing people to get tax refunds if they gave up to 75 per cent of their income to charity, something you can't afford to do unless you make a lot of money or have just sold something valuable. Before the change people could only write off up to 20 per cent of their income. Then, in 1997, Ian Robertson reported that the federal budget introduced another tax rule that allowed people who donated stocks or mutual funds to double their tax break.

But, as always with charity, it was the donor who had the power. Let's see, will my donation go to the opera, the ballet? To cancer research? To a homeless shelter? To educate East Europeans about the free market system (this is what Seagrams does with some of its "charitable" giving)? Who is the most deserving? What kind of donation will make my corporation look the best, give me the biggest tax break? With a charity instead of a human rights-based social system, the poor depend for their basic necessities on decisions like these by corporations, the rich, and by other people who have a little bit of extra cash to donate.

While the federal government was encouraging charitable giving, provincial governments like Alberta were encouraging non-profit charities to provide the services that government used to fund. "The public out there can do a better job than government, and given the opportunity they will," said Alberta Social Services Minister Mike Cardinal at a dinner to raise funds for a day-care centre for children at risk of abuse. At the time his government was planning to cut $108 million from its 1994-95 social services budget. For the province's charities to equal what the government was cutting from social services, they would have to more than triple their annual revenue of about $30 million.

Provinces that were slashing welfare rates were also bringing in so-called Good Samaritan laws. These laws say that people or companies who donate food are not liable for damages if the food causes injury or death to the poor person who eats it unless the food was unfit for human consumption and the donor acted recklessly or intended to injure or kill the person who ate the food. Bev Brown was outraged. "It just means it's a class system for human rights and for health and safety protection," said Brown. The food donation law means "fewer health protection standards for people who eat donated food, which makes charity part of a legal thrust to poor-bash."

Earlier in the decade, Imagine was looking for individual donors. "Can most of us ever do more than a little?" asked Imagine in a 1991 newspaper supplement. "All we've got are drops in the bucket," claimed the ad. "But those drops add up. That's the power of we. And the potential." That's the kind of thinking Imagine wanted ordinary Canadians to do. Actually, some people have a lot more than drops in the bucket. In 1999 *Canadian Business* reported that Ken Thomson was worth $20.97 billion, the three Irving brothers had $6.67 billion, and Galen Weston had

$5.37 billion. It's true, drops in the bucket are all *most* people can contribute as individuals, but collectively we could use our democratic power to get politicians to make changes in tax, wage, and social program laws, changes that could shift billions from the rich to the poor. But that's not how Imagine's government and corporate funders wanted us to think. They'd prefer each of us to throw in our own little drop. That's right, said Imagine, "Giving makes you feel good."

Drops in the bucket will not make up for the flood of government cuts to programs that used to protect basic human rights. And if a feel-good donation to charity helps you ignore a system that forces nearly one-fifth of the people to live in poverty, you're not respecting those people.

How to help out without poor-bashing

After Sheila Baxter and the "grovellers" finished their skit outside the 1991 Taste of the Nation feast, and after the anti-poverty workers had handed out their leaflets to the limo occupants flocking to sample Vancouver's finest cuisine, Debbie Ellison stood in front of ELP's banner, which said, "Charity is a band-aid, not a solution."

"We challenge people who aren't poor to ask hard questions about charity," said Ellison, who was on ELP's board of directors. "Does charity meet the needs of poor people? How many people fall through the cracks of charity? How many don't use food banks because they would rather be hungry than humiliated? Will charity end poverty? Or will it let people think that the hunger problem is solved when it is growing instead? Do we want a society where the poor subsist on leftovers from the rich?"

Ellison continued, "We challenge people who aren't poor to listen to people who are poor. We don't want to live in a society where one group is powerful and another powerless. We want to have a relationship of equality and citizenship. We don't want handouts and humiliation. We want jobs and adequate incomes.

"We challenge people who aren't poor to join with us in rejecting American-style social programs where food and housing are provided for the poor at the whim of the rich. We need jobs, housing, higher minimum wages, higher welfare. Canada has the resources to provide a decent life for everyone. We challenge people who aren't poor to demand that our politicians work for a just society, where people are more equal and where the poor don't have to depend on leftovers from the rich to subsist." The assembled anti-poverty activists gave Ellison a big cheer. The elegant diners were inside, oblivious to the message they should have been hearing.

Most Canadians are involved in charity in some way, as receivers, as donors or volunteers, as people who wish they had enough to donate, as people who wonder if they should donate, or feel guilty when they don't. What should we do about charity if we want to help out, but don't want to poor-bash? Here's my attempt to answer that question.

1. *Don't feel better than the person you're donating to, or make distinctions between so-called deserving and undeserving people.* To help out with this, make a list of all the ways in which you are lucky, or have had privileges in your life. When you live in a system that tolerates and even causes official unemployment rates of up to 20 per cent, the people with the poorest luck and the fewest privileges are likely to be the hardest hit. Have you had to face racism or other kinds of discrimination? Have you been abused as a child, poor as a child or adult, had an education, good health, and people around to help you out? Check out the distribution of wealth and income in Canada described in the Introduction. Think about whether this is right and learn more about how to make the distribution more equal. Think about your own economic security. Are you closer to Ken Thomson, the richest man in Canada, or to a person on welfare? What would have to happen in your life to make you need charity, if you don't need it now?

2. *Don't let corporations use you for their image and benefit.* The big corporations are firmly behind cuts to social programs and policies that cheapen labour and make people poorer. They fund lobby groups to demand these policies and push for them on their own. They donate to politicians who promise to implement these policies. They should change these policies, not get to look good because of measly donations that help them keep power and wealth.

3. *Set some criteria for the charities that you work with or donate to.* Make sure they

- try to meet the needs of people they serve, as defined by the people they serve;
- include or are controlled by low-income people;
- fight for basic human rights and work in solidarity with people who are poor and advocate for justice with them—even if this means "getting political";
- respect people who are poor and treat them with dignity as equals.

If the charity you work with does these things, it may not be a registered charity, or it could risk losing its tax-deductible status because the government doesn't like registered charities to engage in political action. So be prepared to donate just to help out, and not for what you'll get back on your taxes.

4. *Don't let charity work replace justice work.* If all the people who work for and donate to charity were working for a more equal society, with laws that reduced poverty, we'd have a much better chance of ending it. If ending poverty is a priority to you, focus on working for more income and power equality. If you donate to, say, a food bank, take an extra step and write a letter to your elected representatives. Tell them that you've made a donation, but what you really want is political action to end poverty.

"We need to get back to the concept that we're all part of the community," Michelle Forest said when I interviewed anti-poverty workers in Winnipeg. Forrest had a job advocating for people on welfare. "We need to stop making ourselves feel better because we can afford to donate and start thinking of our common interests. We need to stop thinking of poverty as a one-on-one thing. Poverty is not a sin. As a culture we have to deal with it because it breaks down our community if we don't."

Chapter 9

Bashing yourself: Clashing silently with privilege

After a while we start to believe the messages
and we feel worthless even to ourselves.
We feel shame and the shame stops us from speaking out.

Vicki Columbaris

"It's like oxygen," Rose Brown said, "like a natural thing flowing through your whole body."

"Rose, Rose," said Linda Moreau, empathizing with Brown's heavy feelings.

"It's ever-present," Brown said.

"Like wearing grey-coloured glasses. Everything you experience, including your thoughts, is clouded with this perception that you are wrong; the other person is right; you are stupid; the other person is smart; you are a follower, and they're a leader," added Moreau.

"You don't make sense, but they do," Brown said. "You don't know what you're talking about."

"Your take on things is wrong and theirs is right," Moreau said.

"And the hopelessness is another whole thing," added Brown.

"It's very isolating," said Moreau.

I was interviewing Rose Brown and Linda Moreau for their thoughts on internalized poor-bashing, a phrase that more and more people are using to account for the way in which people who are poor feel intense shame and blame about their poverty. Brown and Moreau thought it was crucial that people who are poor—and people who aren't—begin to think about and discuss the subject.

"I was quite young when I realized that we were the poorest people that I knew," Moreau told us. "That in itself wasn't a bad thing if we were on our own," she continued. "It was an okay way to live. We were renting lots of land and we had chickens. We definitely got enough to eat every day. My parents gave us the freedom to be outside a lot. There were some parts that were a little tough, but there were no big hardships. The hardships came in the contrasts with how other people were living and how they saw us as lesser. Our clothes weren't new. On my first day in high school my dress was mended. In a poorer country, that would have been normal. People wouldn't even have looked at the mending marks.

"So it was the contrast," Moreau continued. "That's what started my internalized oppression, thinking, 'Why are we like this? Why can't my parents be like other parents?' It wasn't like, 'Oh, we're different and that's okay.' It was like, 'Oh, we're different and that's really not okay.' We were the ones to blame, not the ones that were snobby and showing off their wealth, and greedy. The good values were on them, and the bad values were on us. That started out this process of noticing the differences and blaming myself and my parents. There's a lot of blame in internalized oppression, blaming and shaming, and that was the basis. We were never on welfare when I was a kid. But the blaming and shaming locked into place when I went on welfare as an adult with my two kids. That was the clincher. There was the stigma of welfare, over a layer of poverty that had been there most of my life, in the sense that whatever collection of circumstances you're calling poverty had a judgment on it. It doesn't need to have a judgment on it. It could be a fairly neutral way to grow up in another setting, but it had a negative judgment on it. I labelled it low self-esteem or being shy. I never labelled it in a political way."

"The attitude hurled against the poor" causes many "to internalize their oppression." Vicki Columbaris was reading from the paper she had prepared for a forum on wealth and poverty in Vancouver in 1999. She was explaining to the mostly middle-class listeners how people on welfare are treated and how that treatment affects their ability to participate with others in a social environment. She had heard comments such as "we should stop complaining, we should pick ourselves up by our bootstraps, we're getting too comfortable on welfare," Vicki continued. "After a while we start to believe the messages and we feel worthless even to ourselves. We feel shame and the shame stops us from speaking out." Columbaris was fighting the shame by speaking out.

She described this incident:

> A close friend of mine, a single mom on social assistance, had her two children registered for swimming through a city subsidy. During the course of the lessons, she created friendships with the other moms who were not on income assistance. When the course ended there were only three places left for the next level, so she and another one of the moms went immediately to register their children. At this point my friend became very embarrassed because she had to let the receptionist know she needed a subsidy in front of the other mom. Out came the bright orange sheets. She was then abruptly told by the receptionist to go to the end of the counter to fill them out. In the meantime a woman came in off the street and asked the same receptionist if there was any room for her daughter for swimming. The receptionist replied that indeed there was room and proceeded to register her in one of the two remaining spots. The forms completed, my friend went back to the counter to finish the registration process. The receptionist told her that the classes were now full and she'd have to wait until the following month. Angry, but not wanting to make a scene, my friend asked the receptionist why she registered another child in the class when she knew she was registering her children. The receptionist said the supervisor wasn't there to sign the forms and if she wasn't happy, she should take it up with the directors. At that point, my friend left quietly, humiliated and angry.
>
> If this had happened to a Black person, it would scream of racism and discrimination. The messages that we are bombarded with every day in society and through public policy legitimized the receptionist's behaviour. She had no qualms about telling this woman to sit at the back of the bus.

Jean Trickey got excited about the similarities between poor-bashing and racism when I talked to her in Ottawa. As one of the first Black students to integrate Little Rock High School in Arkansas back in the 1950s, she knew about racism. She had also been unemployed and poor in Canada but was now the director of the Tungasuvvingat Inuit Centre. Trickey told me that poor-bashing is "the most like racism in how internalized it is on the part of the poor. They don't know what hit them. They blame each other. They blame themselves. I'm actually learning more about racism because I've seen this process and how it works."

Melanie at first wanted me to use her real name but then decided it would be a bad idea because she didn't want to increase the chance of her children being taunted for being on welfare. "I try to say it's okay where we're at," she told me as we drank tea in the kitchen of her one-bedroom apartment. "Poor-bashing probably affects me in that I suppose I don't feel that we're as deserving as people who have money. I know logically that's not right, but emotionally that's how I feel about it," she added. "We're easy targets for people's anger. I guess I carry that around with me." Melanie had felt that anger in conversations with other moms when volunteering at her children's school—moms who didn't know her situation and were making judgmental comments about people on welfare. "Maybe they have a legitimate point," Melanie said, even though, she realized, "Poor people are not the downfall of this country."

People who are poor do not feel shame and inadequacy because they are guilty of a crime, because they really are inadequate as human beings or parents, because they did something wrong, or because they receive money from government, as the Fraser Institute would have us believe. They feel these emotions because poor-bashers constantly discriminate against them, stereotype them, and treat them as less worthy.

In a 1994 statement to the federal government's Standing Committee on Human Resources Development, Dave, who didn't want his last name used, made the following comparison of attitudes faced by two people who get nearly the same amount of money from the government: "I am looking for work. I am on welfare and get $482 a month. A person in the top tax bracket who buys $1,000 worth of RRSPs per month gets $481 a month taken off his taxes. This person doesn't have to pass a needs test. I do. People in the top tax bracket who invest in RRSPs are not accused of fraud daily in the press. People on welfare are. People in the top tax bracket are not scrutinized to determine if they are using their $481 productively or simply squandering it on foreign vacations. The media raises questions about what people on welfare do with our money nearly every day. People in the top tax bracket are not put under a microscope to determine if that $481 a month they get from government contributes to their 'incentive to work.' Yet I am being scrutinized to see if the same amount keeps me from working."

Dave identified at least four bad messages he has to put up with, from government, the public, and media—just because he's on welfare and not "on RRSP." In addition he has to try to survive on an amount of money that doesn't begin to cover normal living expenses.

A study of the way in which subtle and blatant poor-bashing in schools run by mostly middle-class people is internalized by poor children could be the subject of an entire book. Earlier in this book, Donia Naffaa told how she always denied being on welfare because she didn't want to be "pushed around, called names, bums, welfare" by other students. In Chapter 5, Abjullahi Barre related that other children at school told his child, "You live on welfare. You take our money." These expressions can't help but contribute to internalized feelings of shame and blame that make poor children want to escape from school.

John Clarke gave me an example of more subtle poor-bashing at his son's school in a poor area of Toronto where, he said, about 80 per cent of the children are people of colour and about the same number live in public housing. "The other day I went to a Canada Day celebration," Clarke told me when I interviewed him in his Ontario Coalition against Poverty office in Toronto in 1997. "They put on this film about Canada. I thought the kids there must have been thinking, 'This Canada is a very nice place. I wish I lived there.'

"It was all people having barbecues, skiing, and things that had nothing to do with the lives of any of these kids, and yet that's held up for them as what they are supposed to be. That can't help but just cut into them and it can't help but make them think when they go home, that 'My mum is just a failure. There's something wrong with her. She's not providing the things that are supposed to be provided.' I think a lot of the war between the generations that people in poverty experience is promoted in schools. Often what people are trying to do is help," Clarke said, "but whenever the middle class tries to help the poor, they have a way of making them feel shitty." He added, however, that there are "all kinds of people who do a good job."

Leigh Donahue of Vancouver told me about how he experienced classism in high school: "I hung out with a guy whose mother was a teacher. No doubt in his mother's mind that he'd go to university. They split us up. I was seen as a poor kid. We got in trouble together. The school phoned my mother and I got shit. When they phoned his, she was at the school in twenty minutes. Wanted to know what was going on. They kept trying to put me into vocational. 'Let's get him a job as an auto mechanic.' That's a form of poor-bashing. Even the teachers that liked me, condescended to me. They treated me as a victim. They'd feel sorry for me if I came to school beat up by my old man. But they didn't do anything. They'd think, 'Oh, he comes from a poor family.'"

Research shows that poverty is the underlying cause of illiteracy and so-called failure in school. How many subtle and blatant messages about failure and inadequacy do poor children face and internalize in school? Poor parents often talk about the pressure to buy expensive brand-label clothes, about their children being excluded from field trips, about books, supplies, and lunches in public schools costing way too much for them to afford. When low-income students do poorly in school, they get messages about not working hard, being lazy and stupid. They go home to families and neighbourhoods whose realities are not mirrored in school curriculums and blame their parent(s) for not having what others have. I believe poverty and internalized poor-bashing are good places to look for answers to illiteracy and school dropout rates.

Government policies and propaganda contribute to internalized poor-bashing too. The B.C. Ministry of Human Resources' official slogan in the last part of the 1990s was "Making work a better deal than welfare." This ignores the lack of jobs for all who need them, and that many of the jobs that are available pay poverty-level wages—or less. Every time poor people hear that phrase, which saturates Ministry policies and propaganda, they are being told that they are somehow to blame for not having a paid job.

The policies "tell people they are dependent, abusers and need to be self-reliant," Bev Brown explained. She calls welfare rates as low as $92 a month for people who board with relatives in Newfoundland a form of "class hatred."

Low welfare rates contribute even more to internalized poor-bashing for single parents when their kids go to school. "Even though the income that government programs provide is inadequate, people blame themselves for not providing for their kids. Or they feel incompetent when they run out of cash.... They internalize this as not being an adequate parent. Mothers get stressed out worrying about things like, 'When the kids come home from school, will they ask for anything that costs money?' The stress shortens your life."

How much do these feelings of inadequacy, blame, and shame

depend on attitudes that society has towards people who are poor, and how much on other factors such as racism, sexism, an abusive upbringing, or discrimination based on a disability? Rose Brown lived in an orphanage for most of her childhood. She grappled with this question in examining her own life. "We were dirt poor before I went to [the orphanage] and I can vaguely remember things that made me feel it was okay even though we were poor. I had two parents who loved me." The impact on Brown of "just being considered one of five hundred kids in one institution broken down into houses that held about twenty-four kids, and never being spoken to," is crucial, she explains. "The different way that you're raised does produce a different kind of internalized oppression."

But in a sense, explained Brown, "that was classism because that was the way that society dealt with poor children who couldn't live with their own families. It is a very heavy thing in today's society—the internalized oppression that comes from class. I think it colours your life unless you're actually thinking about it."

In some ways, poor-bashing is an extension of our society's harsh attitudes towards working people who aren't poor enough to need welfare or unemployment insurance. Leigh Donahue was raised in a working-class neighbourhood in Vancouver; he described the first time he realized that people were treated differently simply because of their class. He was a seventeen-year-old busboy and took a shine to a waitress. She invited Donahue to her house, which turned out to be a mansion in a rich neighbourhood. "That was the first time I knew there was a big economic difference. I never felt so uncomfortable. I had to go in the back door. They had a tennis court. I didn't even know how to play tennis. I was in awe and in a state of shock. Her parents were terrible. They looked at me and I felt objectified. I wasn't invited to join them in the yard. I was so uncomfortable I said I was going. The girl asked me to stay but the mother kept saying 'Let him go.'

"I was ashamed and embarrassed, confused, scared. I felt cheap; that I wasn't good enough to be their friend, or their daughter's boyfriend." All the same, Leigh acknowledged that he had an easier time in life than women and people of colour. For them, jobs were a lot harder to get.

I met Sandra Pronteau, a mother raising four young children with her partner, when she started volunteering at ELP, and then again when she helped organize a campaign to get more teachers in her children's school—a campaign that included camping out on the lawn of the school board offices. Pronteau has faced a lot of negative messages in her life:

"I'm an Aboriginal woman. They think we're all drunks. They think we're messy, dirty," she told me. "Being in the foster parent system, I was welfare property and had a very judgmental upbringing. Because of my disability, people would say, 'Oh, she's retarded.'"

Pronteau had been on social assistance and in and out of jobs since she was eighteen. When I talked to her, she and her partner both had jobs but their income was so low they were still eligible for a slight amount from welfare. Pronteau didn't like going to the Ministry of Human Resources when she needed welfare because she didn't like to "get shamed or put down." Food banks had sent her more bad messages by making people line up to get a number. "Then you wait another whole hour to get your food. There are remarks about races and lots of judgment there," she added.

As a result of experiences like these, Pronteau said, people bash themselves: "Suicidal thinking, depression, feeling unworthy. We can get clinically depressed because of not having money, and the attitudes people have, and because we can't take our kids out to do things." I remembered the time Pronteau had told me that she and her partner would like to have enough money to afford a car so they could take their kids camping.

"People who are born in a wealthy family," explained Pronteau, who was yearning to go to university, "just have things handed to them. We have to go and get it, to ask for it." Pronteau told me she has "a lot of anger because it's supposed to be the other way around." Aboriginal people would be wealthy if their land hadn't been taken from them, she said. Pronteau is only one of hundreds of thousands of Canadians who experience not only poor-bashing, but also racism and other discriminations all together. It's a miracle that people who deal with so many bad messages can still cope and contribute, as Pronteau does, to their communities.

Internalized poor-bashing can paralyze poor people, Bev Brown explained: "They feel so singled out for discrimination that they can hardly do what they say they'll do. Because their anger is turned to depression, they think nothing will change, so why bother. You feel grandiose and deluded even trying to change the prejudice, because it's so pervasive. All of us go through periods like this," Brown added about people who are poor. "You feel that any hope you have is false." Poor people doing community work have told Brown, "Please don't tell anyone on the committee I'm on welfare. I'm so ashamed." Brown says the emotional trauma of the discrimination is worsened by poverty and "not knowing if you'll be able to eat."

Internalized poor-bashing can also contribute to the isolation that people who are poor often feel: "If you're a lawyer, you want to deal with other lawyers because it brings you prestige or enhances your career," Sara Torres told me. The Ottawa woman had lived on welfare, UI, and wages while being a student, a parent, and doing solidarity work with Latin American countries. She had come to Canada from Colombia thirteen years before I talked to her. "But what do you see that you will gain by being with other poor people? Just to be blamed? I'm talking from my own experience because that happened to me when I realized how I was seen," she went on. "You don't want to be known as poor because then you are part of the whole set of people who are on the sidelines." But this weakens you, Torres explained. "You alienate yourself from the group that can actually give you support. You're on your own, pretending that everything is fine."

To build support for policies that would end poverty, poor people, whether they have paid jobs or not, have to work together. But when internalized poor-bashing makes them continually blame themselves and others like themselves for their poverty, and be ashamed to associate or identify with others in the same situation, it's hard to build a movement.

Several of the anti-poverty activists I interviewed mentioned that people who have precarious jobs, often poor people themselves, are sometimes poor-bashers too. Working at low wages and barely getting by can be very depressing and then, when working people end up needing welfare, they transfer the poor-bashing they had reserved for others to themselves.

Linda Lalonde told me, "If I spent ten years saying that moms who are on welfare are tramps and they don't take care of their kids and they sleep with every Tom, Dick, and Harry and they play bingo and they wear polyester pants and then I'm downsized and become a mother on welfare, I've got two choices. I can say 'Well, obviously that was bullshit and I've been misinformed.' Or I can absorb all of that and not only have to deal with the fact that I've been dumped out of my job, but also have to deal with my own self-image. I wasn't good enough to work, and now I'm scum as well." LaLonde said that people who go through this process can end up with mental health problems because "it's really more than they can deal with. It's such a bash to their self-image."

Elisabeth Ziegler-Simmons's job was advising unemployed people at the HELP centre in Cobourg, Ontario, about their rights to unemployment insurance and welfare. "What's really surprising is that the people that poor-bash the most are the ones most likely to be poor next," she told me. Denying their own vulnerability to poverty is "a useful coping mechanism." People who have paid jobs and are still poor can feel oppressed, trapped, and powerless over their lives, but can reduce their pain, or at least camouflage it, by feeling superior to people who need welfare or unemployment insurance.

Many people who aren't poor don't have a clue what it is to experience life without enough money and as a target of prejudice. They don't know about the paralyzing effects of the feelings of unworthiness and depression. They don't know that people who are poor can feel incapable and ignorant when they're not. They are often also unaware that feelings of confidence and competence come automatically if you have enough money and don't face endless messages that you are less than others.

More and more people are using the phrase "internalized privilege" to describe the consequences of having advantages like good health, adequate income, being heterosexual, being white, and having a good education. Margo Adair and Sharon Howell define privilege as "access to resources and benefits based on who people are, not what they do." In public situations, internalized poor-bashing can silence the poor while internalized privilege gives middle-class people the confidence to make decisions based on their own often inaccurate and discriminatory assumptions. Privilege is invisible to people who have it unless they make a conscious effort to figure it out.

Adair and Howell write that people who have privilege are likely to "take our own ideas more seriously: we are the first to speak; we interrupt others; we are comfortable talking for long periods of time....These patterns keep others locked out, invisible and feeling inappropriate. Women, men of colour, working-class and poor people are forced to accommodate their perspectives and actions in order to gain any measure of acceptance." A person with privilege sees him/herself as normal and others as different. Simply by living in North America, most non-Aboriginal people see it as normal that we use and occupy Aboriginal land. It also seems normal to North Americans that our countries can afford social programs and that we can buy products made with cheap labour in poorer countries.

Arlene Mantle is renowned as a powerful performer, musician, and songwriter who has given hundreds of workshops that help people use music in their struggle for social justice. "I grew up as an adopted kid in a working-class family in a sexually and physically abusive situation. Then I was in a battering marriage for fourteen years. So the first thirty years of my life were pretty awful, and up to age thirty-six, when I was pushed by a social worker to go to school, I didn't think I had a brain. If I can be socialized through my poverty, and through the abuse and the violence perpetrated on me, to believe that I am shit, then it's only logical that some people are equally socialized to believe that they aren't shit. There are people who really think that they know, and they have the answers, and they have the analysis, and they can solve the problems of everybody."

Rande McMurray worked with the Victoria anti-poverty group Together Against Poverty Society and was going to school when she wrote an article about poor-bashing or "classism" in *The Long Haul:*

> Sometimes when I sit in meetings to discuss poverty, I feel all eyes are on me.... Will they know when they talk about how hard it is for poor parents to pay school fees, that I'm one of them? When they talk about how poor mothers have such low self-esteem, do they mean me? When they have money and I don't, when they don't have to bring in child-care receipts to prove they are poor, and I do, I get nervous.

Bev Brown sounded pretty depressed when I talked to her about internalized poor-bashing in March 1999. She had been working with middle-class people who expressed concern about poverty, "People who should be our allies but aren't yet," as Brown put it. The poverty outreach committee of a group of teachers and administrators had asked to meet with her. She started the meeting with a list of words and phrases that had been used by a student teacher group in another workshop to describe people on welfare. They were phrases like "lazy bum," "dependent," "spending money on beer." "They became defensive," said Brown. The committee members claimed that she was insulting them by reading a list that portrayed student teachers as prejudiced. "I was the only unemployed person there," she told me. "I couldn't save the meeting." Then she added, "It was discouraging. I haven't been able to take the next step, even though they've identified themselves as being interested in poverty. The constant challenge of fighting poor-bashing is a very big struggle. It's every day if you go out ... It should end."

On the other side of Canada, Linda Moreau and Rose Brown were telling me of similar experiences with middle-class people. Most middle-class and wealthy people don't feel they have to "explain themselves and excuse themselves, and justify every action they do and every thought they have," Moreau explained. "Most of them think they're right. Their privilege is inherent. They don't think of it as privilege. They think of it as things their parents gave them or things they worked hard to get."

I realized Brown and Moreau could have been talking about me a few years ago. Although I have been poor and poor-bashed, my childhood was pretty middle class and I didn't have to face endless messages about being less than other people because of my clothes or income or housing. I'm white and I had a university education. In other words, I had more privilege in my background than a lot of other people do. As a result, I do think I'm an inherently good person. I have talked way too much at meetings, thinking that what I had to say was pretty important. I never thought of all this talk as taking up space that other people could use to express their thoughts. I have wondered why people didn't speak up and assumed, I'm ashamed to say, it was because they had nothing to say or because they agreed with what was being said by others. Even I, working in the anti-poverty movement for years, never stopped to think that years of poor-bashing had silenced some people, made them think their thoughts were unworthy or would be put down. I certainly never thought that the relatively privileged upbringing I experienced was the reason I was making all those assumptions.

"If I do something wrong," I said to Brown and Moreau, "I think of it as a mistake. I apologize. I don't think, 'I'm a worthless person.'"

"Which we feel a lot," said Brown.

A revolt at ELP when I worked as co-ordinator helped me under-stand that I needed to make a conscious effort to do more listening to and less assuming about the people I worked with. My job, as I understood it, was to supervise the other staff and make sure the work of the organiza-tion got done. I assumed that I would be the one to deal with the media, give the speeches, and talk to the politicians. The other workers, who mostly came from poor backgrounds, wanted more say and a more public profile with the organization. They got together and said that they want-ed a collective, not a hierarchy with me at the top. What they said was hard for me to take and hard for them to say, very hard. I had no idea they felt this way. I thought I was a good person to work with, allowing lots of flexibility around hours and trying to get their wages as high as I could. They explained that they hadn't been telling me of their feelings because of internalized poor-bashing, and I hadn't been seeing it because of inter-nalized privilege. It took a lot of courage because they felt their jobs were at risk for challenging me. But their message seemed correct to me: we should be sharing power in the organization, like we should be sharing power in the country. Since the change, ELP has become more of a coalition *of* low-income people than *for* low-income people.

Women's centres, activist groups in low-income neighbourhoods, and anti-poverty groups—nearly every group that tries to include people who are poor and people who aren't—often wonder what's happening to them as conflicts develop, or the poor participants, feeling uncomfortable within the group, stop coming. When this happens, it deprives anti-poverty work of the insights and the hard work of people who are poor. It takes the urgency out of anti-poverty work. And it shifts the focus to goals that middle-class people have. Goals that poor people usually have, like decent jobs, or adequate welfare rates, are often ignored. The silent clash between middle-income people who care about poverty and the poor who live it prevents the two groups from uniting into a big enough power to challenge the forces that create the problem.

If these well-meaning people would go to people who are poor and ask, "What can we do to support your work and your lives?" the projects they would end up working on would be a lot more useful. The next chapter outlines some ways of equalizing power between poor and more privileged people, and Appendix C has some pointers from the U.S. group Tools for Change.

Becoming unbashable

Arlene Mantle gave us the word we need. Talking to Jo Grey and me, she said, "Ultimately, if we want to end poor-bashing, we have to become unbashable. We have to just not take it on. This is *your* shit. This is not about me. This is about *you* and what *you* believe and who *you* are."

Rande McMurray made the same point in her *Long Haul* article. After she started going to school, Rande explained, she started thinking more about the discrimination she faced as a person on welfare. "People who have more money than they need and feel superior because of it are the problem," she wrote. "I am learning to wear what I like, look how I want, feel proud when I walk with my children. I am learning to speak up, fight for enough money to live on and a decent place to live. I have stopped trying to 'better myself' and stopped feeling inadequate when I felt I couldn't. I am finding out my worth does not hinge on not being poor. I am beginning to understand I am not the one with the problem. Classism is what other people do. They are the ones with the problem.

"Stop telling me how to raise my children," McMurray continued, "how to dress them; where to go. I can challenge people who patronize me, or think less of me. I can challenge people who think I don't have any power because I don't have any money.... It's my power. I am going to use it. I am going to keep saying, 'What's *your* problem?'"

After Mantle invented the word, I started asking people who were poor if they could become unbashable. A lot of them said that understanding what causes poverty helps a lot.

"If you're going to become unbashable you have to learn that your poverty is not your fault," Deb O'Connor said. She believes it's easier for women to understand that poverty is caused by outside forces than it is for men who "see it as a personal failure because of that whole breadwinner expectation. But it's not enough to get educated, you also have to break down the isolation. Then you can work towards becoming unbashable," she said.

Jo Grey said she has "felt fairly unbashable for a long time because I know that I can see a much bigger picture, and I'm a part of the bigger picture, and I've also seen the process of other women coming to that realization and becoming a lot stronger and a lot less bashable." Grey thinks it's vital that poor people understand that government policies and corporate decisions are increasing poverty, and her organization, Low Income Families Together, works to build this understanding. A book about poor people's movements helped Grey feel "so much better," she explained. The book showed that during the depression people realized poverty was "a system problem and took action and that's when we got our social programs. I've got some facts I can draw from, some historical backup."

In the early 1990s ELP held workshops on the corporate agenda with low-income people throughout British Columbia and also in other places in Canada. The organizers travelled to communities, sometimes small, sometimes large, and met in community centres, churches, or union halls, mostly with people and were poor who wanted to learn how to work against poverty. The workshops started by asking participants what corporations wanted governments to do. "Reduce corporate taxes," one person would say. "Reduce wages," another would shout out. "Cut social programs," someone else would chime in. Then there would be a short silence while people were thinking. "Bring in free trade," the next person would say, and the groups would go on listing what they knew from their experiences. Then the participants went into small groups to read and discuss newspaper clippings that confirmed what they had said. There were further discussions of how corporations got what they want and what the results of this were for the poor and the rich. As a person who helped develop the workshops and facilitated many of them, I would often be discouraged just realizing over and over how powerful the corporations were and how often they got what they wanted. But many low-income people who participated had a more liberating reaction. Towards the end of the workshop, people would be looking at all the flip-chart paper taped to the walls and someone would ask incredulously, "You mean poverty is not my fault?" Then we'd have a discussion about that awareness and the relief it brought.

Bev Brown says that the act of challenging poor-bashing helps poor people to see that poverty is not their fault. "If poor people say, 'Okay, I'm going to challenge poor-bashing every time I hear it,' and see how that works, you come to an understanding of how prejudicial it is. It helps you decide that poor-bashing is like racism or sexism; that it's structural rather than individual, and that, in itself, is a big help."

I began this chapter with a conversation I once had with Linda Moreau and Rose Brown. A year later Brown had become more optimistic. "I believe we can make progress against internalized oppression," she told me. "I continue to get stronger and feel better about myself. As I work to help stop poor-bashing and for legislative change, I blame myself less; I like myself more and the deep feelings of shame and worthlessness are slowly replaced by competence and happiness."

"It's always gonna hurt," Kate in Ottawa told me about internalized poor-bashing. The single mother had just published a book about living in poverty and being a drug addict and was about to start a new job she was excited about. She didn't want me to use her real name. "With information comes awareness and with awareness comes anger and with anger comes action," she said. "I didn't even know what voting was a few years ago," she continued, "or why it was important or that my voice would even count. A lot of people are the same in my circle. They feel hopeless, like their voice won't matter anyway. Why bother? Understanding does make a difference."

"I don't know if [internalized poor-bashing] is completely analogous to an abusive relationship," Elisabeth Ziegler-Simmons told me in an interview in Toronto, "but a person who's being abused takes a lot of time to figure out it's not their fault, and they do have rights, and once they do find out, they get angry and empowered. All these unemployed people should be getting angry and not blaming themselves and feeling hopeless. They should turn anger into votes—assuming there's a political party out there that one should vote for."

"When a woman wants to get out of a battering situation it's the same thing [as becoming unbashable]," Sara Torres told me, making the same comparison as Zeigler-Simmons. "Poor people have to understand it is not their fault. Politics is powerful. I guess we need it. Maybe that would be the way [to become unbashable]. Do more politicizing. Politics gives us the tools to analyze our situation."

Jean Trickey thought the key to becoming unbashable is to stop focusing on your own personal poverty. "People need the analysis of what is going on because the internalized thing is 'It's my fault' and therefore 'It's my problem' and therefore 'I'm worthless.' And 'I can break my neighbour's window because I'm very angry.'"

You may never entirely get rid of internalized poor-bashing if you're poor. But you can learn to control it by understanding how poverty is not your fault, challenging the bashers, and getting together with other poor people to work for a better society.

Across Canada people who are poor are working to control their internalized poor-bashing. Here is a list of some ways they do it.

- Name it. You're bashing yourself because you have heard so many prejudiced, bashing messages, not because you are a bad or shameful person. You are just as good, capable, and intelligent as anyone else, if not better. The bashers should change, not you.

- Learn the economic and political basics about what causes poverty. (See the next chapter and Appendix B for information and where to get more.)

- Find ways to be proud of yourself as a working-class or impoverished person. Read stories by working-class or poor writers. Listen to music from the labour movement. Discuss the good things you do, your strengths as a human being and/or parent and community member.

- Get together with other poor people and talk about internalized poor-bashing. See how your experiences are similar and different. Think about who benefits from internalized poor-bashing.

- Learn about the movements and history of other people who have struggled for more power and equality. Learn about the struggles of people of colour, labour, women, Aboriginal people, and people with disabilities, to name a few.

- Work with other poor people in local social justice organizations, or create your own. Organize to fight for laws and programs that make income and wealth distribution more fair.

- Make a commitment to yourself to challenge poor-bashing when you hear or read it. This won't be easy. But it can be exhilarating. Experiment with different approaches. Explain poor-bashing to your neighbours and relatives.

- Remember, your experience and knowledge as a poor person are crucial to developing anti-poverty plans that really work (but you'll still have to fight hard for them).

When Linda Moreau and Rose Brown facilitate workshops for people who are poor they often ask people what keeps them strong. Some of the things people say, Moreau told me, include knowing my family needs me, reading, meditation, keeping in touch with nature, exercise, music, learning, not wasting, and trying to keep the environment clean. Some people also said that working for justice helps make life worthwhile.

"It's not good to not have the things you need to keep healthy," Moreau told me. But, "If poverty doesn't damage or kill you," she said, "it can make you stronger, and help you realize what's important in life."

"What do we do to celebrate, build, and make us stronger?" Arlene Mantle asked Jo Grey and me in her Toronto kitchen. "That to me is ultimately the only thing that's going to change things: when we take our own power."

Chapter 10

Challenging poor-bashing within and around us

We all do this. We're all racist and sexist and we all poor-bash. We're programmed. What we have to do is realize it and try to stop it and help each other stop.

Leigh Donahue

More and more poor people are finding that challenging poor-bashing is a good way to confront internalized messages of shame and blame for poverty. Challenging poor-bashing can also stop the basher, raise awareness about poor-bashing, and help organize poor and other people to fight poverty. In the long run, I believe, challenging poor-bashing can help people see more clearly what's causing poverty and pave the way for actions that will reduce it, even bring a new system that could end it.

Poor-bashing is so embedded in our thinking, not just in family, friends, neighbours, politicians, and the media, but in how our individual brains, our communities, organizations, provinces, and country work, that it's difficult even to name all the ways in which poor-bashing occurs, let alone come up with ways to challenge each instance of it. The work of challenging poor-bashing can be a stressful, tiring, full-time job without pay. Poor people need allies, and together we need information and ideas about how to do it.

Expose the systems and laws that cause poverty

Here are some key pieces of information that can help people understand that the poor aren't to blame for poverty.

1. There is enough wealth to end poverty if that wealth were distributed fairly. This is true in Canada and the world.

Canadian Business magazine, July 30 1999, gave these examples of extreme wealth in Canada:

- Newspaper owner Ken Thomson had nearly $21 billion in personal wealth in 1999. (According to an estimate by Armine Yalnizyan, in 1997, when he had only $14 billion, it was more than the poorest third of Canadian households put together.)

- The Irving family fortune, made from Irving Oil in the Maritimes, is $6.67 billion, and Galen Weston's wealth (groceries, real estate) is $5.37 billion.

Peter Munk, Chairman and Chief Executive Officer of Barrick Gold Corporation, raked in Canada's biggest paycheque in 1998: $38.4 million. I hesitate to say that he "earned" that much or "made" that much. It would take about 1,370 workers making the 1995 average full-time wage to earn the same amount.

Our economic system operates in a way that enables these people to become extremely rich while others sleep in the streets. To keep on top of these inequities, flip through the business pages of daily newspapers and clip articles about high profits and CEO compensation, so you can refer to them when talking with others.

2. Minimum wage isn't enough to get people out of poverty, even with full-time work.

While Peter Munk's compensation was about $18,000 an hour if he worked a regular workweek, thousands of others in Canada drudge for a minimum wage that ranged, in 2000, from $5.50 an hour in Newfoundland to $7.60 in British Columbia, according to a Canadian Council on Social Development survey. Even working thirty-five hours a week at the highest minimum wage in the country, a single worker in a city would be about $1,500 below the poverty line. A family on minimum wage would be in deep poverty. For example, at $7.15 an hour, a full-time worker could earn $14,872 before UI, CPP, taxes, work expenses, and day care are paid for. The National Council of Welfare low-income line for a two-person family in a city in 1998 was $22,453. Of course, many low-paid jobs now are not full-time or permanent. Nearly a million part-time workers, mostly women, would take full-time jobs if they were available, according to a report from the Canadian Labour Congress in the winter of 1997-98.

3. Poverty in Canada is caused by laws and government policy.

Increasing the legal minimum wage could end poverty for thousands of people and not cost taxpayers a cent. Many people are poor because they survive on welfare rates that are far below the poverty line. Changing the regulations to increase welfare rates could reduce or end their poverty. Of course, the corporate lobby would say that wages need to be low so that we can be competitive. That's why we need a different system, a system in which people co-operate to reduce poverty, not one in which they are forced to compete to see who can survive on the lowest wage.

People who live in poverty have to pay hundreds, even thousands, of dollars in income and other taxes. They pay the GST or HST in Atlantic Canada, provincial sales taxes, and part of their landlord's property tax in their rent payments. They pay income taxes if their incomes are over about $7,000 a year, although politicians are talking about increasing this amount. In 1998, for example, a single person with a poverty-line income of about $16,000 a year paid over $2,200 in income tax. Changing tax laws like these could reduce poverty.

Unemployment insurance used to protect nearly 90 per cent of unemployed people. Then government changed the law and now "employment insurance" covers only from 27 to about 40 per cent of unemployed people (depending on the province and the month). For thirty years the Canada Assistance Plan required provincial governments who wanted federal money for welfare to provide social assistance to all people in need. In 1996 the Liberal government ended this law and provinces began denying welfare to people in need. Changing these programs increased poverty, hunger, and homelessness.

4. Corporations and rich people don't pay their fair share of taxes.

A good source of information on this is the Ontario Federation of Labour's biannual report *Unfair Shares,* which shows how much taxes corporations don't pay. For example, Thomson Corporation made U.S.$674 million in 1996 and paid only $45 million in corporate income tax, a mere 6.7 per cent. This is about half the rate paid by a single person earning a poverty-level income of $16,000 in 1999.

Who doesn't pay taxes in Canada?

- Amoco Canada Petroleum: profits U.S.$378 million; corporate income tax zero
- Brascade Resources: profits $51.4 million; corporate income tax zero
- Crown Life Insurance: profits $103 million; corporate income tax $4 million (a lower percentage than many people living in poverty)
- Ford Motor Company of Canada: profits nearly half a billion in 1996; corporate income tax zero
- General Motors of Canada: profits $679 million; corporate income tax zero
- Renaissance Energy: profits $291 million; corporate income tax zero

Source: Ontario Federation of Labour, *Unfair Shares,* 1998. The figures are for 1996.

If corporations can't avoid income tax altogether, they can defer it. By 1996, six huge corporations had deferred over a billion dollars each in corporate income taxes. This is like having an interest-free loan from the government that you may never have to pay back. Seagrams, owned by the fourth-richest Canadian family, had deferred nearly U.S.$2.5 billion in Canadian corporate taxes by 1997. There are lots of other loopholes that benefit the rich, such as being able to deduct half the price of so-called business lunches and corporate hockey boxes from taxable income.

5. There aren't enough jobs for all who need them.

According to the Caledon Institute, in 1997 Canada had about 400,000 job vacancies and 1.4 million unemployed people. "If every unemployed person were able to fill every job vacancy," said Caledon, "that would still leave one million without a job." Caledon says that about 70 per cent of unemployment is due to lack of jobs and "only 30 per cent to a mismatch between the available jobs, and the skills and geographical location of the unemployed." A 1999 report by the Canadian Centre for Policy Alternatives says that the real unemployment rate in the country, counting discouraged workers, underemployed people, and part-timers who want full-time work was 18 per cent, not the 7.8 per cent that the government claimed. How can people in a country that does not provide enough jobs for all then go on to condemn the jobless?

6. Welfare policies intentionally promote cheap labour and working poverty.

Welfare rates have been cut and rules changed to force recipients to compete fiercely for any available jobs. But, as the National Council of Welfare pointed out in 1993, if wages started at $10 or $11 an hour, there would be no talk about the impact of welfare on the "incentive to work."

On a world scale, if our so-called global economy were organized more fairly, 447 individuals would not be allowed to exploit the resources of the world and the labour of the people in it to accumulate more wealth than the combined incomes of the poorest half of the world's population, while nearly a billion people lack access to food and over a billion lack safe water.

Rose Brown explained to me how learning this kind of information can give power to people who are poor: "When the inequities are just vaguely inside us, it shuts us down....When we understand the inequalities, it gives us power. We understand that one reason the rich are rich is because governments help them. It's not that we're just jealous. We have real reasons." (See Appendix B for a list of resources on the causes of poverty.)

Challenging poor-bashing within yourself

In his autobiography, Nelson Mandela tells a story of boarding an airplane and noticing that the pilot was Black: "I had never seen a Black pilot before, and the instant I did, I had to quell my panic," he wrote. "How could a Black man fly an airplane? But a moment later I caught myself: I had fallen into the apartheid mind-set, thinking Africans were inferior and that flying was a white man's job." Here was a person who fought racism so fiercely he had been jailed for decades, yet even he had been programmed with a racist thought.

I'm a person who has been poor for decades, been on welfare and unemployment insurance, and worked for five years to expose and combat poor-bashing, but during the time I was writing this book I blurted out to a co-worker a sentence that implied that people who live on the street are less capable of delivering a brief to city council than others. That statement contradicted my own experience of hearing very articulate, passionate, and urgent comments made to city council by people who live on the street as well as very confused and boring briefs presented by people with advanced degrees, but I made it. Most of us have been programmed by a culture formed through hundreds of years of poor-bashing before us as well as throughout our own life. It takes a conscious and ongoing effort to stop poor-bashing, just as it takes this kind of effort to stop racism and sexism. Whether you're poor, rich, or in between, if you don't have any poor-bashing thoughts or actions, you are unusual. Here are some ways you can make sure that you don't poor-bash. This list is mostly for people who aren't poor, but may be useful for people who are poor too.

- Assume that you poor-bash and try to figure out how. You may not poor-bash much, but start from that assumption and you'll probably find something.

- Check out the language, myths and assumptions about poor-bashing outlined in other parts of this book and don't use them. Be critical of popular phrases used to discuss poverty or poor people, like "needing incentive." Stop and think about them before you repeat them. Learn the facts about poor-bashing so you can explain them to others.

- Use the advice about equalizing power, found in Appendix C.

- Work with groups that low-income people can afford to participate in. Decide that the group, not individuals, will pay for transportation and child care. Do this in a non-stigmatizing, respectful way.

- Hold workshops, conferences, dances, dinners, celebrations, and yes, even fundraisers, that are free for people who don't have money. Don't require them to ask (grovel) individually or know someone on the organizing committee to be able to attend. The best invitation I've ever seen said, "We desire your presence more than your money." Advertise the price, whether $10 or $50, then add "or what you can afford" and don't question what people give.

- Treat everyone with respect. Don't act surprised when people who are poor show that they are capable and intelligent.

- Don't talk more than your share at meetings. As a rule, for example, if there are ten people at the meeting, talk one-tenth of the time. Or take time to "go around" and invite everyone to say what they think about what's being discussed, with an opportunity to "pass" if they want.

- If you are working on poverty issues in a middle-class or wealthy group, check out your focus and goals with local anti-poverty groups. Are you working on something that poor people want and need or something that your group *thinks* poor people need? Better still, ask the anti-poverty groups what their most important issues are and what you can do to help them work on these issues without taking them over.

- Work for political changes that will make income, wealth, and power distribution more equal.

- Challenge poor-bashing when you read or hear it. Consider the ways of doing this suggested in the rest of this chapter.

Challenge poor-bashing language, assumptions, double standards, and myths

Challenging blatant poor-bashing by family, neighbours, and co-workers can be hard, but it can also be rewarding. How do you do it?

You have to figure out what works for you. Like me, you might start by taking a deep breath. Then you can name what has been said as poor-bashing and tell the person what poor-bashing is and that it's similar to racism and sexism because it discriminates and stereotypes people; it's another way of making some people seem less valuable than others; it's a powerful form of exclusion; it's programmed into us by our history and culture; it's a way of cheapening our labour and keeping us from seeing who really has power. If you believe the poor-bashing is done unconsciously, you can explain that we have been programmed by these thoughts so it's important to really think about what we are saying so we have control over the words that come out of our mouths. If you believe the poor-bashing is being done on purpose, you can state that this is unacceptable to you and why and what you are going to do about it. Then you can replace the basher's incorrect information with correct information.

If people don't realize they have been poor-bashing, they may be more willing to listen to you and accept what you say if you have a softer approach, acknowledging that they're not poor-bashing on purpose. But subtle poor-bashing is actually developed and promoted, as we saw in Chapter 4, by corporate interests who want cheaper workers, slashed social programs, and more billionaires. So try not to get depressed if poor-bashers don't acknowledge their problem immediately.

Sometimes you have to really think critically about what you have seen or heard or read to understand its poor-bashing messages. In addition to the language of poor-bashing (Chapter 5), there are other subtle kinds of poor-bashing

Poor-bashing assumptions

Some common poor-bashing assumptions and the non-poor-bashing answers to them are:

All poor people need training. While some might need training, most need jobs to be available.

All poor people need budgeting lessons. Most are experts in making a dollar stretch.

Jobs are available for all who need them. See the unemployment statistics earlier in this chapter.

Welfare and UI are generous. Call up your local welfare office or anti-poverty group and ask what the rates are. Could you live on them?

People on welfare are lazy. This is a stereotype that could also be applied to wealthy people who take lots of vacations, or make profits while sleeping.

Poor-bashing assumptions often aren't stated bluntly, but hidden in what is said or written. For example, it's common to hear, "Why doesn't he get a job?" about single men on welfare. The question assumes that jobs are available. Or, "Single parents will have more self-esteem if they get a job." This assumes that single parents don't place a high value on the job of raising their children.

Poor-bashing and the double standard

Theresa Tresidder placed a high value on her job as mother to her three daughters. "Rich people or two-parent families–people say it's good for the mother to stay home and take care of the children, but poor people— if they do it, people say they have no incentive, no personal goals," she told me, remembering the poor-bashing she had faced for insisting on being an at-home mother after she left her abusive husband. In the early 1990s, Tresidder had sued the government for the right to take care of her own children and not be forced to take a minimum-wage job. "Being here with my kids is benefiting the world ten years from now," she explained. "They're telling me I don't have a valid job. But if I was still here with their dad, what a good mother I'd be. That bugs me big time." When she sued the government over its rule that forced her to look for work, her story became public and she received vicious poor-bashing phone calls until she changed her number. Strangers called her a parasite and a baby machine. "The kids have lost their father," Theresa said. "I don't want them to lose me too."

But now the C.D. Howe Institute is making a conscious effort to promote at-home parenting for two-parent families, while pushing for policies that force single parents on welfare to work at sub-poverty minimum wage.

This poor-bashing double standard crops up in every conceivable situation: media treatment of fraud; the right to sue people who provide food that harms you; and what you have to do to get government money, to name a few. The double standard should be exposed when it happens, and fighting it should be part of our work to end poor-bashing.

Poor-bashing myths

Some poor-bashing myths have been named in other parts of the book, but here are some more:

Poverty doesn't affect me. In fact, more and more people are at risk of becoming poor in this age of low-wage, part-time, short-term jobs. Spouses leave, accidents and sickness happen. If you don't have the resources to protect yourself from these events, poverty could affect you directly.

In a larger sense, everyone is hurt by poverty. By not acknowledging the suffering that poverty creates, even wealthy people are dehumanized, a number of low-income people told me. Rose Brown said that in her mind, being human includes working to realize the total, full potential of every person, their mental and physical health, their creative and co-operative abilities.

Welfare is a way of life passed on through generations. Welfare is the income that people who have no other means of support have to rely on. People need welfare when they get laid off, can't find a job, already have a job raising children, have disabilities that make it hard to work in this economic system, lose their spouse, lose their health. In 1994, about one in four people in British Columbia were on welfare at some point during the year. Most people who are on welfare get off as soon as they can find a job, finish raising their children, or regain their health.

Too many people are on welfare. Rules for getting welfare have been tightened a lot in the last decade. But if a country has an economic system that does not supply jobs for all, and an unemployment insurance system that disqualifies over half of unemployed people, it must have welfare. Ideally, the welfare system would be designed to help protect workers' wages and rights.

Our country can't afford welfare. This is what the corporate think-tanks want us to believe. They tell us we can afford to reduce income taxes for the rich; we can afford RRSP tax exemptions that cost the economy about the same as welfare does. So why should we believe we can't afford to provide basic needs for people in poverty?

People want to live on the street. Most people that I've talked to who live on the street don't want to. Others live on the street because they are only too aware of their off-street housing options: shelters where 30 per cent of the residents have tuberculosis, where they get beat up or have their things stolen, or are thrown out at 7 a.m.; or a scuzzy room that costs so much there is not enough money left for food. In the summer of 1998, some homeless people sleeping on the beach in Vancouver told me they wouldn't have anything to do with welfare because they were "treated like scum" when they did try to get it. I also met a man who has mental illness and says he can't cope with the bureaucracy that is required to look for and maintain housing. With the appropriate help and available and affordable housing, he could live in a home.

People make wrong choices and should live with them. In 1997 I asked a single mom in Ottawa who had left her abusive husband what she thought about this statement. She said, "That's a load of garbage. My choices have been taken away. [Ontario Premier Mike] Harris has made a bigger choice and I'm now floundering on what's left." (In 1995, Harris cut welfare rates by 22 per cent.) "He's put me where my choices are very narrow," she continued. "People don't choose to be poor. Circumstances put us there."

Other people don't choose to be in car accidents that leave them disabled, or choose to be laid off, or choose that the economy will generate too few jobs. Some of those so-called choices are a matter of luck; others result from corporate and government choices, not personal choices of people who are poor.

"People on welfare ..." Any statement that claims that people on welfare or poor people as a group have any particular characteristic is stereotyping. This includes the typical poor-bashing statements that people on welfare are lazy, alcoholic, uneducated, unmotivated, can't budget, have too many children, and are defrauding the welfare system. When we are talking about millions of people who are poor, a few may be in those categories. But many aren't. And people in other income groups have these characteristics too.

"I know someone on welfare who (drinks beer, smokes, works or refuses to work, has too many children ...)." These statements are frequently made and difficult to deal with. Be ready for them if you go on a radio hotline show. The statement could be based on gossip or speculation, rather than knowledge, but people are unlikely to admit that they're basing their statements on gossip. Sometimes the speakers lack knowledge about how the welfare system works. The key point is, why be so judgmental about people on welfare? Everyone knows middle-income people who cheat on their taxes, are poor parents, drink too much, and don't budget wisely. If it's because people on welfare are seen to be wasting "my tax dollars," why aren't they judgmental about richer people wasting money from tax loopholes? You can point out this double standard.

Challenge poor-bashing media and politicians

May McIntyre, an anti-poverty advocate from Salmon Arm, B.C., scours the local papers every week. "We have four papers," she told me. "I read the editorial, letters to the editor, and articles. If I find something that needs to be addressed, I write a letter to the editor. I don't believe I've ever had a letter that hasn't been printed." On June 4, 1997, the *Salmon Arm Observer* ran a prominent story headlined "Stop poor-bashing." The article featured a photo of McIntyre and another advocate, Linne Botrokoff. In it, McIntyre says, "Poor-bashing is a term invented to describe the hostility directed towards the poor because of their poverty. People who need to use income support programs are forced to feel humiliated and despised." McIntyre and Botrokoff give workshops in their community on poor-bashing and other poverty issues.

In September 1997, in Saint John, New Brunswick, local members of NAPO complained about a poor-bashing talk-show host who, they said, called poor people "idiots drawing welfare" and made a number of other poor-bashing remarks. Front-page coverage in the *Saint John Times Globe* wasn't all favourable to the anti-poverty group, but its members were happy because it resulted in a lot of inquiries about poor-bashing and their organization. The host also invited one of their representatives to discuss the issue on the air.

Blatant poor-bashing, like name-calling, is easier to recognize than the more subtle varieties, but the people who do it are not as likely to be receptive to change. Talk-show hosts and newspaper columnists can do the blatant variety of poor-bashing on purpose to increase their ratings. Some politicians will use it as a political strategy to win votes (see Chapter 6).

Still, it can't hurt to inform these people that their poor-bashing is unacceptable to you. If you're getting started, you can practice with the answering machine that most radio and TV stations have for viewer feedback. Then you don't have to actually deal with another person. It's quick and you won't be as likely to put off the call. Or you can ask to talk to the actual poor-basher or his or her supervisor. If you can go on to organize others to protest too, that will be more effective. You can also write to the stations and papers and to their advertisers, threatening not to buy their products if they continue to advertise with poor-bashing media. You can always write letters to the editor, or demand equal time or space to reply to poor-bashing by the media. You may not get it, but it's worth a try. Organizing meetings with editorial boards is another tactic. Be sure to write down the poor-bashing comments, who made them, and the date or time so you can refer to them accurately in your complaint. You can use most of these tactics to challenge poor-bashing politicians too.

As well, you can organize demonstrations in front of the offending poor-basher's office, or occupy it. For occupations, it's a good idea to have a well-thought-out strategy and get advice from reputable groups that have experience doing this.

In Winnipeg, the Community Action Group on Poverty developed a "Macaroni Award," which they presented to poor-bashers for "public display of mean-spirited poor-bashing above and beyond the call of normal venality."

Of course all of these actions will have a lot more effect if lots of people are involved, so organizing groups of poor people and their allies is crucial for a good impact.

Organize to fight poverty

John Clarke is a serious organizer of people who are poor. Working with the Ontario Coalition Against Poverty (OCAP) in Toronto, Clarke, with others, has been been arrested trying to bring attention to the needs of poor people. He is the first to admit that "there are pervasive attitudes of contempt and disrespect and even hatred for the poor. But," he told me during an interview in his tiny Toronto office, "I find that if you

challenge that you can win a lot of respect.... I'm not sure how much
respect you'll win in corporate boardrooms, but among decently paid
working people who own their own homes, who aren't living in poverty
or wealth, I find you can earn a great deal of respect. The panhandling
action we carried out was a case in point." OCAP had organized two hundred poor people to panhandle together through Eaton's department
store in January 1997 to protest the police chief's priorities for the coming year, which included cracking down on panhandlers. A big problem
in Ontario, Clarke pointed out to me, was that people in need were being
refused welfare so they had to panhandle to eat. As the panhandlers
marched through Eaton's, shoppers willingly filled their cups. "No one
got less than $20," said Clarke, and "people felt powerful." The people
who filled the cups said they "supported what we were doing," said
Clarke. "There was a lot more understanding and support and sympathy
for people than we might have immediately assumed.

"When people organize to resist I think that builds respect," Clarke
explained, giving as another example a 1989 anti-poverty march from
Ottawa, Sudbury, and Windsor to the Ontario legislature in Toronto.
"There weren't very many people yelling out, 'You lazy bums' because
it's pretty difficult to tell someone who's slogging 250 or 300 miles down
a highway that they are a lazy bum."

In the past, Clarke recalled, "we had really big movements. The people who resisted the work camps [in the depression of the 1930s] and
demanded relief, didn't consult Decima Research or a whole lot of public
relations experts. They went out and struggled and challenged and were
able to win huge respect among wide sections of the population.... So I
think resistance is the primary question. Passive victims don't generally
get a lot of respect or consideration. People who fight back get noticed
and listened to."

Work for laws to prevent discrimination

"When I moved from Vancouver I looked at thirty houses," Theresa
Tresidder told me. "Twenty-nine of the landlords wanted welfare to pay
them directly or they wouldn't let me rent. I took cancelled cheques
from my previous landlord. No way. They wouldn't give me the benefit of the doubt. That really hurt my pride. No one wants to rent to
people on welfare."

Discrimination against people who are on welfare is rampant in
housing and employment. Some anti-poverty groups are trying to

challenge poor-bashing by getting all provincial—as well as the federal—
human rights codes to forbid discrimination against people who are poor.
Alberta, Saskatchewan, Manitoba, Quebec, Prince Edward Island, and
Nova Scotia forbid discrimination in employment and the provision of
goods, services, facilities, and accommodation based on "source of income."
Quebec and Newfoundland forbid it based on social condition or origin.
Social condition is a broader term than source of income. Human rights
expert Bill Black says it can include "people living in poverty, single parents,
people with certain occupations like domestic workers, people branded as
inferior because they have difficulty reading and writing, and people whose
dress or patterns of speech identify them as coming from the wrong side of
the tracks." British Columbia prohibits discrimination in housing based on
source of income.

The federal human rights code covers people working in industries
regulated by the federal government, such as banking, telephone companies, and the media. It does not offer any protection from discrimination
for people who are poor, in spite of the great need to end rampant discrimination by employers. NAPO and other anti-poverty groups across the
country are lobbying for "social condition" or "source of income" to be
added to the federal Human Rights Act, and have been supported in this
request by the United Nations Committee on Economic, Social and
Cultural rights, and by the chief commissioner of the Canadian Human
Rights Commission, Michelle Falardeau-Ramsey.

On a national and international level, anti-poverty groups took
their complaints about poor-bashing government policies to the same
UN committee. In December 1998 it issued a damning report on
Canada's compliance with the UN Covenant on these rights. It called on
Canada to protect people who are poor against discrimination with
changes to human rights laws and, more importantly, to legislate economic human rights, such as the right to adequate income, housing, and
a freely chosen job. Anti-poverty groups are now pushing to get the government to implement these UN recommendations.

Organize proactive campaigns to challenge poor-bashing

In September 1995, the board of ELP in Vancouver decided that the coalition's main campaign for that year would be about poor-bashing. The
group feared it would become the winning tactic in the upcoming
provincial election, as it had been in the Ontario election. We distributed

"Stop poor-bashing" posters throughout the province. We encouraged people to tell their stories about poor-bashing and published them. And developed a fact sheet about people on welfare.

By February 1996 ELP had produced ten thousand copies of the eight-page flyer, *Speaking out against poor-bashing*. It included stories of poor-bashing by people who were poor, tips on how to recognize and challenge poor-bashing, and some of ELP's thinking about who benefits from poor-bashing and who causes poverty. The flyers and posters were distributed through ELP's member groups in British Columbia and, through NAPO, across Canada. On the good side, I believe this material helped spread throughout the country the phrase poor-bashing and the idea that people who do it should stop. On the disappointing side, while it may have had a slight impact on the name-calling during the B.C. election, it certainly didn't stop the ignoring of the issues of poor people, targeting welfare for massive cuts in campaign speeches, and promising that ending welfare fraud would free up untold millions of dollars.

The B.C. Teachers Federation (BCTF) conducted a two-year campaign on the issue of poverty, including poor-bashing, in 1996 and 1997. They put feature articles in their newspaper and held conferences on poverty, where the federation paid expenses so poor parents could attend and be featured as speakers. The BCTF also produced a resource unit about poverty for teachers, called *Poverty, It's Local, It's Global, and It's All Connected*, written by Sandy Cameron, an ELP volunteer. Blaming the victim, the gap between the rich and poor, and the power dynamics of charity are all explored in the unit. Training on how to use the resource is provided during teachers' professional days. In addition, the teachers' union participates in coalitions that fight welfare cutbacks, and it makes donations to anti-poverty groups. Education about poor-bashing is crucial to reducing and ending it, and could help make a lot more students feel comfortable in school. Low-income people must be involved in designing this education if it is to be effective.

Work with unions to explain how poor-bashing hurts people with jobs

"Whenever I get the opportunity to speak at a union education meeting, I always try to explain the link between the attack on the poor and the attack on the broader working class population," John Clarke told me. "There's a link between undermining welfare and attacking wage levels. People respond to that."

In British Columbia, the Hospital Employees Union (HEU) has included, in their shop-steward training, information about how anti-poverty struggles affect their workplace. "Poor-bashing by governments won't work if voters don't support it," said the union's secretary business manager in *The Long Haul*. "That's why unions must confront the poor-bashing that takes place within their own memberships." Staff from HEU the B.C. Nurses Union and ELP developed a workshop on poor-bashing to be used at union training sessions.

In my dreams, unions would make the fight against poor-bashing an integral part of their member education services, similar to and in solidarity with strengthened campaigns against racism and sexism, which also cheapen labour.

Challenge racism and sexism too

At the end of 1999, over four hundred poor people from China were in B.C. jails for seeking a better life in Canada. They had arrived in decrepit boats and were taken into custody and jailed while their refugee claims were processed. B.C.'s women's paper, *Kinesis*, ran a front-page collage of the racist headlines that greeted the immigrants: "Go Home," "Enough already," "Disease-carrying immigrants post health risk to Canadians," "Migrants siphon funds needed for our youth." Even some of the poor people who wrote letters to the editor of *The Long Haul* got into the racist act, saying the government shouldn't give welfare to these migrants from China. It should improve welfare and disability pensions for "Canadians" instead. Racism was disguising who really had power. It wasn't the desperate Chinese refugee claimants who made the decision to keep welfare low and to deny it to people in need. They didn't have any power. Nor were the boat-people-bashers taking into account that the Canadian government was actually pressuring China to privatize many of its industries and lay off people, making them poor; that it was encouraging free trade zones within the country, places where people worked for sub-poverty wages.

So long as the idea exists that it's okay for some people to be poor because of their race, sex, the country they live in, or some other category, every powerless person in the world is also at risk. We won't understand what's causing our economic insecurity if we're blaming it on people of colour or women or people in other countries or people on welfare or panhandlers. If we don't understand its causes, then we won't be able to struggle effectively against it. So, a huge part of challenging poor-bashing is also to challenge the racism and sexism that is used to justify poverty, conceal power, and cheapen labour here in Canada and all over the world.

In short, there are myriad things you can do to challenge poor-bashing. Every time you do it, you're working on the cutting edge of a larger movement that's struggling for justice for people who are poor. Besides, it can feel so very very good, just saying with a straight back and a dignified, matter-of-fact tone, "That's poor-bashing."

Conclusion

Poverty in Canada kills more people than cancer does, according to the Ontario Medical Association. But there is a big difference between the two killers. While we don't yet know how to end cancer, we do know how to end poverty in the world, and especially in Canada. There are plenty of resources to do it and we don't need any high technology. At the world level, the United Nations says it would take only 4 per cent of the combined wealth of the 225 richest people (who have about one trillion dollars' worth of wealth) to pay for basic education, basic health care, reproductive health care, adequate food, safe water, and sanitation for all.

In Canada at the end of 1999 the federal government projected huge budget surpluses amounting to $95.5 billion over five years. This is enough to end poverty for everyone in Canada. Using the money for that purpose would have been a great way to enter the new millennium.

Instead of erasing poverty, however, Canadian federal and provincial governments, as we have seen, passed new poor laws that take us back to the beginnings of capitalism in the sixteenth century. On the world level, our government was working through the World Trade Organization to give corporations more rights and to speed up the competition for below-poverty-level wages throughout the world.

Just a few months before the budget surplus announcement, the mayor of Toronto was upset that the Ontario Coalition Against Poverty (OCAP) was planning to set up a safe park for homeless people. We won't have people defecating in parks, or leaving their condoms and syringes lying around, he poor-bashed on an August 8, 1999, radio news program I heard in Vancouver

Premier Mike Harris followed the mayor's homeless-bashing by introducing laws to severely restrict panhandling and outlaw squeegee-ing, the often helpful practice of washing car windows at traffic lights for a donation. The money that could end the suffering of homeless people and the need to panhandle and squeegee was sitting right there in the federal budget. But it wasn't being used for that. In fact, politicians were not only bashing the poorest people, but were also making them into criminals for doing what they had to do to survive. Ontario politicians were announcing to the world, as Disraeli did in 1837, that poverty was a crime.

History was repeating itself for the rich too. Canadian corporations and their lobby groups wanted tax cuts for people in the highest tax bracket, those with incomes ranging from about $60,000 to millions a year. Just like the elite in the eighteenth century, the elite in the 1990s invented a way of portraying themselves as better than the poor. They called people in the highest tax bracket "brains" and "our best and brightest," and claimed the so-called brains were about to "drain" out of the country because of high taxation.

Since feudalism changed to capitalism in Europe, the elite have defended their wealth in the midst of poverty with myths, language, and patterns of thinking that justified treating Aboriginal people and women as cattle, people of colour as savages, the poor as "vicious" and lazy, and themselves as "civilized" and "virtuous." A huge part of justifying personal wealth is treating the people who don't have it, or the people it's taken from, as lesser human beings.

In the 1990s, as governments and corporations used trade deals to speed up the race to the bottom for low wages, poor-bashing, along with racism and sexism, made it seem almost natural that even more human beings had to work in "the most servile, the most sordid, and the most ignoble offices in the community," as one of the British elite said two centuries earlier.

I believe the big corporations have to take a huge responsibility for poor-bashing. *They* own the media that spread gossip and lies; that accuse people who use welfare and UI of being fraudulent. *They* funded the think-tanks that promote blatant, as well as more insidious, poor-bashing. *They* fund the think-tanks' efforts to circulate their views to politicians, government officials, and the media, as well as the public. *They* keep changing the subject from poverty to "incentive to work" at low wages and part-time jobs. *They* want poor-bashing policies like low or no minimum wages, welfare cuts, no government job creation, and trade deals that give corporations more rights.

Politicians in power have to take responsibility too. *They* bash the poor to get elected; save their political skins by calling the poor names; pass laws that deprive the poor of basic rights and needs—or keep silent when their colleagues do these things. *They* are working with the corporations to replace the human right to food and shelter with the inadequate provisions and unequal power relations of charity. *They* help corporations take advantage of the cheap labour of very poor people in this and other countries.

But we can't blame the whole problem on corporations and politicians. Nearly all of us, including people who are poor, have been programmed with almost five hundred years of poor-bashing ideas and behaviours. It takes a conscious and continuous effort to recognize and root out those ideas and behaviours.

If we are not Aboriginal and live in North America, most of us benefit from bashing even if we're not in the corporate or political elite. We occupy land that was stolen from Aboriginal people, who were dehumanized to justify the theft. We buy coffee grown on land that people in the Third World need for food. We may be members of unions or professions that have a history of excluding people of colour. Our country's politicians take Team Canada trips around the world to set up Canadian corporations in free trade areas in poorer countries where wages, taxes, and environmental standards are low. We buy the cheap products made by these exploited workers, and then some Canadians object when these workers try to move to Canada to seek the same kind of living conditions that we take for granted.

Ending poor-bashing is a crucial part of a much larger world struggle to realize what the Universal Declaration of Human Rights proclaimed, in 1948, as the "inherent dignity" and "equal and inalienable rights of all members of the human family." It's a crucial part of this struggle because, like racism and sexism, poor-bashing is used to justify the inequality. "Our system is really okay," our programming tells us. "It's those lazy, alcoholic poor people with too many children who have to change their behaviour to get out of poverty." Or, "It doesn't cost as much to live in a poor country, therefore it's all right that the people there earn below poverty level wages." Or, "People of colour are better at doing that kind of stuff than people here, therefore their low wages are acceptable." In reality there is no justification for treating some groups of people as needing or deserving less than others.

Ending poor-bashing is an essential part of the struggle for justice because poor-bashing insidiously drives working people to demand the kinds of policies that cheapen their own paid work. "Those people on welfare have to be forced to work at any job so I won't have to support them with my taxes," says the programming. "Welfare rates should be too low to live on so the people who get it will be forced to take any low-wage job." In fact, as we have seen, welfare programs can help protect the wages and working conditions of working people *only* when they provide adequate benefits, don't force the unemployed to take degrading jobs or workfare jobs, and treat recipients with dignity.

Ending poor-bashing is also critical in the struggle for a just world because, like racism and sexism, it conceals who really has power. If we don't see who is powerful and how they use their power to create great wealth alongside poverty, we can't very well work effectively for more equality. While our country is ruled by an elite, we still have a vote that we can, theoretically, use to get politicians who will do what we want. But if voters get focused on the poor as simply bad individuals who cause their own poverty, on immigrants of colour whom they accuse of "taking all the jobs," or Aboriginal people whom they see as wanting too much land, they won't see how the elite is working to enrich itself. They won't see how laws and practices like low minimum wages, tax reductions for the rich, welfare cuts, interest rate policies, refusal to settle Aboriginal land claims, and free trade deals are what really cause poverty and economic insecurity, not the groups of people they've learned to blame.

Will we ever end or even reduce poor-bashing and achieve the ideals in the Universal Declaration of Human Rights? I think we can be cautiously hopeful. Some of the building blocks of a huge movement for justice are coming into place. One positive sign is that more and more people are talking about poor-bashing. It's been named. As people who are poor learn to identify poor-bashing, they are losing their fear of speaking out against it, and refusing to accept it. While there is still a lot to learn about poor-bashing, more and more Canadians are now working to stop it.

Another good sign is that more people and organizations are finally getting serious about combining work against poverty and poor-bashing with work against racism and sexism and other oppressions. I'm an example of someone who has been slow to act on this understanding: racism, sexism, and poor bashing are all part of the same system of exclusion that sees some people as less valuable than others so that the elite can justify and conceal its wealth and power and cheapen labour.

This work to fight racism, sexism, poor-bashing and poverty together won't be easy because of how we've been programmed and how most of us, even those who are not among the powerful elite, benefit in some ways from a system that exploits others. It will be important for white people in this movement to figure out and acknowledge their privilege. Most of us need to learn more about the histories of racism, sexism, and poor-bashing—not just *what* happened, but also *why* and *who benefits*.

People who aren't poor will need to do a lot of listening, be willing to learn, leave space for others, and actively work to end poverty. If we can do this with respect, it could bring together a lot of people who have been separated in the larger struggle for worldwide justice.

It has given me hope to see the number of thoughtful, active, committed people who are making their lives a struggle for justice. Probably none of them will get an Order of Canada or any other famous prize. Fay Blaney is a living example of how to challenge poor-bashing by uniting it with education against racism and sexism too. She sees building a broad coalition to work for justice as a matter of life and death, which it is, especially for the poor, Aboriginal people, people of colour, and people in poor countries. Not only is she raising two children, and working to support them, but she also volunteers with women's and Aboriginal groups working for justice.

Marlene Vieno of Winnipeg takes a special pride in her birthday, December 10th, International Human Rights Day. "I've always believed in equality, social justice, and fairness for everybody," Marlene told me. She has battled the mental health and welfare systems for about forty years, working in different anti-poverty and other groups.

Other people featured in this book have devoted decades to anti-poverty and coalition work, much of it unpaid. And there are thousands more across the country, trying to cope on totally inadequate incomes and, at the same time, working in little groups and larger ones to raise poverty, poor-bashing, and social justice issues. People like John Clarke of OCAP, and others, have been arrested for their beliefs, and I suspect a lot more of us will be jailed as our struggle continues.

There is a growing anger in Canada among people who have been made poor since the Canada Assistance Plan was abolished and the attacks on poor people increased. Time and again, people who return from humiliating, useless visits to welfare and unemployment insurance offices have broken down and made the same simple statement to me: "I'm human too." I'm hopeful that learning about poor-bashing and its role in promoting a society of greed and poverty will help to keep people from turning that anger inward at themselves, or at their spouses or children, or at other oppressed people who may be in a different group from them. I'm hoping that we can build an anti-poverty movement that focuses that anger at the system that causes the poverty of all people in the world.

I believe that we can use the strength and intelligence of people who are poor, the understanding that people who are poor have of what's really important in life, to build power with, not over, all oppressed people. An understanding of poor-bashing, racism, and sexism can help unite Canadians with others concerned about the environment,

peace, workers' rights, and social and economic justice into a huge solidarity movement. Eventually, we will build a world in which everyone's
needs are met, and in which the systems and structures we set up are
based on co-operation and human caring, not competition and greed.

Appendix A

How you can tell when the media poor-bash

Sometimes poor-bashing is obvious. Calling people on welfare names like cheats or criminally inclined opportunists is blatant poor-bashing. But subtle poor-bashing can be just as devastating. You must read or listen critically to make sure you're not being taken in by it.

Newfoundland anti-poverty activist Bev Brown asks these questions about media coverage of poverty issues when she gives workshops on poverty and the media:

What's left out of the story?
Issues usually left out of articles about welfare and UI are the high unemployment rate, the poor quality of jobs that are available (when they are), an explanation of who benefits from poverty, information about the laws that cause poverty (like low welfare rates and minimum wages), and information about who has the funds or could create the jobs or pay the wages to reduce poverty.

Who is speaking?
Do poor people or groups that represent poor people have any voice in the story? Do we hear directly from people in poverty or only from people who work for agencies or charities or from researchers who theorize about them?

Is the story based on false assumptions?
Is it assumed that jobs are available when they aren't? That welfare is generous? That people on welfare are lazy? That welfare is easily available? That people on welfare and UI don't have to look for work? That single moms aren't productive? That people have to be forced to look for work? That training programs will create enough jobs for all who need them?

What are the subtle messages of the story?
Does it suggest—without clearly stating— that people who have paid work are better than people who have unpaid work (caring for children, for example)? Does it imply that people on welfare prefer this to a range of other options?

Does the story use facts, or gossip and insinuation?
Are sources named? Are the sources right-wing think-tanks that have a vested interest in policies that cut the taxes and reduce the wages that their member corporations pay? Are the sources "authorities" who promote the typical stereotypes about people on welfare or UI? Would a similar standard of accuracy apply when reporting about a person or group with a lot of power?

Does the story use the social policy newspeak words?
Does it use words or phrases like dependent, incentive, disincentive, and others (described in Chapter 5) that blame the poor and take the pressure off the rich?
Brown recommends these supplementary questions:
   Does the story ask how to end poverty, or does it merely expose the suffering of poor individuals?
   Does it ask who benefits from poverty?
   Does it investigate what laws cause poverty instead of focusing on individual characteristics of poor people?
   Does it deal with the morality of poverty in the midst of great wealth?
   If a publication includes stories advising upper-income people how to use RRSPs, does it also print stories advising poor people how to use welfare and UI? If there are stories about welfare fraud, are there any about tax fraud, or corporate fraud?
   Does the story assume charity is the only way to deal with poverty?

A final test: how would it sound if the statements about poor people were made about women or people of colour? Would it be okay to say that women are "criminally inclined opportunists"? That would be sexist. Would it be okay to say that people of colour are "criminally inclined opportunists"? No, that would be racist. Then it's poor-bashing to say that people on welfare are "criminally inclined opportunists."

Appendix B

Resources for learning about poverty and the economy

National Anti-Poverty Organization. *NAPO News*. A newsletter published several times a year. A subscription, $2 if you are a low-income person, includes membership in NAPO. From NAPO at 440-325 Dalhousie Street, Ottawa, Ont. K1N 7G2; phone 1 800 810-1076; fax 613 789-0141.

B.C. Teachers' Federation. *Poverty: It's Local, It's Global and It's All Connected.* Written by Sandy Cameron as a resource for students and teachers. Includes material for instruction on poverty in British Columbia and on what poverty is; includes a critical look at poor-bashing articles in the media and suggests learning activities. Obtainable from B.C. Teachers' Federation at 604 871-2283 or <http://www.bctf.bc.ca>.

Armine Yalnizyan. *The Growing Gap*. The Centre for Social Justice, 836 Bloor St. West, Toronto, Ont. M6G 1M2; phone 416 516-0009, fax 416 531-3197. This 128-page book is written in plain language and analyzes the growing income and wealth gaps between the rich and poor in Canada. It costs $10. Ask your local public library to obtain a copy.

Canadian Centre for Policy Alternatives. *The CCPAMonitor*. This report comes out ten times a year and includes articles about the economy, globalization, poverty, the environment, and politics from a progressive point of view. $25 a year for low-income people. From CCPA at 410-75 Albert St., Ottawa, Ont. K1P 5E7; phone 613 563-1341, fax 613 322-2458. Ask your local public library to subscribe.

The Alternative Federal Budget. Published annually by the CCPA (see address above) and CHO!CES, a Manitoba social justice coalition. Demonstrates the federal policy decisions that would reduce poverty. Obtainable from CCPA or CHO!CES if you live in Manitoba. Ask your local public library to obtain a copy.

End Legislated Poverty. *The Long Haul*. ELP's monthly newspaper includes information about poverty, how low-income people are thinking about it, and what they are doing about it. It focuses on British Columbia, but also has a national and international perspective. From ELP at 211-456 W. Broadway, Vancouver, B.C. V5Y 1R3; phone 604 879-1209, fax 604 879-1229. Free to low-income people. Ask your library to subscribe.

United Nations Committee on Economic, Social and Cultural Rights. Report on Canada's compliance with the International Covenant on Economic, Social and Cultural Rights, Dec. 8, 1998. Get this from NAPO or ELP, addresses above.

Social Planning Council of Metro Toronto and the Ontario Social Safety Network. *Workfare Watch*. Project and newsletter to monitor and report on Ontario's workfare policy. Contact Workfare Watch at <http://worldchat.com/public/tab/> or phone 416 351-0095.

Appendix C

To equalize power among us*

We need to keep ourselves in check in whatever ways we have privilege.
Margo Adair & Sharon Howell

In the Ways We've Been Oppressed
In addition to keeping ourselves in check regarding whatever ways we possess privilege, it is vital that we stop constraining ourselves—stop keeping ourselves in check, in the particular ways that relate to how we have experienced being an "outsider." We have to take the risk of putting our experience into the centre. We can no longer afford to collude with our own oppression by accommodating and/or not acknowledging our own power. It is our experience that is needed to inform and shape decisions.

It is also important to remember that offensive behaviour is not necessarily calculated to protect power. It is often simply a result of ignorance. Those with privilege have never needed to understand the experience of others. They are frequently oblivious of how their behaviour reinforces the status quo.

Despite our best intentions we find, more often than not, that we duplicate the patterns of power we find so abhorrent in dominant culture. Following are some guidelines to help us equalize relations. *Privilege is invisible to those who have it.* To create a context which embraces diversity, in which no one is marginalized, a conscious and ongoing effort is required. By noticing and changing what we take for granted, we make room for everyone's contributions. This list is offered as a way to help privileged group members reflect on their own behaviour.

Don't interrupt.
Don't unilaterally set the agenda.
Don't patronize.
Don't assume you're more capable.
Don't trivialize the experience of others.
Don't challenge tone, attitude or manner.
Don't assume anyone is more "suited" for anything.
Don't take responsibility for, think for, or speak for others.
Don't assume someone is exceptional compared to the "average" person of
     their group.
Don't assume an individual speaks for or has the same opinions as others
     from their group.

---

* Reprinted from *Breaking old patterns, weaving new ties*, published by Tools for Change, 2408 East Valley, Seattle, WA 98112; e-mail: <Madair@toolsforchange.org>.

Don't be the only one controlling the organization's resources.

Don't reduce difficulties to personality conflicts.

Don't assume the root of a problem is misunderstanding or lack of information.

Don't ask others to explain, prove, or justify themselves.

Don't mimic other cultural traditions or religious practices.

Don't expect to be treated as an individual outside of your group's history.

Don't flaunt how you may be different than others of your group.

Don't take up all the space or always speak first.

Don't ignore or minimize differences by emphasizing similarities.

Don't overlook history and equate all oppressions as equal.

Don't expect "others" to educate you about their group's history, conditions or sensibilities.

Don't expect others to be grateful.

Don't defend mistakes by focusing on good intentions.

Don't take everything personally.

Don't assume everyone has the same options you do.

Don't try to guess what's needed.

Don't assume that the visible reality is the only one operating.

Don't expect to be trusted.

Do take responsibility to learn about the history, culture and struggles of other groups as told by them.

Do make sure the context welcomes everyone's voice and listen.

Do appreciate efforts to point out mistakes. (You must be doing something right, or no one would bother to tell you what's wrong.)

Do expect discomfort when relating to people different from yourself.

Do address the many dimensions of accessibility, including such things as money, space, transportation, childcare and language.

Do notice what you expect from and assume about others, and note what experiences formed your ideas.

Do name unacknowledged realities, so that the parameters of the situation expand to include everyone's experience.

Do remember that others speak about more than the conditions of their own group.

Do regard people as whole human beings with families, interests and ideas beyond those of the particular task.

Do take responsibility for equalizing power.

Do name dominating behaviour when you see it.

Do encourage pride in your own and other's ancestry and history.

Do understand individuals in the context of their social history.

Do look for political differences rather than personality conflicts.

Do ask questions.

Do struggle over matters of principle and politics.

Do respect disagreements.

Do make accessible all information so others can decide if they are interested.

Do appreciate the risk a person takes in sharing their experience with you.

Do take risks.

Do trust others.

Sources

Introduction

Craig, Susanne. "Millionaires' Club triples to 220,000." *Globe and Mail* 11 Nov. 1997, p.A1.

Federal, Provincial and Territorial Advisory Committee on Population Health. *Toward a Healthy Future: Second Report on the Health of Canadians.* Charlottetown, 1999, p.26.

Katz, Michael B. *The Undeserving Poor.* New York: Pantheon, 1989, p.7.

Osberg, Lars. "Canada's Economic Performance: Inequality, Poverty and Growth." In *False Promises*, ed. Robert C.Allen and Gideon Rosenbluth.Vancouver: New Star, 1992, p.49.

Yalnizyan, Armine. *The Growing Gap.* Toronto: Centre for Social Justice, 1998, pp. 9, 11, 19.

Chapter 1
What poor people say about poor bashing

Harcourt, Mike, with Wayne Skene. *A Measure of Defiance.* Vancouver/Toronto: Douglas and McIntyre, 1996, p.133.

Newman, Peter. *Titans: How the New Canadian Establishment Seized Power.* Toronto: Viking (Penguin), 1998, p. 49.

Westcott, Craig. "How many unemployed? It depends on the stats." St. John's *Evening Telegram* 11 Dec. 1994, p.7.

Chapter 2
History: Making the rich better than the poor

Bainton, Roland H. *Here I Stand: A Life of Martin Luther.* New York: Abingdon Press, 1991, pp.234-237.

Barstow, Anne Llewellyn. *Witchcraze.* San Francisco: Pandora, 1994, pp.25, 26, 100, 104.

Berkhofer, Robert F. *The White Man's Indian.* New York and Toronto: Random House, 1978, p.11.

Berger, Justice Thomas R. "Native rights in a new world." An address to the Canadian Ethnology Society at Banff Park Lodge in Alberta, 24 Feb. 1979, pp.2, 4.

Cameron, Sandy. "What the Luddites can teach us." *The Long Haul* February 1995, p.10.

Carniol, Ben. *Case Critical.* 2d ed. Toronto: Between the Lines, 1990, p.28.

Driver, Felix. *Power and Pauperism.* Cambridge: Cambridge University Press, 1993, pp.115, 117.

Edsall, Nicholas C. *The Anti-Poor Law Movement.* Blue Ridge Summit, PA: Rowman and Littlefield, 1971, p.17.

Garrison, Janine. *A History of 16th Century France 1483-1598.* London: Macmillan, 1995, pp.11, 20, 61-65.

Guest, Dennis. *The Emergence of Social Security in Canada.* 2d ed. Vancouver: UBC Press, 1985, p.11.

Hanson, F. Allan. "Why don't we care about the poor anymore?" *The Humanist* November /December 1997, p.11.

Korten, David C. *When Corporations Rule the World*. West Hartford, Conn.: Kumarian Press, and San Francisco: Berrett-Koehler Publishers, 1995, p.249.

Miles, Robert. *Racism After "Race Relations."* London and New York: Routledge, 1993, pp.90-97.

Malthus, Thomas Robert. *On Population*. New York: Random House, The Modern Library, 1960, pp.31-34.

Piven, Frances Fox and Richard A.Cloward. *Regulating the Poor*. New York: Vintage, 1971, pp.28, 34, 35, 38.

————. "The Historical Sources of the Contemporary Relief Debate," in Block, Fred et al., *The Mean Season*. New York: Pantheon Books, 1987, pp. 36, 37.

Tawney, R.H. *Religion and the Rise of Capitalism*. Gloucester, Mass.: Harcourt Brace, 1926, p.46.

Thompson, E.P. *The Making of the English Working Class*. London: Penguin, 1984, pp.60-69, 246-48.

Webb, Beatrice and Sidney. *English Poor Law History*. London: Frank Cass, 1963, *Part I*, pp.4, 86, 110, 111, 151; *Part II, Volume 1,*. pp. 8,9.

Weber, Max. *The Protestant Ethic and the Spirit of Capitalism*. New York: Charles Scribner's Sons, 1958, pp.162, 177, 178, 182.

Chapter 3
History: Keeping the myth alive

Adams, Ian, William Cameron, Brian Hill, and Peter Penz. *The Real Poverty Report*. Edmonton: Hurtig, 1971, p. 68.

Allen, Richard, ed. *The Social Gospel in Canada*. Ottawa: National Museums of Canada, 1975, pp.10, 13, 190.

Barlow, Maude and Bruce Campbell. *Straight through the Heart*. Toronto: Harper Collins,1995, pp.20, 27.

Canada. Chief Electoral Office of Canada. *A History of the Vote in Canada*. Ottawa: Ministry of Public Works and Government Services, 1997, pp.63, 75.

Canada. Senate Committee on Poverty. *Poverty in Canada*. Ottawa: Information Canada, 1971, pp.viii, ix, xii.

Canadian Conference on Social Work. *Proceedings of 6th Annual Conference,* 1938, p.9.

Carniol, Ben. *Case Critical*. 2d ed. Toronto: Between the Lines, 1990, pp.25, 29, 31.

Drover, Glenn and Allan Moscovitch, eds. *Inequality*. Toronto: University of Toronto Press, 1981, p.199.

Francis, R. Douglas, Richard Jones, Donald B. Smith. *Origins: Canadian History to Confederation*. 2d ed. Toronto: Holt, Rinehart and Winston, 1988, pp. 138, 158, 229.

Grayson, L.M. and Michael Bliss, eds. *The Wretched of Canada*. University of Toronto Press, 1971, pp.5, 41.

Guest, Dennis. *The Emergence of Social Security in Canada*. 2d ed. Vancouver: UBC Press, 1985, pp.10, 13, 29, 36, 37, 49-63, 69, 104, 109, 116.

Leier, Mark. *Where the Fraser River Flows*. Vancouver: New Star, 1990, p.26.

Liversedge, Ronald. *Recollections of the On to Ottawa Trek*. Toronto: Carleton Library, McClelland and Stewart,1973, pp.viii, ix.

Lovick, L.D., ed. *Tommy Douglas Speaks*. Vancouver: Douglas and McIntyre, 1979, p.30.

Manuel, George and Michael Posluns. *The Fourth World*. Don Mills, Ont: Collier-Macmillan,1974, pp.17, 22.

Porter, John. *The Vertical Mosaic*. Toronto: University of Toronto Press, 1965, p.307.

Struthers, James. "A Profession in Crisis" in *The "Benevolent" State*, Allan Moscovitch and Jim Albert, eds., Toronto: Garamond Press, 1987, pp.114-20.

Swankey, Ben and Jean Evan Sheils. *Work and Wages*. Vancouver: Trade Union Research Bureau, 1977, pp.14, 15

Wilson, Myron. "The New Brunswick Slave Trade." *Weekend Magazine* 8 June 1974, pp.8, 10.

Chapter 4
History: Justifying the race to the bottom

Anderson, Ronald. "Tough decisions needed to survive wave of change." *Globe and Mail* 19 Feb. 1985, B2.

Business Council on National Issues. *A Submission to the Royal Commission on the Economic Union and Development Prospects for Canada*, December 1983, p.ii.

———. *On the Mulroney Government's Agenda for Economic Renewal*, April 1985, pp.iv, vii.

Canada. Ministry of Employment and Immigration. *Income Security for Canadians*. Ottawa: 1970, pp.1, 3, 6, 9, 16, 17, 22, 23, 53.

———. Human Resources Development Canada. *Improving Social Security in Canada*. Ottawa: Ministry of Supply and Services, 1994, pp.8, 9, 10, 22, 25, 29, 31, 33, 35, 43, 72.

———. Human Resources Development Canada. *Social Security Review Communications Strategy*. Ottawa: 3 August 1994, p.8.

———. National Council of Welfare. *Poverty Profile 1992*. Ottawa: Ministry of Supply and Services, 1992, p. 7.

———. National Council of Welfare. *Poverty Profile 1985*. Ottawa: Ministry of Supply and Services, 1985, p.70.

———. National Council of Welfare. *Welfare Incomes, 1994*. Ottawa: Ministry of Supply and Services, 1994, pp.27, 28.

———. *Royal Commission on the Economic Union and Development Prospects for Canada*. Volume 2. (Donald S. Macdonald, et al.) Ottawa: Ministry of Supply and Services, 1985, pp.541, 542, 588, 612.

Canadian Union of Public Employees. "The Policies of Depression." *CUPE Facts*. Ottawa: February 1983, p. 6.

Clarke, Tony. *Silent Coup*. Ottawa and Toronto: Canadian Centre for Policy Alternatives and Lorimer, 1997, pp.12, 15, 21.

Collins, Sheila. *Let Them Eat Ketchup!* New York: Monthly Review Press, 1996, pp.66-70.

Covington, Sally. "How Conservative Philanthropies and Think Tanks Transform US Policy." *Covert Action Quarterly* Winter 1998, p.9.

Drache, Daniel and Duncan Cameron. *The Other Macdonald Report*. Toronto: Lorimer, 1985, p.xi.

Gilder, George. *Wealth and Poverty*. 2d ed. Oakland, CA: Institute for Contemporary Studies, 1993.

Herrstein, Richard J. and Charles Murray. *The Bell Curve: Intelligence and Class Structure in American Life*. New York: Free Press, 1994.

Katz, Michael B. *The Undeserving Poor*. New York: Pantheon Books, 1989, pp.151, 152.

McQuaig, Linda. *Behind Closed Doors*. Toronto: Penguin, 1988, p.183.

———. *Shooting the Hippo*. Toronto: Viking, 1995, p.221.

Mead, Lawrence. *Beyond Entitlement: The Social Obligations of Citizenship*. New York: Free Press, 1985.

Murray, Charles. *Losing Ground: American Social Policy 1950-1980*. New York: Basic Books, 1994.

Piven, Frances Fox and Richard A.Cloward. "The Historical Sources of the Contemporary Relief Debate." in *The Mean Season*, ed. Fred Block et al., New York: Pantheon Books, 1987, p.50.

Westbrook, Robert B. *John Dewey and American Democracy*. Ithaca and London: Cornell University Press, 1991, p.551.

Chapter 5
Using language to corrupt thought

Beeby, Dean. "Plan to get Nova Scotians past welfare to jobs fails." *Vancouver Sun* 14 Jan. 1998, p.A9.

Bradbury, Bruce. "Disarming the poverty trap?" Sydney, Australia: *Social Policy Research Centre Newsletter* May 1999, p.1.

British Columbia. Premier's Forum on New Opportunities for Working and Living. *Report from the Forum*. Victoria: 1995, pp. 2, 4, 19, 80.

Cameron, Sandy. "Stop the hate literature." *Carnegie Newsletter*. Vancouver: Carnegie Community Association, Oct.1, 1995, p.1.

Canada. Human Resources Development Canada. *Improving Social Security in Canada*. Ottawa: 1994, p.29.

———. Human Resources Development Canada. *Social Security Review Communications Strategy*. Ottawa: 1994, p.7.

———. Human Resources Development Canada and Government of Nova Scotia. Strategic Initiatives Evaluation. *Nova Scotia Compass Report*. Ottawa: 1997, p.1.

C. D. Howe Institute. *Annual Report, 1995*. Toronto, pp.2 and 6.

———. *Annual Report, 1994*. Toronto, p.6.

Courchene, Thomas J. *Social Canada in the Millennium*. Toronto: C. D. Howe Institute, 1994, pp.324-327.

———. *Social Policy in the 1990s*. Toronto: C. D. Howe Institute, 1987, p.181.

Dooley, Martin D. et al. *Family Matters*. Toronto: C. D. Howe Institute, p.228.

"Howe Institute applauds Alberta's welfare reforms." *Vancouver Sun* 10 April 1997, p.A8.

International Monetary Fund. *Canada, selected issues.* IMF Staff Country Report 99/14, Washington, D.C.: 1999, pp. 50-55.

"Job clubs blame jobless for unemployment." *The Long Haul* May 1998, p.7.

Newfoundland and Labrador government. *Meeting the Challenge.* St. John's: 1994, p.21.

Organization for Economic Co-operation and Development. *The OECD Jobs Study.* Paris: OECD, 1994, p.39.

O'Neil, Peter. "US studios lobby against change in tax shelter." *Vancouver Sun* 22 Oct. 1997, p.A6.

Orwell, George. *Nineteen Eighty-Four.* New York: Penguin Books,1983, pp.242, 244, 248.

Osberg, Lars. "Canada's Economic Performance: Inequality, Poverty and Growth" in *False Promises*, ed. Robert C. Allen and Gideon Rosenbluth. Vancouver: New Star, 1992, pp.41,49.

Richards, John and Aidan Vining, eds. *Helping the Poor.* Toronto: C.D. Howe Institute, 1995, pp.vi, xiv, 29, 148.

Richards, John. *Retooling the Welfare State.* Toronto: C.D. Howe Institute, 1997, pp.258, 260, 261.

Sarlo, Christopher. *Poverty in Canada.* Vancouver: Fraser Institute, 1992, pp. 2, 191, 171.

————. "Poverty in Canada—1994." *Fraser Forum Critical Issues Bulletin.* Vancouver: Fraser Institute, 1994, pp. 53, 54.

Streifel, Dennis. "Poor are escaping trap of welfare dependency." *Vancouver Sun* 13 Jan. 1998, p.A11.

Swanson, Jean. "NAPO board discusses social policy reform experiments." *NAPO News* Summer 1994, p. 4.

United Nations. *Human Development Report, 1997.* New York: Oxford University Press, 1997, p.110.

Watson, William G., John Richards, and David M. Brown. *The Case for Change.* Toronto: C.D. Howe Institute, 1994, pp. 2, 5, 9.

York, Geoffrey. "Grits vow radical social reform." *Globe and Mail* 1 Feb. 1994, p.A1.

————. "UI system destroying incentive to work, Axworthy says." *Globe and Mail* 26 Feb. 1994, p.A6.

Chapter 6
The media and politicians: poor-bashing through the 1990s

"Anti-poverty groups fight welfare policies." *The Long Haul* April 1994, p.5.

"'Beth' misrepresented in welfare story." St. John's *Evening Telegram* 14 March 1998, p.10.

Cameron, Sandy. "Article is gossip, not research." *The Long Haul* September. 1995, p.7.

Canada. National Council of Welfare. *Welfare Incomes, 1991.* Ottawa: Ministry of Supply and Services, 1991, p.24.

————.Statistics Canada. "Historical statistical supplement, 1996/7." *Canadian Economic Observer* 1997, p.31.

Cleary, Ryan. "Annie's song." St. John's *Evening Telegram* 9 March 1998, p.9.

————. "Cheque in..." St. John's *Evening Telegram* 10 March 1998, p.1.

————. "Poverty by the numbers." St. John's *Evening Telegram* 11 March 1998, p.1.

Crosby, Louise. "Minister shoots down report on welfare fraud." *Vancouver Sun* 13 Nov. 1993, p.A1.

Eurchuk, Reed. "The anti-welfare bandwagon." ELP *Action Line* September 1993, p.12.

Farrow, Moira. "Welfare scam 'buying arms for Somalia.'" *Vancouver Sun* Oct. 1993, p.A1.

————. "Suspect in welfare fraud subject of bench warrant." *Vancouver Sun* 25 Nov. 1993, p.A1.

————. "Warlord's welfare scam confirmed." *Vancouver Sun* 4 March 1994, p.A1.

Francis, Diane. "Welfare system economic suicide." *Financial Post* 15 April 1991, p.2.

————. "The shame of 'poverty pimps.'" *Financial Post* 29 April 1991, p.2.

————. "Welfare beats work in Ontario." *Financial Post* 10 April 1992, p.3.

Girard, Daniel and Patricia Orwen."Harris sorry for 'beer' crack." *Toronto Star* 17 April 1998, p.A1.

"Harcourt: 'I see the hurt you have experienced.'" ELP *Action Line* December 1993, p.1.

Hunter, Justine. "Half of 669 complaints of welfare fraud in March were valid, statistics show." *Vancouver Sun* 9 June 1993, p.B2.

Jiwa, Salim. "Stop the Scam" and "We're legitimizing fraud, police say." *Vancouver Province* 3 Dec. 1993, pp.A1, A5.

Kimberly, Todd. "Reforms open to change—Klein." *Calgary Herald* 28 March 1993, p.1.

Leslie, Colin. "McLeod predicts $1 billion saving in welfare plan." *Toronto Star* 22 May 1995, p.A9.

Lindgren, April. "Revenue Canada ready to close book on $4.2 billion fiasco." *Ottawa Citizen* 27 March 1996, p.A5.

"McLeod, Harris clash on welfare." *Toronto Star*, 25 May 1995, p.A1.

Ogilvie, Clare. "Four convicted in $17.5 m fraud free pending appeal." *Vancouver Province* 9 Jan. 1994, p.A16.

"Ontario tests waters on parenting classes." *Vancouver Sun* 25 July 2000, p.A6.

"Overwhelmed by response, single mom urges action." St. John's *Evening Telegram* 12 March 1998, p.1.

Piven, Frances Fox and Richard A. Cloward. *Regulating the Poor*. New York: Vintage, 1971, p.34.

Power, Jonathan. "The critical role of governments in communal hatred." *Vancouver Sun* 1 May 1995, A12.

Progressive Conservative Party of Ontario. *The Common Sense Revolution*. Toronto: 1994, pp.10, 11.

Sinclair, Gordon Jr. "False accusations clog welfare line." *Winnipeg Free Press* 26 July 1994, p.1.

Social Assistance Review Committee Network. Unpublished critique of article in *The Financial Post* 10 April 1991.

Tait, Kathy. "Honesty ought to matter." *Vancouver Province* 19 June 1995, p.A14.

———. "A druggies' tale" and "Alcohol, drug abuse shoot up welfare costs." *Vancouver Province* 9 July 1995, p.A16.

———. "Weed out welfare abuse and aid the truly needy." *Vancouver Province* 17 July 1995, p.A11.

"Taxpayers support cheats." *Financial Post* 5 Dec. 1992, p.S1.

Vipond, Robert. "The two Mike Harrises" *Globe and Mail* 29 April 1998, p.A27.

Walkom, Tom. "There is something going on among voters." *Toronto Star* 27 May 1995, p.B1.

York, Geoffrey. "Foes jump on remark by Chrétien." *Globe and Mail* 22 April 1994, p.A4.

Chapter 7
The new poor laws: helping employers; cheapening labour

Anderson, Tom. "Human dignity is the issue." *The Long Haul* March 1998, p.2.

Baines, David. "Growing number of Canadians to do business offshore." *Vancouver Sun* 4 Oct. 1997, p.F8.

Barrett, Tom. "Bad economy leads to loss of full-time work." *Vancouver Sun* 18 March 1998, p.A2.

Beatty, Jim. "Labor Minister stirs anger by saying workfare like tough love." *Vancouver Sun* 2 Nov. 1995, p.B1.

Blackwell, Tom. "Firms can use workfare free." *Globe and Mail* 9 July 1998, p.A4.

Boyd, Bernie. "Will microwave ovens that seat hundreds be next?" *The Long Haul* March 1998, p.2.

British Columbia. *BC Benefits: Renewing Our Social Safety Net.* Victoria: 1995.

———. Premier's Forum on New Opportunities for Working and Living. *Report from the Forum.* Victoria: 1995, p.4.

———. "Welfare caseload down, Clark releases independent report projecting savings of $350 million to $470 million." Government news release. Victoria: 22 April 1997.

Buchanan, Carrie. "Region penalized for welfare successes." *Ottawa Citizen* 29 Nov. 1999, pp.B1, B2.

Canada. Human Resources Development Canada. *Improving Social Security in Canada.* Ottawa: 1994, p.10.

———. Human Resources Development Canada. *The National Child Benefit.* Ottawa: 1997, p.7.

———. National Council of Welfare. *Myths and Realities.* Ottawa: Ministry of Supply and Services, 1998, p.3

Canadian Labour Congress. "Creating more and better jobs through reduction and redistribution of working time." *The Economy* Winter 1997-98, p. 21.

Chow, Wyng. "Ottawa simplifies reporting of foreign assets." *Vancouver Sun* 21 Aug. 1998, p.A1.

Courchene, Thomas J. *Social Canada in the Millennium*. Toronto: C.D. Howe
     Institute, 1994, pp. 326, 327.
Ekos Research Associates Inc. *Child Poverty Focus Groups Final Report*. Toronto:
     1997, pp.5, 20.
————. *Memorandum on Child Poverty Focus Groups: Revised Conclusions*. Toronto:
     1997, pp.3, 7.
"Family bonus similar to workfare." *The Long Haul* August/September 1996, p.1.
"The federal budget: great words; disgusting actions." *The Long Haul* March
     1997, p.7.
Greenspon, Edward. "More funds sought for child benefit plan." *Globe and Mail*
     7 Oct. 1997, p.A6.
Hunter, Justine. "Victoria wants Ottawa to kill asset disclosure." *Vancouver Sun*
     14 Jan. 1999, p.A5.
"Job clubs blame jobless for unemployment." *The Long Haul* May 1998, p.7.
"Jobs program undermines wages." *The Long Haul* February 2000, pp.1, 10.
King, Romana. "Toronto to get $622,000 for promoting workfare." *Toronto Star*
     6 June 2000, p.A5.
Klein, Seth and Barbara Montgomery. *Depressing Wages: Why Welfare Cuts Hurt
     Both the Welfare and Working Poor*. Vancouver: Canadian Centre for Policy
     Alternatives, 2001.
KPMG. *A Review of the Impact of BC's Social Safety Net Reforms on Income
     Assistance Caseloads and Savings*. Toronto: 1996, p. 7.
"Man pleads guilty to feed children." *The Long Haul* November 1997, p.1.
McCrate, Elaine. "Hitting bottom." *Dollars and Sense* September/October 1997,
     pp.4,5.
Social Planning Council of Metropolitan Toronto. "Minimum wages and ade-
     quate income." *Social Infopac* April 1987, p.7
National Anti-Poverty Organization. *Changes to Social Assistance and Services*.
     Ottawa: March 21, 1997.
Naylor, Nancy. "A National Child Benefit Program" in ed. Dooley, Martin D. et
     al. *Family Matters*. Toronto: C.D. Howe Institute, 1995, pp.218, 232.
O'Connor, Deborah. Personal Interview. 1999.
Ontario. Ministry of Community and Social Services. "Ontario announces
     expansion of workfare program." Press release. 22 Nov. 1999.
————. Ministry of Community and Social Services. *Summary of Ontario Works
     Program*, August 1996, p.1.
"People on welfare said ..." *The Long Haul* February 1997, p.7.
Roberts, David. "Single people on welfare target of Manitoba cutbacks." *Globe
     and Mail* 13 March 1996, p.A6.
Salutin, Rick. "An unvarnished gem from the mouth of a squeegee kid." *Globe
     and Mail* 6 June 1997, p.C1.
Shragge, Eric. "Workfare in Quebec" in Eric Shragge, ed. *Ideology for a New
     Under-Class*. Toronto: Garamond, 1997, pp.61, 71.
Singhania, Lisa. "Gates tops list of billionaires." *Vancouver Sun* 16 June 2000,
     p.F5.
Sklar, Holl and Chuck Collins. "*Forbes* 400 World Series." *The Nation* 20 Oct.
     1997, pp.6, 7.

Uchitelle, Louis. "Welfare recipients taking jobs often held by the working
  poor." *New York Times* 1 April 1997, p.1.
Community Social Planning Council of Toronto and the Ontario Social Safety
  NetWork. *Workfare Watch* August 1996, pp.1-3; January 1998, p.8.

Chapter 8
Substituting Charity for Justice

Beauchesne, Eric. "UI recipients should take available jobs, council says."
  Vancouver Sun 21 June 1995, p.D5.
———. "Record low proportion of unemployed collect from jobless fund."
  Vancouver Sun 23 April 1998, p.D7.
Block, Walter. *On Economics and the Canadian Bishops*. Vancouver: The Fraser
  Institute, 1983, p.17.
Canadian Centre for Philanthropy. *More Than Charity: A New Agenda for
  Corporate Citizenship*. Toronto: 1998, pp.5, 6, 14, 33-36.
Cellini, Adelia. "Man with cancer struggles to lead normal, active life." *Montreal
  Gazette* 20 Dec. 1995, p.A3.
Cohen, Marjorie. "Deconstructing the Welfare State." Unpublished paper.
  Photocopied. Vancouver: 1995, p.9.
"Comox paper poor-bashes food bank users." *The Long Haul* January 1999, p.4.
Drohan, Madeleine. "Tax cuts council's ticket to popularity." *Globe and Mail* 25
  Sept. 1999, p.B2.
Edmonton Gleaners Association. Code of Ethics of Canadian Food Banks. 1998.
Ellison, Debbie. Speech at Taste of a Nation Event. Records of End Legislated
  Poverty, Vancouver, 25 April 1991.
Fabar, Lynn. "Letter from a person who uses the food bank." *Action Line*.
  September 1991, p. 3.
Frank, Jeffrey and Stephen Mihorean. "Who gives to charity?" *Canadian Social
  Trends* Winter 1996, p.9.
Fraser, Graham. "Unemployment insurance changes hit poor hardest, study
  says." *Globe and Mail* 8 July 1989, p.A9.
Gold, Marta. "Klein asks charities to work with government." *Edmonton Journal*
  4 Oct. 1994, p.A7.
Gram, Karen. "Food bank regular gets a taste of how the elite eat." *Vancouver
  Sun* 16 April 1993, p.3.
"Heirs and community reap tax benefits of estate planning." *Leave a legacy BC*.
  Supplement to *The Globe and Mail* 2 Oct. 1999, p.F3.
Hobbs, Karen, et al. *The Waste of a Nation*. Vancouver: End Legislated Poverty,
  1992, pp.8, 11-17, 20, 21, 45.
"Imagine's new program: It's about more than just charity." *Imagine*.
  Supplement to *The Globe and Mail* 6 Nov. 1998, C6.
"Imagine the difference we can make." *Imagine*. Supplement to *The Vancouver
  Sun* 30 May, 1991.
Kane, Marion. "Charity harvests funds at tasteful event." *Toronto Star* 28 April
  1993, p.C1.
Lippert, Owen. *Response to Improving Social Security in Canada*. Vancouver: Fraser
  Institute, 1994, pp.4,17.

McQuaig, Linda. *The Quick and the Dead*. Toronto: Viking, 1991, p.26.

Means, Marianne. "Charities can't pick up the Gingrich slack." *Vancouver Sun* 5 June 1995, p.A10.

Noel, Albert. "Father scours garbage to make ends meet." *Montreal Gazette* 1 Dec. 1995, p.A3.

"People on welfare said..." *The Long Haul* February 1997, p.7.

"Performance 2000." *Canadian Business* 25 June 1999, p.72.

"Policies force worker to deny help." *The Long Haul* February 1997, p.6.

"Poverty statistics at a glance." Information sheet. Ottawa: National Anti-Poverty Organization, December 1997.

Robertson, Ian. "Planned charity pays dividends." *Vancouver Courier* 7 Feb. 1999, p.19.

Saleh, Antoinette. "School charity backfires." *Action Line* December 1992, p.6.

Save our Strength web site, 5 Oct. 1998.
http://www.strength.org/programs/taste—about.html

Seagram Company Ltd. *Annual Report*. Montreal: 1992, p.3.

Stewart-Patterson, David. "A Community of Enterprise" in Caledon Insitute of Social Policy. *Perspectives on Partnership*. Ottawa: 1998, p.33.

Todd, Douglas. "Poorest people the most generous." *Vancouver Sun* 22 Jan. 1999, p.B3.

"The rich 100." *Canadian Business*. 30 July 1999, pp. 65, 66.

Waters, Morgan. "Acts of many kind people disprove notion that we're all alone." *Montreal Gazette* 31 Dec. 1995, p.C3.

Chapter 9
Bashing yourself: clashing silently with privilege

Adair, Margo and Sharon Howell, *Breaking Old Patterns, Weaving New Ties*. San Francisco: Tools for Change, 1994, pp.8, 10.

"Dave's statement to social policy committee." *The Long Haul* March 1994, p.1.

McMurray, Rande. "Classism: It's your problem, not mine." *The Long Haul* January 1995, pp.6, 7.

Chapter 10
Challenging poor bashing within and around us

Battle, Ken and Sherri Torjman. *Good Work: Getting It and Keeping It*. Ottawa: Caledon Institute, 1999, pp.10, 21.

Beauchesne, Eric. "Report calls low jobless rate false." *Vancouver Sun* 14 April 1999, p.D5.

Black, Bill. *Report on Human Rights in British Columbia*. Vancouver: Ministry Responsible for Multiculturalism and Human Rights, 1994, p.170.

Cameron, Sandy. *Poverty, It's Local, It's Global, and It's All Connected*. Vancouver: British Columbia Teachers' Federation, 1998.

Canada. National Council of Welfare. "Estimates of Statistics Canada's low-income cut-offs for 1998." Fact sheet.

———. National Council of Welfare. *Incentives and Disincentives to Work*. Ottawa: Ministry of Supply and Services, 1993, p.37.

————. Human Rights Commission. "Prohibited grounds of discrimination in Canada." Leaflet. Ottawa: December 1998, pp.3, 5.

Canadian Council on Social Development. "Minimum wage rates for experienced workers." Fact Sheet. Ottawa: 2000.

Canadian Labour Congress. "Creating more and better jobs through reduction and redistribution of working time." *The Economy* Winter 1997-98, p. 21.

Kinesis. (Newsletter of Vancouver Status of Women.) October/November 1999, p.1.

Mandela, Nelson. *Long Walk to Freedom.* Boston: Little, Brown, 1994. pp.254, 255.

MacKinnon, Bobbi-Jean. "Shocked by jock talk" *Saint John Times Globe* 9 Sept. 1997, p.1.

MacKinnon, Mark. "Canada's biggest paycheques." *Globe and Mail* 26 April 1999, p.B1.

Old, Mike. "Hospital union confronts poor-bashing." *The Long Haul* October 1997, p.7.

"Speaking out against poor-bashing." *The Long Haul* February 1996, pp.S-1 – S-4.

"Stop poor-bashing and create jobs." *The Long Haul* July 1997, p. 4.

"The rich 100." *Canadian Business* July 1999, pp. 65, 66.

Ontario Federation of Labour. *Unfair Shares 1998*, pp.18, 32.

United Nations Committee on Economic, Social and Cultural Rights. *Concluding Observations of the Committee on Canada's Report.* Geneva: 1998.

United Nations Development Programme. *Human Development Report, 1997.* New York: Oxford University Press, 1997, p.110.

Yalnizyan, Armine. *The Growing Gap.* Toronto: Centre for Social Justice, 1998, p.11.

Conclusion

Battle, Ken. *Poverty Eases Slightly.* Ottawa: The Caledon Institute, 1999, p.4.

Baxter, Sheila. *No Way to Live.* 2d ed. Vancouver: New Star, 1995, p.73.

Cordon, Sandra. "Surpluses to bring tax cuts, Martin says, seeking input." *Vancouver Sun* 3 Nov. 1999, p.A1.

United Nations Development Programme. *Human Development Report, 1998.* New York: Oxford University Press, 1998, p.30.